AF529092

WBT

WORK, INCOME AND STATUS OF RURAL WOMEN

WORK, INCOME AND STATUS OF RURAL WOMEN

Edited by :

Dr. Thota Jyothi Rani

Professor of Economics

Kakatiya University

Warangal - 506009 (A.P.)

SERIALS PUBLICATIONS

NEW DELHI

© Dr. Thota Jyothi Rani

First Published - 2005

ISBN : 81-86771- 93-X

All rights reserved with the Publisher, including the right to translate or reproduce this book or parts thereof except for brief quotations in critical articles or reviews.

Published by

Head Office : **SERIALS PUBLICATIONS**
4, B.S.S. Hall, Khyber Pass Market
Civil Lines, Delhi-110054 (India)
Phone : 23245225
Fax : 91-11-23272135
E-mail: serials@satyam.net.in

Branch Office : 4830/24, Prahlad Street, Ansari Road
Darya Ganj, New Delhi-110002 (India)

Acknowledgement

I would like to express my thanks to University Grants Commission, New Delhi and all the concerned officials for the sanctioning of financial assistance under the scheme of Major Research Project to take up the present inquiry.

I am thankful to esteemed professor C.K. Kokate, Former Vice-Chancellor, Kakatiya University, Prof. T. Bhaskar Rao, Former Registrar of Kakatiya University for their constant encouragement for the timely completion of the project.

I am also grateful to Respected Prof. V. Gopal Reddy, Vice Chancellor Kakatiya University, Prof. S. Jagannatha Swamy, Registrar and Prof. G. Damoder, coordinating officer, UGC unit, Kakatiya University for their constant encouragement.

I am also thankful to all the faculty members of the Dept. of Economics, Kakatiya University especially to Prof. N. Linga Murthy, Prof. T. Papi Reddy, Dr. Burra Ramulu and Dr. C. Renuka for their encouragement and help.

I will be failing in my duty if I don't express my gratitude to my friends Prof. K. Katyayani and Dr. H. Girija Rani.

I am also grateful to DRDA officials of Khammam, Warangal and Karimnagar districts, all the 820 respondents and my project Associate Mr. K. Ravinder Reddy, Mr. S. Vidya Sagar for their timely help, assistance and cooperation.

I am indebted to Dr. L.S.R. Prasad and Yugandhar for their help in selection and the finalization of cover design. I am also thankful to Sri Yele Laxman whose cartoons are used for cover design.

I will be failing in my duty if I don't express my deep sense of gratitude to my husband Sri. Bajjuri Rajaiah, my children B. Sandeep and B. Spandana for their constant cooperation and encouragement with which I could complete the project easily.

I am thankful to Serials Publications, New Delhi for publishing the present inquiry.

Prof. T. JYOTHI RANI

Contents

1

Introduction & Methodology

"Development must be redefined as an attack on the chief evils of the world today: malnutrition, diseases, illiteracy, slums, unemployment and inequality. Measured in terms of aggregate growth rates, development has been a great success. But measured in terms of jobs, justice and the elimination of poverty, it has been a failure or only a partial success".

Paul P. Streetan, *Director,*
World Development Institute.

Unemployment, chronic poverty and consequent hunger remain serious problems inspite of economic growth in third world countries. Development at the aggregate level offered little or no relief to the poor. Till 1960's, development was always seen as an economic phenomenon in which rapid gains in overall and per capita GNP growth would either 'trickle down' to the masses in the form of jobs and other economic opportunities or create the necessary conditions for the wider distribution of the economic and social benefits of growth. The actual experience has revealed that even though a large number of third world nations did achieve the overall UN growth targets but the levels of living of the masses of people remained for the most part unchanged. In this context, Prof. Dudley Seers rightly put forward three fundamental questions to determine in regard to the development of that nation viz. what has been happening to unemployment? What has been happening to inequality? What has been happening to poverty? In all the third world countries almost all of these problems are growing unabated. India is no exception in this regard.

In view of the seriousness of the problem of poverty, improving the lot of poor has become an increasingly important aspect of World Bank's activities. Poverty alleviation became core objective of World Bank's lending. Still, the prescriptions of World Bank has not benefited the poorest people as well as the poor countries. More than one fourth people of the developing countries still live in poverty as measured by Human Poverty Index (UNDP 1997). India is no exception to these trends.

Since the benefits of development did not change the living standards of the poor i.e., trickle down theory is a failure, public action is needed to eliminate poverty. From the late 1960's Govt. of India have been implementing target group oriented approach for creating employment opportunities and distributing renewable assets among the poor. The emphasis has also been laid on women because they are more vulnerable to the consequences of poverty as a marginalised section of the society.

Anti-Poverty or Income Generating Programmes

The deficiencies in the process of growth, demographic pressures, inability of the organised sector to absorb growing work force, failure in the implementation of land reforms have resulted in agrarian tensions on the one hand and rise in the absolute and relative poverty on the other. In order to reduce the incidence of absolute poverty i.e., to provide basic needs to the people. Govt. of India have been formulating various Rural Development Strategies and Approaches at different points of time.

During the first three Five Year Plans, the method of Community Development had been used as a means to attain rural development. The Planning Commission of India opines that the Community Development is a method through which the Five Year Plan seeks to initiate a process of transformation of the social and economic life of the village. It has been launched on 2nd October, 1957 and described that it is directed against the triple enemies-hunger, disease and ignorance. However, the programme could benefit only rich farmers which had resulted in the widening of disparities among different sections of the rural people. Its noteworthy contribution was the establishment of administrative set-up across the country for implementing future rural development programmes.

The emphasis had been shifted from Community Approach to Area Approach during Third Five Year Plan in view of the failure of Community Development Programme to reach the weaker section of rural people.

The programme of IADP of 1960, IAAO of 1964, the Drought Prone Area Programme (DPAP), the Desert Development Programme (DDP) and the Command Area Development (CAD) Programme of late 1970 were started under the Area Approach. The main objective of these programmes was to raise food production by applying HYV based Agricultural Modernisation Programme. They had their inherent quality of pro-rich which did not do any benefit to the poor. In view of this, the Rural Development Strategy had been transformed from Area Approach to Target Group Approach.

The target group approach aims at making the family economically viable and self-sufficient. In the case of Small and Marginal Farmers where farm holding is of uneconomic size, income is supplemented by the subsidiary occupations like dairy, poultry, sheep breeding and other agricultural allied activities. For landless labourers, rural artisans and crafts-persons, various self-employment ventures based on animal husbandry, cottage and small scale industries and other occupations are provided in the programme and suitable assistance is also given for this purpose. The multiplicity of schemes has resulted in over- lapping of the area of operation and therefore target group programmes were combined and made into one programme called IRDP.

The Planning Commission in the draft Sixth Five Year Plan had visualised integrated plan of development at the block level within the beneficiary oriented programmes for the poor will be approximately integrated. As a comprehensive strategy and approach for translating these objectives into specific programme, the IRDP now involves a multi-pronged direct attack on rural poverty, integrated covers four principal dimensions viz. integration of sectoral programmes, spatial integration of social and economic processes and the policies with a view to achieving a better fit between growth, removal of poverty and employment generation. More specifically, it involves a sharp focus on target groups comprising Small, Marginal Farmers, Agricultural Labour and Rural Artisans including women.

The Anti-Poverty Programmes which have been operating throughout the country have brought under one single agency called "District Rural Development Agency - DRDA" for the purpose of implementation.

Four important approaches which are being operated though distinctive in nature, which can be regarded as complementary approaches constituting a direct attack on the problem of rural poverty. These are the Training of Rural Youth for Self-Employment (TRYSEM), supply of improved tool-kits to Rural Areas, Development of Women and Children in Rural Areas (DWCRA) and Integrated Rural Development Programme (IRDP). All these four programmes are being implemented through a single agency called DRDA.

The employment generating programmes are intended to provide income and thereby maintain consumption level of the different sections of the rural poor. On the other, the IRDP aims at promoting self-employment through the provision of productive assets that would generate an income stream, so that the beneficiaries are enabled to cross the poverty line on a permanent basis. Thus, there has been a two-pronged attack on poverty since 1980 - an employment oriented approach and an asset oriented approach.

Poverty is gender-specific and it is not gender neutral because women suffer from systematic social injustice due to their gender. They are exploited and oppressed not only as human beings but also as women. Their economic subjugation and dependent position is the result of a rigid distinction in men's and women's roles in society and leads to exploitation. Mahatma Gandhi once observes that "Today the sole occupation of a woman amongst us is supposed to be to bear children, to look after her husband and otherwise to drudge for the household—not only is the woman condemned to domestic slavery, but when she goes out as a labourer to earn wages, though she works harder than man she is paid less".

The Human Development Report-95 recognises that the process of development itself is not gender-neutral. It states "For too long, it was assumed that development was a process that lifts all boats, that its benefits trickled down to all income classes and that it was gender neutral in its impact. Experience teaches otherwise. Wide income disparities and gender gaps stare us in the face in all societies... moving towards gender equality is not a technocratic goal-it is a political process. It requires a new way of thinking-in which the stereotyping of women and men give way to a new philosophy that regards all people, irrespective of gender, as essential agents of change. The relentless struggle for gender equality will change most of today's premises for social, economic and political life".

Though poor women the world over bear a disproportionately large share of the family's work burden - apart from the formally counted productive work, there is also the incessant struggle to collect some of the critical resources for family survival such as food and water, fuel and fodder, their work remains unpaid, unrecognized and under valued. Women's work has not been recognised inspite of its intrinsic use value or human value only on the ground that it is not captured by exchange value. The failure to value most of their work reduce women to virtual non-entities in most economic transactions. Status in contemporary society is often equated with income earning power, women suffer a major under valuation of their economic status. If women's unpaid work were properly valued, it is quite possible that women would emerge in most societies as the main bread winners or at least equal bread winners-since they put in more hours of work than men.

In most of the third world countries, poverty accentuates the problems faced by women. In these countries, gender relations are influenced by traditional hierarchies based on patriarchy, caste and ethnicity and compounded by inequalities of wealth and power. Women in the lower strata are not only exploited economically but are also socially oppressed. The excess burden of poverty has been borne by women because the responsibility of the survival of the household rests on the shoulders of the woman. That the families fed, clothed and cared for is the women's concern since it ties up with her share of work as per the gender based division of labour. Under these conditions, woman has to work for longer hours - paid as well as unpaid and cut down her own consumption. Further, excess burden of poverty on women is the result of existing patriarchal intra-household gender specific disparities in distributive rules with respect to income, resources, consumption and time.

Formulation and implementation of relevant strategies are needed to face the challenge of feminisation of poverty. This can be attained through (i) the boosting of productivity in women's paid and unpaid work (ii) the expansion of women's employment opportunities (iii) the raising of income levels in women's jobs and (iv) the mobilisation of women into participatory groups.

To attain this, public action is needed. Moreover, the policies of our government are always towards the achievement of gender equality. Further, the policies towards women have been shifted from women's welfare to women's development and at present, the emphasis is on women's empowerment.

The Gender Empowerment Measure (GEM) developed in the UNDP's HDR seeks to determine the degree to which women and men participate actively in economic, professional, and political activity and take part in decision making. This is measured on the basis of:

(i) power over economic resources depicted by per capita income;

(ii) access to professional activities and participation in economic decision making based on share of jobs in the professional, technical, managerial and administrative category, and;

(iii) political opportunities and decision making reflected by share of parliamentary seats.

Women's Empowerment can be viewed at two levels - household level to overcome intra-household inequality and at the societal level to over come inequalities at that level.

Need For Specific Anti-poverty Programmes For Women

Despite the positive policies and action programmes of the government to uplift women, their problems have been accentuated by land alienation, environmental degradation, increasing agricultural poverty, concentration of resources in a few hands, increasing polarisation of the rich and the poor and polarisation between urban and rural areas. The Sixth Five Year Plan Document also recognises that inspite of the development measures, the constitutional legal guarantees, women have lagged behind in almost all sectors.

Majority of labouring women can be found in the self-employed and informal sector. They do arduous work as wage earners, piece-rate workers, casual labour and paid and unpaid family labour, still their economic and social conditions are dismal.

The labour market is also not gender - neutral. It favours men against women. Gender inequalities exist in almost all sectors. Unskilled, nurve and back breaking and low paid work will usually be done by women. One can notice the prevalence of wage discrimination. In addition, feminisation of jobs can also be seen where the operations that fetch higher wages are male preserves and work of arduous nature bringing in lower wages is done by women. Gender inequality is also manifests in acquiring educational and vocational skills. Inspite of the impressive increase in total number of literate women, the male -female gaps remain large, and a slow rate of progress of women's education is noted with a virtual stagnation in the area of technical education.

Women, who are working in the informal sector of economy, operate in a vicious circle of subsistence, deprivation and survival. They are largely asset less and do not own any productive assets in relation to their work. Even when some of these assets are held by the family, women's own access to and control over these assets have been marginal. Therefore, provision of productive assets in the hands of women who are working in the informal sector will result in the qualitative improvement in their lives over a period of time given other inputs such as knowledge, skill, organisation and confidence. Moreover, the government policies are towards the attainment of women's empowerment. Thus, there is a need for the formulation and implementation of programmes that specifically benefit women, while recognising this need, the Govt. of India have launched Development of Women and Children in Rural Areas (DWCRA) in September, 1982 as a sub-scheme of IRDP. The main objective of the programme is to improve lot of rural women through the creation of income generating activities. The programme envisages formation of groups of rural women as thrift groups and each group will be sanctioned a revolving fund. So that, they carry income generating activities. In recent years, DRDA is extending Integrated Rural Development Programmes directly to DWCRA groups. Several studies have revealed that the performance of schemes given to DWCRA groups are relatively successful.

Need For A Separate Study on DWCRA

Though DWCRA is a sub-scheme of IRDP, it has a broader objective of raising the economic status of women there by boosting up their social status too. As HDR-95 rightly remarks moving towards gender equality is not a technocratic goal, it is a political process.

As women are marginalised section of poor and more vulnerable to small deterioration in the living conditions of family, simple rise in the income and employment generation cannot automatically raise their status because of the rigidity of cultural norms and attitudes. However, no one can deny that the rise in income of women is a pre-condition for raising their status. But, it is not a sufficient condition. Therefore, a critical analysis is required as to what extent these programmes affect the intra-household disparities in regard to control over resources, income, consumption and decision making. This is one of the important aspects underline in women empowerment.

Moreover, under DWCRA, women are encouraged to form groups. These economic groups also act as social groups. This makes them more conscious of their status and makes them aware of the causes for their subordination. Whether this awareness enable them to organise themselves to combat the problems that are associated with the gender based division of labour responsibilities and attitude of society towards women is another basic question which has to be enquired. In addition, formation of women groups may give impetus to their leadership qualities and make them to derive the benefits of team work. This may raise their political opportunities and participation in the political decision making in the society. In view of all this, there is a serious need for a separate study on DWCRA programme which affects the status of women at large.

Objectives of the Study

The main objective of the study is to assess the impact of DWCRA on the work, income and status of rural women. Further, the study intends to:

(i) ascertain the success of scheme in economic terms viz. generation of more work, income, rise in consumption expenditure-change in the nutritional value of food, purchase of consumer durables, purchase of productive assets, expansion of the activity of venture, repayment of loan as well as old debts, provision of educational opportunities to children and expenditure on health;

(ii) examine the socio-economic background of the respondents;

(iii). inquire the success in terms employment and income generation with respect to scheme, caste, category, educational qualifications and age of the respondents.

(iv) explore the causes of failure.

(v) examine the impact of scheme on the patriarchal intra-household gender specific disparities in distributive rules with respect to control over resources, control over income, change in the distribution of consumption in favour of women;

(vi) findout the effect on work-burden i.e., domestic work in view of the gender based division of labour;

(vii) ascertain the impact on the domestic violence in the form of harassment, humiliation, and wife beating;

(viii) observe the result of scheme on the state of autonomy and independence of women in terms of taking decisions related to trade and family;

(ix) analyse the participation of respondents in social as well as political decision making;

(x) make suggestions on the basis of inquiry to improve the socio-economic status of women in order to ensure the broader objective of women's empowerment.

Hypotheses of the Study

The hypotheses of the study are formulated as follows:

(i) There is a direct relationship between success of trade and economic status of women;

(ii) Success of trade in economic terms positively affects intra-household gender specific distributive rules in favour of women;

(iii) Higher the success of scheme, higher will be the political participation of women.

Methodology

The present study is based on primary as well as secondary sources of data. Studies on anti-poverty programmes in general and on DWCRA in particular at the level of individual researches, voluntary organisations and concurrent evaluation studies conducted by respective DRDAs are taken as background information. In order to elicit the information in regard to the socio-economic impact of DWCRA on women, a structured questionnaire is administered to selected sample. In addition to the administration of structured questionnaire, observation and interview methods are also be used to elicit the information pertaining to the inner realities of women's lives.

Sample Design

Three staged stratified random sampling technique is adopted where three districts of North Telangana region of Andhra Pradesh have been chosen first. They are Khammam, Warangal and Karimnagar. In Khammam district, 300 respondents from 23 villages representing 19 trades are chosen. (Details of sample characteristics are presented in Chapter-III).

In Warangal district, 300 respondents from 20 villages representing 24 trades are chosen. (Details are presented in Chapter-IV).

In Karimnagar district, 220 respondents from 18 villages representing 19 trades are chosen. (Details are represented in Chapter-V).

Thus, total selected respondents are 820 covering three districts. The sample respondents are selected in such a way to cover all the castes - Forward Castes, Backward Classes, Scheduled Caste and Scheduled Tribe. Table-1.1 represents caste-wise distribution of sample.

Table-1.1 : Caste-wise Distribution Of Sample

Caste	*Districts*			
	Khammam	*Warangal*	*Karimnagar*	*Total*
F C	75	34	17	126
B C	157	207	128	492
S C	21	47	65	133
S T	47	12	10	69
Total :	**300**	**300**	**220**	**820**

Source : Field Study.

Out of 820 selected respondents 492 belonged to Backward Classes while 133 belonged to Scheduled Castes and 126 belonged to Forward Castes where as least place is occupied by Scheduled Tribe respondents. They are only 69 in number. The relative positions of various castes in Warangal and Karimnagar districts are in line with the total position but variance can be found in Khammam district.

The sample respondents are also elicited in such way to cover various economic categories. The relevant information is shown in Table-1.2.

Table-1.2 : Category-wise Distribution of Sample

Category	*Districts*			
	Khammam	*Warangal*	*Karimnagar*	*Total*
Small Farmer	53	53	37	143
Marginal Farmer	87	94	51	232
Agricultural Labour	41	12	58	111
Non-Agri. Labour	19	11	9	39
Rural Artisan	61	56	46	163
Others	39	74	19	132
Total	**300**	**300**	**220**	**820**

Source : *Field Study.*

It can be seen from table-1.2 that out of 820 respondents selected, first position is occupied by Marginal Farmers with 232 and 2nd place is occupied by Small Farmers while 'Other's occupy third position and Non-Agricultural Labourers stand last in regard to their relative position in the total sample.

In Khammam district, first position is occupied by Marginal Farmers while Rural Artisans stand 2nd and last position is occupied by Non-Agricultural Labourers.

In Warangal district also Marginal Farmers stand first in terms of their number while second position is occupied by 'others' and last position can be seen for Agricultural Labour. where as they stand first in Karimnagar district while last position is occupied by Non-Agricultural Labourers as in the case of Khammam district. Thus, inter-district variation is observed in regard to economic category-wise distribution of sample.

Chapterisation

The present report has been divided into eight chapters including the present one i.e., 'Introduction and Methodology.

The Secondary data related to DWCRA groups in selected three districts of Khammam, Warangal and Karimnagar are presented in Chapter-II.

The impact of DWCRA on Work, Income and Status of Women in Khammam district has been analysed in Chapter-III. While the effect of DWCRA on Work, Income and Status of Rural Women in Warangal district is examined in Chapter-IV. Where as the impact of DWCRA on Rural Women in terms of employment and income generation as well as improvement in their status in Karimnagar district is discussed in Chapter-V.

A comparative analysis of selected three districts is made to assess relative performance in terms of employment and income generation so as to affect their pattern of consumption is examined in Chapter-VI.

The relative performance of three districts in terms of attaining improvement in the status of rural women is discussed in Chapter-VII.

Lastly the conclusions drawn on the basis of present inquiry are presented as Chapter-VIII.

2

Performance of DWCRA—An Overview

This chapter has been divided into two sections for the purpose of convenience. Section-I will be devoted to discuss the experience of poor women groups in various countries and India. Thus, an overview of literature that analyse in regard to the achievements of women groups will be presented in section-I. As the present study covers three districts of Telangana region of Andhra Pradesh viz.,Khammam, Warangal and Karimnagar, the analysis pertaining to the performance of DWCRA in these three districts is warranted. Therefore, the performance of DWCRA in terms of number of groups formed, number of beneficiaries, matching grant sanctioned and revolving fund provided will be discussed in Section-II.

SECTION-I

In the Post-Independence period India has achieved significant progress on the industrial and economic fronts. Still the progress did not trickledown to the rural areas, poor people and women. Consequently, widening disparities can be noticed between urban and rural sectors, upper classes and disadvantaged low classes and between men and women. Women have failed to get their proportionate share in the achievement of progress. Though, every one talk about the need to empowerment of women, this has not resulted in any specific, workable or sustainable measures that would assist in the creation of a social order based on gender justice.

In terms of Human Development, the rank of Andhra Pradesh is 11 in the female in literacy, 7 in life expectancy, 7 in infant mortality rate and 8 in percapita income[1].

Majority of women, can therefore, be seen in the unorganized sector. In 1971 census, 93.84 percent of women workers are found in unorganized sector. This is increased to 93.87 percent in 1981 and further increased to 95.79 percentage in 1991[2]. This clearly shows the economic status of women in India. However, this condition is existing even in other Third World countries. Therefore, the women who could attend Fourth World Conference on women at Beizing 1995 have demanded the governments for an agenda for development that will empower people, eradicate poverty, create sustainable livelihoods, build stable lives and healthy communities and promote peace on a long term basis. Therefore, policy and planning are no longer content with women's absence as substantive subject of development and as social agents in poverty eradication programmes. It is now increasingly understood that the goal of development is not simply one of increasing income (or GDP) but one of transforming economic and social relations, in particular, gender relations.

The Asia division of IFAD is playing a vital role in supporting Grameena Banks micro credit for women since the early 1980's. Since then, it has continued its concern for rural and indigenous women's advancement. A workshop was organised by Asian Institute of Technology, Thailand to define IFAD, Asia divisions gender analyses approach in May, 2000. In which 5 case studies from Lao PDR, Nepal, India and China were presented. Almost all the case studies have a common feature of women subordination. They opined that the women have capabilities to transform societies. They also stated that, micro credit has broadened that arena of women's decision making and improved women's well-being[3].

The Bangladesh Rural Advancement Committee (BRAC), one of the World's largest NGO's, has organised over one million women into over 30,000 village level organizations. One of the distinctive component of BRAC's Integrated Rural Development Programme is it's sub-sector approach to promoting economic opportunities for women where by BRAC collaborates with both village women and Govt. of the Bangladesh to build the necessary infrastructure and provide the necessary services to promote large scale employment opportunities in key sub-sectors of the economy. The poultry and textiles constitute a large segment of the programme. In the case of poultry, village women are involved as the providers of key services while the govt. of Bangladesh necessary inputs and infrastructure. In the case of textiles, BRAC directly creates jobs for rural women in garments and embroidery production centres and establishes necessary backward and forward linkages to raw-material sources and markets. Further, they gain awareness and confidence through social awareness and legal literacy courses and begun to participate meaningfully in community life[4].

In Srilanka, thousands of poor rural women have turned local societies into a net work of rural women's development societies and rural bank which can assist them to overcome economic hardships. The individual banks which have changed their lending system on that of the Grameena Banks in Bangladesh are giving women access to credit. This enabled them to establish small enterprises which resulted in the creation of more income. This increased ability to contribute to family income has raised their esteem with in the family and the community and lead to an increase in women's self-confidence[5].

On similar lines, women's empowerment programme is implemented with work book approach in Nepal. It caused the establishment of thousand rural banks. Women's empowerment in Nepal has not only resulted in the upliftment on economic front but also made them aware of the social problems. Women, as a group, have been fighting against dowry, sale of girls, domestic violence, child marriage etc[6].

The Government of India have initiated Integrated Rural Development Programme in 1975 to create rural employment in general and employment to rural women in particular. The percentage of women beneficiaries to total family assisted had increased from 9.90 percent in 1985 - 86 to 33.13 percent in 1996-

97. During 6th Five Year Plan, the ministry for Rural Development has started Development of Women and Children in Rural Areas (DWCRA), an exclusive programme for women. The Seventh Plan added 'equity and empowerment' to rural women's development, inculcating confidence among women, generating awareness about their rights and privileges but the National Perspective Plan admits that progress in all there has been slow and marginal.

The study made by Bala Saheb Vikhas Patil and Guru Charan Singh has pointed out that Integrated Rural Development Programme (IRDP) has failed to eliminate poverty and employment because of lack of proper implementation, technical expertise, awareness among the poor households[7].

D. K. Ghosh also observes that the implementation of IRDP Scheme was not satisfied because of poor awareness of beneficiaries[8].

A concurrent evaluation study conducted by T. Jyothi Rani (et. al) has observed that the role of middle men should be eliminated because in many cases they are misdirecting the people in regard to the selection of scheme and repayment of loan. The study recommended that in sanctioning of a particular scheme, the skills of the beneficiary, it's relevance to the locality and viability should be considered seriously. The measures should be taken to minimise the gap between sanction of scheme and it's grounding. Insufficient funds is another problem which come in the way of generation of more income. However, problems differ from scheme to scheme and village to village. Therefore, proper identification of problems is necessary to take appropriate measures to correct them[9].

Adverting the attention to DWCRA, N. Prem Kumar and A. Rahul have identified that marketing is a major problem coming in the way of success of scheme[10].

The study made by M. Shivashankaraiah and P. Ramappa also identifies raw-material and marketing problems by the beneficiary of DWCRA[11]. P. Sunderam and D. Ṣuman Singh opines that lack of co-operation among the group members, finance, motivation, poor quality of packing are the main problems of the beneficiaries[12].

Several evaluation studies conducted at the State and National levels have identified certain short comings of the DWCRA such as:

1. Wrong selection of group activities (skill, attitudes, and local conditions).
2. Lack of co-operation, zeal among the group members.
3. High cost of Raw-material.
4. Lack of Demand.
5. Inadequate provision of backward and forward linkages.
6. Lack of managerial skills.
7. Low quality of goods (Comparatively big companies).
8. Poor qualities of packing.
9. Inadequacy of revolving fund.

On the basis of these deficiencies they make certain suggestions to make DWCRA more effective. They are:

1. Women extension functionaries at the block level should be involved in the selection of beneficiaries.
2. District Block Development officials should have discretion to change the group activities which become dead or non-functional.
3. Interest
4. Investment and technology.
5. Training
6. Amount
7. Marketing societies
8. Middle men should be eliminated
9. Raw-material
10. Marketing surveys
11. Supervision[13]

Thus, the studies on DWCRA concentrated on the achievement in terms of income alone. Therefore, there is a need to have a study on DWCRA to analyse it's impact not only on economic front but also on their position in the family as well as in the society. The present study tries to fill up the gap in the existing literature.

SECTION-II

As the main aim of the present inquiry is to examine the impact of DWCRA on rural poor women, the discussion as to the performance of DWCRA in selected districts of Khammam, Warangal and Karimnagar of Telangana region of Andhra Pradesh is necessary. The information in this regard is presented in this section.

DWCRA In Khammam District

The trends in the formation of DWCRA groups indicate the views of rural women towards the programme. The information in regard to number of DWCRA groups formed and revolving fund sanctioned is presented in Table-2.1.

It can be observed from Table-2.1 that the number of DWCRA groups formed during 1993 and 2000 has been 3867

Table 2.1 : Dwcra Groups And Revolving Fund In Khammam District

(Revolving fund in Rs.)

Year	*No. of Groups*	*Revolving Fund*
1992-'93	317	41,50,980
1993-'94	729	92,92,260
1994-'95	740	98,19,570
1995-'96	456	65,53,000
1996-'97	363	56,18,500
1997-'98	342	52,52,500
1998-'99	915	2,28,00,002
1999-2000	5	1,25,000
TOTAL	3867	6,36,11,812

Source : Records of DRDA, Khammam.

and the amount of revolving fund sanctioned is as high as Rs. 6,36,11,812. The number of DWCRA groups formed in each year from 1993 to 2000 is not uniform and it has varied in a wide range of 5 in 2000 and 915 in 1999. In line with the variation in the number of DWCRA groups formed, the amount sanctioned as revolving fund also varies. However, it can be observed that in every year, the formation of DWCRA groups is present which indicates the significance of the programme in the opinion of rural women.

The caste-wise distribution of DWCRA members in Khammam district is presented in Table-2.2. This is categorised on the basis of the caste of the group leaders.

It can be observed from the table that the percentage share of Backward Class members is highest at 33.02 percent while last place is occupied by Minorities in this regard with 1.28 percent. The percentage share of Scheduled Caste members is 30.08 percent whereas for Scheduled Tribes, it is 28.26 percent and the percentage share of Forward Caste respondents is 7.37. Moreover in the year 2000 only Backward Class and Scheduled Caste groups are formed. Highest number of DWCRA members at 11,288 can be found in 1998-'99 but immediately it fall down to 65 in the subsequent year 1999-2000.

Table 2.2 : Caste-wise Distribution of DWCRA Members in Khammam District

Year	*F C*	*B C*	*S C*	*S T*	*Minority*	*Total*
1992-'93	148	1288	1363	974	63	3836
1993-'94	550	2899	2599	2687	135	8870
1994-'95	450	2901	3248	2549	104	9252
1995-'96	566	1965	1979	1328	102	5940
1996-'97	399	1548	1614	1089	16	4666
1997-'98	531	1616	864	1231	58	4300
1998-'99	909	3701	2772	3768	138	11288
1999-2000	—	3	63	—	—	66
TOTAL	3553 (7.37)	15921 (33.02)	14502 (30.08)	13626 (28.26)	616 (1.28)	48218 (100.00)

Source : Records of DRDA, Khammam.

Dwcra in Warangal District

The data in regard to number of groups formed in Warangal district from 1992-93 to 2001-2002 have been shown in Table-2.3.

Table 2.3 : Trend In The No. of DWCRA Groups Formed in Warangal District

Year	*Groups*
1992-'93	27
1993-'94	167
1994-'95	557
1995-'96	1004
1996-'97	628
1997-'98	2118
1998-'99	4414
1999-2000	11139
2000-'01	1544
2001-'02	43
TOTAL	21641

Source : Records of DRDA, Warangal.

It can be observed from Table-2.3 that the number of DWCRA groups formed has increased continuously from 27 in 1992-93 to 11,139 in 1999-2000 but later on decreased to 1544 in 2000-'01 and 43 in 2001-'02. On the whole, by the year 2001-2002, the number of DWCRA groups formed has reached to 21,641.

Table-2.4 indicates the sanction of revolving fund to DWCRA groups in Warangal district. By the end of 1999-2000, the amount to the tune of Rs. 6.73 crores to 3353 groups. The number of DWCRA groups which have been sanctioned Revolving Fund has varied between 983 during 1994-'95 and 156 during 1998-'99. While the amount of Revolving Fund sanctioned has varied between Rs. 39 lakhs in 1998-'99 and Rs. 2.25 crores in 1999-2000.

Table-2.5 denotes that from 1997-'98 to 2000-'01 i.e., over a period of four years, 3,710 DWCRA groups have been

Table 2.4 : Revolving Fund Sanctions to Dwcra in Warangal District

(Revolving fund in Rs.)

Year	*Groups*	*Revolving Fund*
1994-'95	983	1,43,75,000
1995-'96	296	44,34,450
1996-'97	705	1,75,20,000
1997-'98	310	45,00,000
1998-'99	156	39,00,000
1999-2000	903	2,25,75,000
TOTAL	3353	6,73,04,450

Source : Records of DRDA, Warangal.

Table - 2.5 : Matching Grant Sanctions To Dwcra Groups in Warangal District

(Maching Grant in Rs.)

Year	*No of Groups*	*Matching Grant*
1997-'98	357	30,74,869
1998-'99	355	31,67,213
1999-2000	1361	1,08,00,988
2000-'01	1637	1,55,48,200
TOTAL	3710	3,25,91,280

Source : Records of DRDA, Warangal.

sanctioned Rs. 3.25 crores of Matching Grant in Warangal district. The year 2000-'01 stands first in terms number of groups which have been sanctioned Matching Grant as well as the amount of Matching Grant sanctioned where the former is 1,637 while the latter is RS. 1.55 crores. Moreover, the number of groups which were given Matching Grant as well as the amount of Matching Grant sanctioned is on the rise continuously from 1997-'98 to 2000-'01.

Table-2.6 explains the caste-wise distribution of DWCRA members in Warangal district. The Backward Class members stand first in terms their percentage share in the total with 58.45 and they are followed Scheduled Caste respondents whose percentage share in the total is 20.64 and it is 14.48 percentage for Scheduled Tribe respondents while last position is occupied by Forward Caste respondents whose percentage share is only 6.44.

Table 2.6 : Caste-wise Distribution of Dwcra Members in Warangal District

Caste	*DWCRA Members*
F C	19,102 (6.44)
B C	1,73,384 (58.45)
S C	61,214 (20.64)
S T	42,940 (14.48)
TOTAL	2,96,640 (100.00)

Source : Records of DRDA, Warangal district.

Dwcra In Karimnagar District

Table-2.7 indicates the number of DWCRA groups formed and amount of Revolving Fund sanctioned in Karimnagar district. It is to be noted that from 1992-'93 to 1998-'99 i.e., over a period of seven years, the number of DWCRA groups formed is 49,163 and the Revolving Fund sanctioned is Rs. 91.59 crores. The number of groups formed has varied between 20,796 in 1993-'94 and 1,782 in 1992-'93. Similarly, the amount of Revolving Fund sanctioned has varied between Rs. 31.24 crores in 1993-'94 and Rs. 2.67 crores in 1992-'93.

Table-2.8 explains the caste-wise distribution of DWCRA groups is Karimnagar district. It is on the basis of the caste of the group leader. The caste-wise distribution of DWCRA groups indicates that Backward Class groups stands first in terms of their percentage share in the total groups with 45.82 percentage and 2nd place is occupied by Scheduled Caste groups with 44.39 percent. It is to be noted that the percentage share of Scheduled Tribe groups is 4.60 while for Forward Castes, it is 3.65 and

Table 2.7 : Number of Dwcra Groups Formed & Amount of Revovling Fund Sanctioned In Karimnagar District

(in Rupees)

Year	*No. of Groups*	*Revolving Fund*
1992-'93	1782	2,67,30,000
1993-'94	20796	31,24,25,400
1994-'95	7142	10,71,30,000
1995-'96	6641	16,60,25,000
1996-'97	3353	7,42,05,000
1997-'98	5017	12,04,62,000
1998-'99	4437	4,08,00,000
TOTAL	49163	91,59,77,400

Source : Records of DRDA, Karimnagar.

0.21 per cent for Minorities and 1.33 percent for Others. Thus, Backward Class and Scheduled Castes together occupy 90.21 percent of the total groups.

Table-2.8 : Caste-wise Distribution Of Dwcra Groups in Karimnagar District

Year	*F C*	*B C*	*S C*	*S T*	*Minority*	*Others*	*Unknown*	*Total*
1992-'93	25	430	897	71	28	10	321	1782
1993-'94	801	10592	8400	857	62	2	82	20796
1994-'95	106	2378	4101	504	9	3	41	7142
1995-'96	263	2569	3335	425	2	–	47	6641
1996-'97	83	1316	1782	150	–	–	22	3353
1997-'98	182	2833	1738	202	1	–	61	5017
1998-'99	332	2409	1570	52	2	–	67	4432
TOTAL	1792	22527	21823	2261	104	15	641	49163
	(3.65)	(45.82)	(44.39)	(4.60)	(0.21)	(0.03)	(1.3)	(100.00)

Source : Records of DRDA, Karimnagar district.

Comparative Analysis of DWCRA In Selected Three Districts

Table-2.9 indicates that Karimnagar district stands first in terms of number of DWCRA groups formed as well as amount of Revolving Fund sanctioned with 49,163 groups and Rs. 91.60 crores Revolving Fund. It is to be noted that Khammam district occupies 2nd place in terms of number of DWCRA groups formed with 48,217 while Warangal district occupies 2nd place in terms of amount of Revolving Fund sanctioned with Rs. 6.73 crores. Thus, inter-district variation is noticed in this regard.

Table 2.9 : Comparative Analysis of No of Dwcra Groups Fromed And Revolving Fund Sanctioned

Selected Districts	*No.of Dwcra Groups Formed*	*Amount of Revolving Fund Sanctioned (Rs. in Crores)*
Khammam	48217	6.36
Warangal	21647	6.73
Karimnagar	49163	91.6

Source : Records of DRDA of Selected districts.

Table-2.10 explains the caste-wise distribution of DWCRA groups in selected three districts. It can be observed that in all the three selected districts of Khammam, Warangal and Karimnagar, Backward Classes stand first, Scheduled Castes, Scheduled Tribes and Forward Caste occupy 2nd, 3rd and 4th place respectively in terms of number of DWCRA groups formed. Thus, no inter-district variation is observed. However, a close examination of the table reveals that Backward Class and Scheduled Caste respondents together occupy 90.21 percent in Karimnagar, 79.09 percent in Warangal and 63.10 percent in Khammam district. Similarly, the percentage share of Scheduled Tribe respondents is 28.26 in Khammam, 14.48

Table 2.10 : Comparative Analysis of Caste-wise Distribution of Dwcra Groups

District	*F C*	*B C*	*S C*	*S T*	*Minority*	*Others*	*Total*
Khammam	7.37	33.02	30.08	28.26	1.28	–	100.00
Warangal	6.44	58.45	20.64	14.48	–	–	100.00
Karimnagar	3.65	45.82	44.39	4.6	0.21	1.33	100.00

Source : Records of DRDA of selected districts.

percent in Warangal and 4.60 in Karimnagar districts. Moreover, Minorities can not be found in Warangal district. Thus, inter-district variation is observed in regard to caste-wise distribution of DWCRA groups.

FOOTNOTES

1. The Deccan Herald (Banglore) 22 Oct, 1995.
2. Census of India, Registrar General and Commissioner, Census operations, Government of India, New Delhi. 1971, 1981 and 1991.
3. Workshop Report, Defining IFAD, Asia divisions gender Analysis approach, Gender, Technology and Development, Vol. IV, No. 3, Sept-Dec, 2000, pp - 495-514.
4. Marielyn, Car, Marthachen, Renena Jahabvala (ed) 'Speaking Out' Women's Economic Empowerment in South Asia, Vistar Publications, New Delhi. 1997, pp. 1-10.
5. W.M. Leela sena and Chitrani Dhammika, Op-Cit., Ibid., pp. 127-142.
6. Vismaya : A New Approach to Women's Empowerment Programme, Bhoomika, A Feminist magazine (Telugu), May - August, 2001, pp. 54-56.
7. Balasaheb, Vikhe Patil and Gurucharan Singh, Implementation IRDP, effectively, Kurukshetra, Vol. XXXIX, No. 10, July, 1991, pp. 26-28.
8. D.K. Ghosh, Awareness of IRDP beneficiaries; A study, Kurukshetra, Vol. XXXIX, No. 12, Sept, 1991, pp. 15- 19.
9. T. Jyothi Rani (et al) Evaluation of Integrated Rural Development Programme, 1996-97 in Khammam district A.P. Report submitted to the DRDA Khammam. April - 1998.
10. N.Premkumar and A. Rahul: How Does DWCRA Scheme Operate? Kurukshetra, Vol. XL, No. 5, Feb - 1992. pp. 24-29.
11. M. Siva sankaraiah and P. Ramappa: Impact of DWCRA on Rural Areas, Kurukshethra, Vol. XLI, No. 10, July, 1993, pp. 11-14.
12. A. Sunderam and Suman Singh : Assesment of DWCRA Programme on modalities of operation, Kurukshethra, Vol. XLIII, No. 11, August, 1995, pp. 96-99.
13. D.S. Dhillon and B.N. Hansra : On making DWCRA effectively, Kurukshethra, Vol. XXXIX, No. 12, Sept, 1991, pp. 15-17.

3

Employment, Income & Status of Rural Women–Part-I

This chapter analyses the impact of DWCRA on rural women in Khammam district in terms of providing employment, generating income and improving the status of women. Therefore, the present chapter is divided into two sections. The economic impact of DWCRA on rural women is presented in Section I while the impact on status of women is discussed in Section II.

Characteristics of Selected Respondents

(i) ***The relationship between village and trade is shown in Table-3.1.***

It can be observed from Table-3.1 that 23 villages representing 19 trades are selected to assess the impact of DWCRA on rural women in Khammam district. The selected villages are Koratlagudem, Burangutta Thanda, Pusalapadu, Nayakangudem, Jeevanchi Pally, Garla, Bayyaram, Balapeta Thanda, Teldarpally, Balapeta, Enkur, Pandurangapuram, Karepally, Gampalagudem, Jakkepally, Perika Singaram, Jeella Cheruvu, Kesavapuram, Gopavaram, Muthyalampadu, Gattu Singram, Yellandu. The 19 selected trades consists of i) Agriculture and Allied activities such as Vegetable cultivation, Milch Animals, Sheep Rearing ii) Food Processing Activities such as Pickles and making of Edible items, Sambar and Rasam powders iii) Manufacturing activities inclusive of Baniyans

Table 3.1 : Village - Wise Distribution of Trades Under DWCRA in Khammam District

Village	*Baniyans Making*	*Veg. Culti-Vation*	*Milch Animals*	*Pickles/ Edible Items*	*Surf/ Blue/ Phenoil*	*Sambar/ Rasam Powders*	*Petty Coats*	*Woolen Carpets*	*Fish Vend-ing*	*Sheep Rear-ing*	*Candle Making*	*Carpets*	*Basket Mak-ing*	*Cutpiece & Saree Selling*	*Leaf Plate Mak-ing*	*Kiranam/ Sale of Ag. Prod*	*Veg./ Fruit Vend-ing*	*Wire Baskets*	*Others*	*Total*
Koratla Gudem	20	–	–	–	–	–	–	–	–	–	–	–	–	–	–	–	–	–	–	20 (6.7)
Burangutta Thanda	–	7	5	–	–	–	–	–	–	–	–	–	–	–	–	–	–	–	–	12 (4.0)
Pusala Padu	–	–	–	15	–	–	–	–	–	–	–	–	–	–	–	–	–	–	–	15 (5.0)
Nayakan Gudem	–	–	–	–	15	–	–	–	–	–	–	–	–	–	–	–	–	–	–	15 (5.0)
Nelakonda Pally	–	–	–	–	–	14	–	–	–	–	–	–	–	–	–	–	–	–	–	14 (4.7)
Jeevanchi Pally	–	–	–	–	–	–	15	–	–	–	–	–	–	–	–	–	–	–	–	15 (5.0)
Garla	–	–	–	–	–	–	–	5	6	–	–	–	–	–	–	–	–	–	–	11 (3.7)
Bayyaram	–	–	–	3	–	–	–	–	–	18	–	–	–	–	–	–	–	–	–	21 (7.0)
Balapeta Thanda	–	–	–	–	–	–	–	–	–	–	8	–	–	–	–	–	–	–	–	8 (2.7)
Teldar Pally	–	–	–	–	–	–	–	–	–	–	–	12	–	–	–	–	–	–	–	12 (4.0)
Balapeta	–	–	–	–	–	–	–	–	–	–	7	–	–	–	–	–	–	–	–	7 (2.3)
Enkur	–	–	–	–	–	–	–	–	–	–	–	–	22	–	–	–	–	–	–	22 (7.3)

Contd....

Table 3.1 : (Contd....)

Village	*Baniyans Making*	*Veg. Culti-Vation*	*Milch Animals*	*Pickles/ Edible Items*	*Surf/ Blue/ Phenoil*	*Sambar/ Rasam Powders*	*Petty Coats*	*Woolen Carpets*	*Fish Vend-ing*	*Sheep Rear-ing*	*Candle Making*	*Carpets*	*Basket Mak-ing*	*Cutpiece & Saree Selling*	*Leaf Plate Mak-ing*	*Kiranam/ Sale of Ag. Prod*	*Veg./ Fruit Vend-ing*	*Wire Baskets*	*Others*	*Total*
Panduranga Puram	–	–	–	3	–	–	5	5	1	–	–	–	–	6	1	3	2	–	2	28 (9.3)
Karepally	–	–	–	–	–	–	–	–	–	–	–	–	–	–	–	–	–	5	–	5 (1.7)
Gampala Gudem	–	–	–	–	–	–	2	–	–	–	–	–	–	–	–	8	–	–	–	10 (3.3)
Jakke Pally	–	–	18	–	–	–	–	–	–	–	–	–	–	–	–	–	–	–	–	18 (6.0)
Perika Singaram	–	–	11	–	–	–	–	–	–	–	–	–	–	–	–	–	–	–	–	11 (3.7)
Jeella Cheruvu	–	4	–	–	–	–	1	–	–	–	–	–	–	–	–	–	–	–	–	5 (1.7)
Keshava Puram	–	4	–	–	2	–	1	–	–	–	–	–	–	–	–	2	–	–	2	11 (3.7)
Gopavaram	–	–	–	–	–	–	–	–	–	–	–	–	–	4	–	1	–	–	1	6 (2.0)
Muthayalam Padu	–	1	–	4	–	–	2	–	–	–	–	–	–	–	1	2	–	–	4	14 (4.7)
Gattu Singaram	–	1	–	–	–	–	2	–	–	–	–	–	–	1	1	–	–	–	–	5 (1.7)
Yellandu	–	–	–	–	–	–	–	–	–	–	–	–	–	–	15	–	–	–	–	15
TOTAL	20 (6.7)	17 (5.7)	34 (11.3)	25 (8.3)	17 (5.7)	14 (4.7)	28 (9.3)	10 (3.3)	7 (2.3)	18 (6.0)	15 (5.0)	12 (4.0)	22 (7.3)	10 (3.3)	18 (6.0)	17 (5.7)	2 (0.7)	5 (1.7)	9 (3.0)	300 (100.0)

Source : Field Study.

making, production of Surf, Blue & Phenoil, Woolen Carpets, Candles, Carpets, Baskets, Wyre Baskets, Leaf Plates iv) Tailoring and v) Business activities inclusive of Fish vending, Vegetable & Fruit vending, sale of cut-pieces and sarees, Kiranam and sale of agriculture products.

The village wise distribution of sample in Khammam district shows that the highest number of respondents of 28 out of 300 is drawn from the village Pandu Rangapuram in which 9 trades are found which is followed by Enkur from which 22 beneficiaries are drawn and all the beneficiaries are only from one trade i.e., Basket making and least number of beneficiaries are from the villages of Karepally, Jeellacheruvu and Gattu Singaram. Thus, the village-wise distribution of beneficiaries has varied between 28 and 5.

The data pertaining to trade-wise distribution of sample respondents from Khammam district indicate that as high as 34 number of beneficiaries are found in the trade Milch animals followed by Tailoring activity and third place occupied by Pickles/ Edible items making while only two beneficiaries are found in the trade of vegetable and fruit vending. Thus, the trade-wise distribution of sample has varied between 34 and 2

(ii) Caste-wise Distribution of Selected Respondents

The data in regard to caste-wise distribution of selected sample in Khammam district have been presented in Table-3.2.

The caste-wise distribution of sample respondents indicates that the highest number i.e., 157 beneficiaries are from Backward Classes followed by 75 beneficiaries are from Forward Castes, third place i.e., 47 beneficiaries are from Scheduled Tribes while 21 are from Scheduled Castes.It can be observed from Table-3.2 that the beneficiaries who belonged to Backward Classes can be found in 17 activities out of 19 selected trades. They are not seen in the activity of carpet making and Wyre Basket making. However, trade-wise distribution of Backward Class beneficiaries is not uniform. The highest number of 23 beneficiaries are found in Tailoring followed by 15 each in Baniyans making and Leaf Plate making

Table 3.2 Trade & Caste-wise Distribution of Selected Respondents In Khammam District

Trade	*F C*	*B C*	*S C*	*S T*	*Total*
Baniyans Making	5 (6.7)	15 (9.6)	–	–	20 (6.7)
Veg. Cultivation	3 (4.0)	7 (4.5)	–	7 (14.9)	17 (5.7)
Milch Animals	14 (18.7)	14 (8.9)	1 (4.8)	5 (10.6)	34 (11.3)
Pickles/ Edible items	15 (20.0)	10 (6.4)	–	–	25 (8.3)
Surf/ Blue/ Phenoil	4 (5.3)	13 (8.3)	–	–	17 (5.7)
Sambar/ Rasam Powders	9 (12.0)	5 (3.2)	–	–	14 (4.7)
Tailoring	2 (2.7)	23 (14.6)	2 (9.5)	1 (2.1)	28 (9.3)
Woolen works	2 (2.7)	8 (5.1)	–	–	10 (3.3)
Fish Vending	–	7 (4.5)	–	–	7 (2.3)
Sheep Rearing	8 (10.7)	10 (6.4)	–	–	18 (6.0)

Contd....

Table 3.2 (Contd....)

Trade	*F C*	*B C*	*S C*	*S T*	*Total*
Candle Making	5 (6.7)	2 (1.3)	–	8 (17.0)	15 (5.0)
Carpets	–	–	12 (57.1)	–	12 (4.0)
Basket Making	–	3 (1.9)	–	19 (40.4)	22 (7.3)
Cut Pieces/Saries Selling	2 (2.6)	8 (5.1)	–	–	10 (3.3)
Leaf Plate Making	2 (2.7)	15 (9.6)	–	1 (2.1)	18 (6.0)
Kiranam/Sale of Agri. products	2 (2.7)	10 (6.4)	1 (4.8)	4 (8.6)	17 (5.7)
Veg/ Fruit vending	–	2 (1.3)	–	–	2 (0.7)
Wire Baskets	–	–	5 (23.8)	–	5 (1.7)
Others	2 (2.7)	5 (3.2)	–	2 (4.3)	9 (3.0)
TOTAL	75 (25.0)	157 (52.3)	21 (7.0)	47 (15.7)	300 (100.00)

Source : Field Study.

and only 2 beneficiaries each are observed in Candle making and Vegetable/ Fruit vending.

The Forward Caste beneficiaries are found in 14 trades out of 19 selected trades. However, 20 percent of them are in the activity of Pickles and Edible items preparation followed by the activity of Milch animals while Scheduled Tribe beneficiaries are found in 8 trades and as high as 40 percent of them are engaged in the activity of Basket making whereas Scheduled Caste beneficiaries are seen only in 5 trades. As high as 57 percent of them are in the activity of Carpet Making.Thus, the scope in terms of number of trades is relatively wider for Backward Classes followed by Forward Castes and last place in this regard is occupied by Scheduled Castes.

(iii) Village And Caste-wise Distribution of Selected Sample

The data in regard to the village and caste wise distribution of selected beneficiaries have been presented in Table-3.3.

It can be seen from Table-3.3, that as high as 28 beneficiaries are selected from the village Panduranga Puram followed by 22 in the village Enkur. The number of beneficiaries only 5 each in the villages Karepally, Jeellacheruvu and Gattu Singaram. Thus, the total number of beneficiaries 300 are distributed in the range of 5 to 28 in the selected 23 villages of Khammam district.

Further, caste-wise distribution of beneficiaries is also varies from village to village. The Backward Class respondents can be found in 19 out of 23 selected villages while Forward Caste respondents can be seen in 14 villages. A close observation of the table reveals that Scheduled Caste and Scheduled Tribe beneficiaries are seen in 5 out of 23 selected villages. Both Scheduled Caste and Scheduled Tribe beneficiaries can be seen in only one village called Gampala Gudem.

(iv) Caste And Category-wise Distribution of Selected Sample

The relationship between caste and category-wise distribution of selected respondents is shown in Table-3.4.

Table 3.3 : Village and Caste-wise Distribution of Selected Respondents in Khammam District

Village	*F C*	*B C*	*S C*	*S T*	*Total*
Koratla Gudem	5 (6.7)	15 (9.6)	–	–	20 (6.7)
Burangutta Thanda	–	–	–	12 (25.5)	12 (4.0)
Pusala Padu	12 (16.0)	3 (1.9)	–	–	15 (5.0)
Nayakan Gudem	2 (2.7)	13 (8.3)	–	–	15 (5.0)
Nelakonda Pally	9 (12.0)	5 (3.2)	–	–	14 (4.7)
Jeevanchi Pally	– (9.6)	15	–	–	15 (5.0)
Garla	–	11. (7.0)	–	–	11 (3.7)
Bayyaram	11 (14.7)	10 (6.4)	–	–	21 (7.0)
Balapeta Thanda	–	–	–	8 (17.0)	8 (2.7)
Theldar Pally	–	–	12 (57.1)	–	12 (4.0)
Balapeta	5 (6.7)	2 (1.3)	–	–	7 (2.3)
Enkoor	– (1.9)	3 (40.4)	–	19 (7.3)	22

Contd....

Table 3.3 : (Contd....)

Village	*F C*	*B C*	*S C*	*S T*	*Total*
Panduranga Puram	4 (5.3)	22 (14.0)	2 (9.5)	–	28 (9.3)
Karepally	–	–	5 (23.8)	–	5 (1.7)
Gampala Gudem	–	7 (4.5)	1 (4.8)	2 (4.3)	10 (3.3)
Jakke Pally	13 (17.3)	4 (2.5)	1 (4.8)	–	18 (6.0)
Perika Singaram	1 (1.3)	10 (6.4)	–	–	11 (3.7)
Jeela Cheruvu	–	5 (3.2)	–	–	5 (1.7)
Keshavapuram	6 (8.0)	5 (3.2)	–	–	11 (3.7)
Gopavaram	2 (2.7)	4 (2.5)	–	–	6 (2.0)
Muthyalam Padu	2 (2.7)	6 (3.8)	–	6 (12.8)	14 (4.7)
Gattu Singaram	1 (1.3)	4 (2.5)	–	–	5 (1.7)
Yellandu	2 (2.7)	13 (8.3)	–	–	15 (5.0)
TOTAL	75 (25.0)	157 (52.3)	21 (7.0)	47 (15.7)	300 (100.00)

Source : Field Study..

Table 3.4 : Caste & Category-wise Distribution of Selected Respondents in Khammam District

Category	*F C*	*B C*	*SC*	*ST*	*Total*
Small Farmers	30	12	3	8	53
	(40.0)	(7.6)	(14.3)	(17.0)	(17.7)
Marginal Farmers	27	38	3	19	87
	(36.0)	(24.2)	(14.3)	(40.4)	(29.0)
Agri. Labourers	9	17	8	7	41
	(12.0)	(10.8)	(38.1)	(14.9)	(13.7)
Non-Agri. Labourers	1	14	22	2	19
	(1.3)	(8.9)	(9.5)	(4.3)	(6.3)
Rural Artisans	—	51	—	10	61
		(32.5)		(21.3)	(20.3)
Others	8	25	5	1	39
	(10.7)	(15.9)	(23.8)	(2.1)	(13.0)
TOTAL	75	157	21	47	300
	(100.0)	(100.0)	(100.0)	(100.0)	(100.00)

Source : Field Study.

The data clearly indicates that the sample is dominated by Marginal Farmers where 87 out of 300 respondents belonged to the category of Marginal Farmers which is followed by Rural Artisans and third place goes to Small Farmers while only 6.3 percent of sample respondents are from the category of Non-Agricultural Labourers.

The data in regard to caste and category of the respondents indicate that 40 percent of Forward Caste respondents are from the category of Small Farmer while as high as 32.5 percent of the Backward Class respondents belonged to Rural Artisans, where as 38.1 percent of the Scheduled Caste respondents are from the category of Agricultural Labour and 40.4 percent of Scheduled Tribe respondents are from the category of Marginal Farmers. Thus, a close relationship is observed between caste and category.

(v) Trade and Category-wise Distribution of Selected Sample

The data are also elicited to find out the relationship between category of the respondent and selection of trade and the relevant data are presented in Table-3.5.

Table 3.5 : Trade and Category-wise Distribution of Selected Respondents in Khammam District

Trade	*S F*	*M F*	*A L*	*N A L*	*R A*	*Others*	*Total*
Baniyans Making	3	5	3	1	7	1	20
	(5.7)	(5.7)	(7.3)	(5.3)	(11.5)	(2.6)	(6.7)
Veg. Cultivation	3	14	–	–	–	–	17
	(5.7)	(16.1)					(5.7)
Milch Animals	12	16	3	–	3	–	34
	(22.6)	(18.4)	(7.3)		(4.9)		(11.3)
Pickles/Edible items	14	6	3	1	1	–	25
	(26.4)	(6.9)	(7.3)	(5.3)	(1.6)		(8.3)
Surf/ Blue/ Phenoil	5	2	–	3	1	6	17
	(9.4)	(2.3)		(15.8)	(1.6)	(15.4)	(5.7)
Sambar/ Rasam Powders	2	7	–	–	2	3	14
	(3.8)	(8.0)			(3.3)	(7.7)	(4.7)
Tailoring	–	7	4	–	13	4	28
		(8.0)	(9.7)	(21.3)		(10.2)	(9.3)
Woolen works	–	–	–	1	2	7	10
				(5.3)	(3.3)	(17.9)	(3.3)
Fish Vending	–	–	2	–	3	2	7
			(4.9)		(4.9)	(5.1)	(2.3)
Sheep Rearing	2	5	4	–	7	–	18
	(3.8)	(5.7)	(9.8)		(11.5)		(6.0)

Contd....

Table 3.5 : (Contd....)

Trade	*S F*	*M F*	*A L*	*N A L*	*R A*	*Others*	*Total*
Candle Making	2	5	6	–	1	1	15
	(3.8)	(5.7)	(14.6)		(1.6)	(2.6)	(5.0)
Carpets	2	2	5	2	–	1	12
	(3.8)	(2.3)	(12.2)	(10.5)		(2.6)	(4.0)
Basket Making	3	6	–	–	13	–	22
	(5.7)	(6.9)			(21.3)		(7.3)
Cut Pieces/Sarries Selling	–	2	1	3	3	1	10
		(2.3)	(2.4)	(15.8)	(4.9)	(2.6)	(3.3)
Leaf Plate Making	–	4	6	3	1	4	18
		(4.6)	(14.6)	(15.8)	(1.6)	(10.3)	(6.0)
Kiranam/Sale of Agri. products	3	4	1	3	2	4	17
	(5.7)	(4.6)	(2.4)	(15.8)	(3.3)	(10.3)	(5.7)
Veg/ Fruit vending	–	–	–	2	–	–	2
				(10.5)			(0.7)
Wire Baskets	–	–	2	–	–	3	5
			(4.9)			(7.7)	(1.7)
Others	2	2	1	–	2	2	9
	(3.8)	(2.3)	(2.4)		(3.3)	(5.1)	(3.0)
TOTAL	53	87	41	19	61	39	300
	(100.0)	(100.0)	(100.0)	(100.0)	(100.0)	(100.0)	(100.00)

Source : Field Study.

It can be seen from Table-3.5 that the distribution of Small Farmers among various trades is in the range of 3.8 and 26.4 percent. Thus, 14 out of 53 Small Farmers have selected the trade Pickles/ Edible items and 12 respondents are found in the trade - Milch Animals. As high as 16 Marginal Farmers have selected the trade Milch animals followed by 14 in Vegetable Cultivation. The category of Agricultural labour is found in 13 trades. However, 6 each found in the schemes of Candle Making and Kiranam and Sale of Agricultural products while 21.1 percent of Non-Agricultural Labourers are also seen in this trade. In the case of Rural Artisans, 26.2 percent of them are in the scheme of Cut-pieces and Sarees selling and which is followed by 21.3 percent in Tailoring.

Thus, in Agriculture and Allied activities like Vegetable Cultivation and Milch Animals, the category of Small Farmers and Marginal Farmers are observed while the majority of Agricultural Labour and Non-Agricultural Labour have selected the schemes related to business activity and the majority of Rural Artisans have selected Tailoring i.e., the activity related to Service sector. Interestingly, all the categories are found only in two schemes Baniyans Making, Kiranam and sale of Agricultural products.

Socio-economic Profile of Selected Respondents in Khammam District

The information in regard to the socio-economic background of selected respondents is presented in Table-3.6.

It can be noticed from Table-3.6 that 43.3 percent of the respondents are in the age group of 20-30 years which is followed by 40.3 percent in the age group of 31-40 years. Only 2.3 percent of the respondents are in the age group of 50 years and above.

The caste-wise distribution of sample reveals that 52.3 percent of the sample belongs to Backward Classes followed by 25 percent to Forward Castes and Scheduled Tribes are in the third place with 15.7 percent and last place goes to Scheduled Castes with 7 percent.

Table - 3.6 : Socio-economic Background of Selected Respondents in Khammam District

AGE	*No. of Respondents*	*% to Total*
20 - 30	130	43.3
31 - 40	121	40.3
41 - 50	42	14.0
Above 50	7	2.3
TOTAL	300	(100.0)
CASTE	*No. of Respondentds*	*% to Total*
F C	75	25.0
B C	157	52.3
S C	21	7.0
S T	47	15.7
TOTAL	300	(100.0)
EDN. QUALI.	*No. of Respondentds*	*% to Total*
Illiterate	116	38.7
Primary	129	43.0
Secondary	42	14.0
Intermediate	11	3.7
Degree	2	0.7
TOTAL	300	(100.0)

Contd....

Table - 3.6 : (Contd...)

MARITAL STATUS	*No. of Respondents*	*% to Total*
Married	274	91.3
Un-married	–	–
Divorced	5	1.7
Seperated	1	0.3
Widowed	20	6.7
TOTAL	300	(100.0)
PRIMARY OCCU.	*No. of Respondentds*	*% to Total*
Agriculture	103	34.3
Agri. Labourers	43	14.3
Non-Agri. Labourers	17	5.7
Rural Artisans	36	12.0
Business	16	5.3
Tailoring	33	11.0
House Wives	26	8.7
Others	26	8.7
TOTAL	300	(100.0)

Contd....

Table - 3.6 : (Contd....)

SEC. OCCU.	*No. of Respondentds*	*% to Total*
Agriculture	37	12.3
Agri. Labourers	94	31.3
Non-Agri. Labourers	19	6.3
Rural Artisans	49	16.3
Business	14	4.7
Tailoring	27	9.0
House Wives	32	10.7
Others	28	9.3
TOTAL	300	(100.0)

Source : Field Study.

The data in regard to educational qualification indicates that 43 percent of the respondents could study upto primary level. As high as 38.7 percent of the sample are illiterates and only 2 out of 300 selected respondents could study upto degree level. On the whole, 81.7 percent of the sample have less than primary level education.

The information as to the marital status of respondents shows that 91.3 percent of sample are married and remaining 8.7 percent are distributed among the marital status of divorced, separated and widowed in the range of 0.3 to 6.7 percent.

It can also be noticed that the primary occupation of 34.3 percent of the sample respondents is Agriculture followed by 14.3 in Agricultural Labourers. The data in regard to the secondary occupation of the sample respondents show that 31.3 percent are in Agricultural Labourers which is followed by the occupation Rural Artisans, while Business occupies least position in the primary as well as secondary occupation.

Relationship Between Caste and Educational Qualifications

The information pertaining to caste and educational qualifications of the selected respondents is presented in Table 3.7.

It can be seen from Table-3.7 that Forward Caste respondents could get the opportunity to have degree level education and no other caste respondents found in this level. Contrastingly, Scheduled Tribe respondents could not go beyond secondary level education. Moreover, 42.9 percent of the Scheduled Caste respondents, 63.8 percent of the Scheduled Tribe respondents are illiterates while it is 37.6 percent in Backward Classes and only 24 percent in Forward Caste. Thus, illiteracy is more pronounced in Scheduled Tribes followed by Scheduled Castes. However, 45.9 percent of the Backward Class respondents could get upto primary level education. Thus, caste plays an important role in the determination of their level of education.

Relationship Between Caste and Family Size

The data in regard to the relationship between caste and size of the family are shown in Table-3.8.

Table 3.7 ; Relationship Between Caste and Educational Qualifications of The Selected Respondents In Khammam District

Caste	*Illiterate*	*Primary*	*Secondary*	*Intermediate*	*Degree*	*Total*
F C	18	37	13	5	2	75
	(24.0)	(49.3)	(17.3)	(6.7)	(2.7)	(100.0)
B C	59	72	22	4	–	157
	(37.6)	(45.9)	(14.0)	(2.5)		(100.0)
S C	9	6	4	2	–	21
	(42.9)	(28.6)	(19.0)	(9.5)		(100.0)
S T	30	14	3	–	–	47
	(63.8)	(29.8)	(6.4)			(100.0)
TOTAL	116	129	42	11	2	300
	(38.7)	(43.0)	(14.0)	(3.7)	(0.7)	(100.0)

Source : Field Study.

Table 3.8 : Relationship Between Caste & Family Size of The Selected Respondents In Khammam District

Caste	*1 - 2*	*3 - 4*	*5 - 6*	*Above 6*	*Total*
F C	9	43	19	4	75
	(12.0)	(57.3)	(25.3)	(5.3)	(100.0)
B C	18	79	53	7	157
	(11.5)	(50.3)	(33.8)	(4.5)	(100.0)
S C	–	10	10	1	21
		(47.6)	(47.6)	(4.8)	(100.0)
S T	4	20	12	11	47
	(8.5)	(42.6)	(25.5)	(23.4)	(100.0)
TOTAL	31	152	94	23	300
	(10.3)	(50.7)	(31.3)	(7.7)	(100.0)

Source : Field Study.

It can be seen from Table-3.8 that the size of the family is in the range of 3-4 for 50.7 percent of the sample followed by 5-6 for 31.3 percent of the sample. The size of the family is 7 and above only for 7.7 percent of the sample.

The caste-wise analysis indicates that 57.3 percent of the Forward Caste respondents are having the size of the family in the range of 3-4 followed by 25.3 percent in the range of 5-6.

Thus, 82.6 percent of the Forward Caste respondents are having the family size in the range of 3-6 and the size of the family is large only for 5.3 percent of them. Similar position can be seen even for the respondents belonged to Backward Classes and Scheduled Caste. However, a different picture can be noticed as regards Scheduled Tribe beneficiaries where 23.4 percent of them are having the large size of the family.

Relationship Between Caste and Economic Assets

The information in regard to the relationship between caste and the house possession of the sample is presented in Table-3.9. It can be noticed from the table that 45 percent of the respondents could possess Pucca houses and 26.3 percent of the sample are having RCC houses while 25.7 of the sample are having only Kutcha houses.

Table 3.9 : Relationship Between Caste & House Possession of the Selected Respondents in Khammam District

Caste	*Kutcha*	*Pucca*	*R C C*	*Rented*	*Total*
F C	20	30	24	1	75
	(26.7)	(40.0)	(32.0)	(1.3)	(100.0)
B C	43	82	24	8	157
	(27.4)	(52.2)	(15.3)	(5.1)	(100.0)
S C	6	8	7	–	21
	(28.6)	(38.1)	(33.3)		(100.0)
S T	8	15	24	–	47
		(17.0)	(31.9)	(51.1)	(100.0)
TOTAL	77	135	79	9	300
	(25.7)	(45.0)	(26.3)	(3.0)	(100.0)

Source : Field Study.

The caste wise analysis indicates that 72 percent of the Backward Caste respondents could possess either Pucca or RCC houses. Similar position can be seen even for remaining caste respondents. It is interesting to notice that 51.1 percent of the Scheduled Tribe respondents could possess RCC houses. Thus, Scheduled Tribes stood first in regard to the possession of RCC houses. Contrastingly, they were the least in regard to Kutcha houses.

The information in regard to the relationship between caste and source of house possession is presented in Table-3.10.

Table 3.10 : Relationship Between Caste & Source of House Possession of The Selected Respondents in Khammam District

Caste	*Parents*	*Govt.*	*Own*	*Others*	*Total*
F C	22	2	50	1	75
	(29.3)	(2.7)	(66.7)	(1.3)	(100.0)
B C	48	17	84	8	157
	(30.6)	(10.8)	(53.5)	(5.0)	(100.0)
S C	3	9	9	–	21
	(14.3)	(42.9)	(42.9)		(100.0)
S T	3	30	14	–	47
	(6.4)	(63.8)	(29.8)		(100.0)
TOTAL	76	58	157	9	300
	(25.3)	(19.3)	(52.3)	(3.0)	(100.0)

Source : Field Study.

It can be observed from Table-3.10 that 52.3 percent of sample respondents could possess the house through own sources while 25.3 percent of the respondents could acquire the house from parents where as 19.3 percent could get the house from government. It can be noticed that 66.7 percent of the Forward Caste respondents could construct the houses through own sources and 29 percent could acquire from parents and only 2.3 percent of them could get the house from the government. The percentage of beneficiaries who get benefit from the government for house purpose is on the rise when we move from Forward Caste to Scheduled Tribes. Thus, 63.8 percent of Scheduled Tribe respondents could get benefit from government. Contrastingly, the percentage of beneficiaries who acquired house either from parents or from own sources is on the decline when we move from Forward Caste to Scheduled Tribes.

The information in regard to the caste and asset position of the sample is placed in Table-3.11.

Table 3.11 : Relationship Between Caste & Assets Position of the Selected Respondents in Khammam District

(Asset value in Rs.)

Caste	*Below 1000*	*1001-3000*	*3001-5000*	*5001-10000*	*10001-15000*	*Above 15000*	*Total*
F C	1	19	15	18	13	9	75
	(1.3)	(25.3)	(20.0)	(24.0)	(17.3)	(12.0)	(100.0)
B C	7	71	38	26	10	5	157
	(4.5)	(45.2)	(24.2)	(16.6)	(6.4)	(3.2)	(100.0)
S C	2	5	9	4	1	–	21
	(9.5)	(23.8)	(42.9)	(19.0)	(4.8)		(100.0)
S T	4	14	16	7	5	1	47
	(8.5)	(29.8)	(34.0)	(14.9)	(10.6)	(2.1)	(100.0)
TOTAL	14	109	78	55	29	15	300
	(4.7)	(36.3)	(26.0)	(18.3)	(9.7)	(5.0)	(100.0)

Source : Field Study.

It can be seen from Table-3.11, that 36.3 percent of the sample respondents are having the assets in the range of Rs. 1001-3000 followed by 26 percent in the range of Rs. 3001-5000. As the asset amount increases, the percentage of respondents who fall in that range decreases. Thus, only 5 percent are in the range of rupees more than 15000. The caste-wise analysis shows that Forward Caste respondents can be seen in all the ranges of asset amount with minor variations while Backward Class respondents are also appeared in all the ranges of assets but the percentage of beneficiaries in different ranges show a wide variation. Therefore, 45.2 percent of them are found in the range of Rs. 1001-3000 and only 3.2 percent of them are found in rupees above 15000 while no Scheduled Caste respondents can be seen in this range and more than 75 percent of the Scheduled Caste respondents are having the assets less than Rs.3001-5000. Similar picture can be seen even in regard to Scheduled Tribe respondents.

Relationship Between Caste and Savings

The information in regard to the relationship between caste and savings position is presented in Table-3.12.

Table 3.12 : Relationship Between Caste & Savings Position of the Selected Respondents in Khammam District

Caste	*Yes*	*No*	*Total*
F C	46	29	75
	(61.3)	(38.7)	(100.0)
B C	52	105	157
	(33.1)	(66.9)	(100.0)
S C	8	13	21
	(38.0)	(62.0)	(100.0)
S T	17	30	47
	(36.2)	(63.8)	(100.0)
TOTAL	123	177	300
	(41.0)	(59.0)	(100.0)

Source : Field Study.

It can be seen from Table-3.12 that 41 percent of the respondents are able to save part of their income. The caste-wise analysis indicates that 61.3 percent of Forward Caste respondents, 33.1 percent of the Backward Class respondents, 38 percent of Schedule Caste respondents and 36.2 percent of Scheduled Tribe respondents are in a position to save some amount.

The information in regard to caste wise analysis pertaining to savings in various sources is depicted in Table-3.13.

It can be seen from Table-3.13 that 39 percent of the respondents are keeping their savings in banks while 37.4 percent are in Chits 17 percent are in Post-Offices and only 6.5 percent are approaching LIC. The priority given to different sources by Forward Caste respondents and Backward Class respondents coincides with the total picture. The data in regard to Scheduled Caste respondents indicate that 75 percent of them are keeping their savings in chits while 25 percent are in banks. Similarly, 47 percent of Scheduled Tribe respondents are also giving preference to chits.

The information in regard to the amount saved by selected respondents is illustrated in Table-3.14.

Table 3.13 : Caste & Savings in Various Institutions of the Selected Respondents in Khammam District

Caste	*Chits*	*L I C*	*Banks*	*Post-office*	*Total*
F C	17	4	18	7	46
	(38.9)	(8.7)	(39.1)	(15.2)	(100.0)
B C	15	3	23	11	52
	(28.8)	(5.8)	(44.2)	(21.2)	(100.0)
S C	6	–	2	–	8
	(75.0)		(25.0)		(100.0)
S T	8	1	5	3	17
	(47.0)	(5.9)	(29.4)	(17.6)	(100.0)
TOTAL	46	8	48	21	123
	(37.4)	(6.5)	(39.0)	(17.0)	(100.0)

Source : Field Study.

It can be seen from Table 3.14 that the amount saved by the selected respondents has varied between less than Rs. 1,000-20,000. However, 86.2 percent of the respondents could save upto Rs. 10,000 only. Of the remaining 13.8 percent, only 4.9 percent could save beyond Rs. 15,000. Except Scheduled Castes all the remaining caste respondents can be seen in this range. However, the percentage of Forward Caste respondents are more followed by Backward Classes respondents.

Table 3.14 : Caste and Amount Saved By Selected Respondents in Khammam District

(Amount in Rs.)

Caste	*Below 1000*	*1001-3000*	*3001-5000*	*5001-10000*	*10001-15000*	*Above 15000*	*Total*
F C	2	8	12	15	5	4	46
	(4.3)	(17.3)	(26.0)	(32.7)	(10.9)	(8.7)	(100.0)
B C	7	18	11	9	6	1	52
	(13.5)	(34.7)	(21.1)	(17.3)	(11.5)	(2.0)	(100.0)
S C	1	4	2	1	–	–	8
	(12.5)	(50.0)	(25.0)	(12.5)			(100.0)
S T	4	2	6	4	–	1	17
	(23.5)	(11.8)	(35.3)	(23.5)		(5.9)	(100.0)
TOTAL	14	32	31	29	11	6	123
	(11.4)	(26.0)	(25.2)	(23.6)	(8.9)	(4.9)	(100.0)

Source : Field Study.

Selection of Trade

As the selected respondents are economically poor, educationally backward and ignorant of economic environment, they will not be in a position to select suitable trade. Therefore, they seek help from different officials VDO, MPDO, DRDA officials, bank officials and others. The relevant information is shown in Table-3.15.

It can be seen from Table-3.15 that only 21.31 percent of respondents could take decision on their own as to the selection

Table 3.15 : Selection of the Trade by the Selected Respondents in Khammam District

Trade	*Own*	*Vdo/ MPDO*	*DRDA Offi-cials*	*Bank Offi-cials*	*Group Leader/ Others*	*Total*
Baniyans Making	–	5	11	–	4	20
Veg. Cultivation	9	7	–	–	1	17
Milch Animals	7	11	4	9	3	34
Pickles/ Edible items	–	3	16	–	6	25
Surf/ Blue/ Phenoil	–	–	14	–	3	17
Sambar/ Rasam Powders	–	–	8	–	6	14
Tailoring	15	10	3	–	–	28
Woolen works	–	–	7	–	3	10
Fish Vending	4	3	–	–	–	7
Sheep Rearing	3	3	–	12	–	18
Candle Making	–	3	10	–	2	15
Carpets	–	–	–	–	12	12
Basket Making	13	5	4	–	–	22
Cut Pieces/ Sarees Selling	4	4	2	–	–	10
Leaf Plate Making	–	–	13	–	5	18
Kiranam/ Sale of Agri. products	5	8	1	–	3	17
Veg/ Fruit vending	2	–	–	–	–	2
Wire Baskets	–	2	3	–	–	5
Others	5	1	2	–	1	9
TOTAL	67 (22.3)	65 (21.7)	98 (32.7)	21 (7.0)	49 (16.3)	300 (100.00)

Source : Field Study.

of trade. The DRDA officials have extended help to as many as 98 respondents out of 300 in regard to the selection of trade & VDO's and MPDO's have extended help to 65 respondents.

The scheme-wise analysis did not show any specific relation between type of trade and recommended agency.

Problems of Trade

The problems in operating the scheme are usually related to two major areas - procurement of raw-materials and marketing of the product. Therefore, the data are elicited in this regard. The information pertaining to problems in the procurement of raw-materials is presented in Table-3.16.

Table 3.16 : Problems in the Procurement of Raw-material by the Selected Respondents in Khammam District

Trade	*Yes*	*No*	*Total*
Baniyans Making	14	6	20
Veg. Cultivation	–	17	17
Milch Animals	7	27	34
Pickles/ Edible items	4	21	25
Surf/ Blue/ Phenoil	11	6	17
Sambar/ Rasam Powders	–	14	14
Tailoring	4	24	28
Woolen works	–	10	10
Fish Vending	2	5	7
Sheep Rearing	–	18	18
Candle Making	4	11	15
Carpets	–	12	12
Basket Making	17	5	22
Cut Pieces/ Sarries Selling	6	4	10
Leaf Plate Making	13	5	18
Kiranam/ Sale of Agri. products	–	17	17
Veg/ Fruit vending	–	2	2
Wire Baskets	–	5	5
Others	3	6	9
TOTAL	85 (28.3)	215 (71.7)	300 (100.00)

Source : Field Study.

It can be seen from Table-3.16 that only 28.3 percent of the sample respondents are facing the problems in regard to the procurement of raw-material. In the case of 11 trades out of 19 selected trades, the respondents are facing raw-material problem. They are Baniyans Making, Milch Animals, Pickles/ Edible Items, Surf/Blue/Phenoil, Tailoring, Fish Vending, Candle Making, Basket Making, Cut-Pieces Selling, Leaf Plate Making and Others. Further, more number of respondents are facing the problem of raw-material in 4 trades - 17 in Basket Making, 14 in Baniyans Making, 14 in Leaf Plate making, 11 in Surf/ Blue/ Phenoil.

Marketing of The Product

To facilitate marketing of the product produced under various schemes of DWCRA, the DRDA organises DWCRA bazars. Therefore, the respondents have the opportunity to sell the product through DWCRA bazars also. The information about this aspect is shown in Table-3.17.

It can be observed from Table-3.17 that 22 percent of the respondents sell their product only through DWCRA bazars. They are 18 in Pickles/ Edible Items, 10 in Sambar/ Rasam Powder 10 in Woolen Works, 12 in Candle Making, 9 in Carpets, 2 in Cut-pieces and Sarees selling and 5 in Wire Baskets. Thus, 66 respondents out of selected 300 exclusively sell their product through DWCRA bazar. It can also be noticed from the table that 127 respondents sell their product on their own. This indicates that these people would not use the opportunity of DWCRA bazars. However, 107 respondents who constitute 35.7 percent of the sample used to sell the product in both ways i.e., DWCRA bazars as well as own.

The information in regard to the marketing problems of the selected respondents is presented in Table-3.18.

Table-3.18 indicates that 191 respondents i.e., 63.7 percent of the sample do not face any problems in regard to the marketing of the product while remaining 36.3 of the sample are facing marketing problem. The information in regard to the nature of the marketing problem is shown in Table-3.19.

Table 3.17 : Marketing of the Product by the Selected Respondents in Khammam District

Trade	*DWCRA Bazar*	*Own*	*Both*	*Total*
Baniyans Making	–	2	18	20
Veg. Cultivation	–	17	–	17
Milch Animals	–	34	–	34
Pickles/ Edible items	18	–	7	25
Surf/ Blue/ Phenoil	–	2	15	17
Sambar/ Rasam Powders	10	1	3	14
Tailoring	–	17	11	28
Woolen works	10	–	–	10
Fish Vending	–	7	–	7
Sheep Rearing	–	18	–	18
Candle Making	12	–	3	15
Carpets	9	–	3	12
Basket Making	–	4	18	22
Cut Pieces/Sarries Selling	2	2	6	10
Leaf Plate Making	–	3	15	18
Kiranam/ Sale of Agri. products	–	9	8	17
Veg/ Fruit vending	–	2	–	2
Wire Baskets	5	–	–	5
Others	–	9	–	9
TOTAL	66 (22.0)	127 (42.3)	107 (35.7)	300 (100.00)

Source : Field Study.

Table 3.18 : Marketing Problems of the Selected Respondents in Khammam District

Trade	*Yes*	*No*	*Total*
Baniyans Making	16	4	20
Veg. Cultivation	–	17	17
Milch Animals	–	34	34
Pickles/ Edible items	9	16	25
Surf/ Blue/ Phenoil	4	13	17
Sambar/ Rasam Powders	5	9	14
Tailoring	3	25	28
Woolen works	10	–	10
Fish Vending	5	2	7
Sheep Rearing	–	18	18
Candle Making	15	–	15
Carpets	2	10	12
Basket Making	13	9	22
Cut Pieces/Sarries Selling	3	7	10
Leaf Plate Making	15	3	18
Kiranam/Sale of Agri. products	–	17	17
Veg/ Fruit vending	1	1	2
Wire Baskets	5	–	5
Others	3	6	9
TOTAL	109 (36.3)	191 (63.7)	300 (100.00)

Source : Field Study.

Table 3.19 : Nature of Marketing Problems of The Selected Respondents In Khammam District

Trade	*Inadequate Demand*	*Transport*	*Quality/Packing*	*Competition*	*Total*
Baniyans Making	2	11	2	1	16
Veg. Cultivation	–	–	–	–	–
Milch Animals	–	–	–	–	–
Pickles/ Edible items	3	–	2	4	9
Surf/ Blue/ Phenoil	3	–	1	–	4
Sambar/ Rasam Powders	2	–	3	–	5
Tailoring	–	3	–	–	3
Woolen works	8	–	–	2	10
Fish Vending	–	5	–	–	5
Sheep Rearing	–	–	–	–	–
Candle Making	11	–	4	–	15
Carpets	–	2	–	–	2
Basket Making	2	8	–	3	13
Cut Pieces/Sarries Selling	–	2	–	1	3
Leaf Plate Making	9	6	–	–	15
Kiranam/Sale of Agri. products	–	–	–	–	–
Veg/ Fruit vending	–	1	–	–	1
Wire Baskets	5	–	–	–	5
Others	1	–	–	2	3
TOTAL	46 (42.2)	38 (34.9)	12 (11.0)	13 (11.9)	109 (100.0)

Source : Field Study.

It can be denoted from Table-3.19 that 46 out of 109 respondents face problems due to inadequate of demand while transport is the problem for 38 respondents and lack of attractive package is creating problems to 12 respondents where as competition is a problem for 13 respondents.

The scheme wise analysis indicates that the respondents who operate Baniyans making scheme are facing all the four types of marketing problems. The respondents who are in the trade of Pickles/ Edible Items, Basket Making are facing problems due to inadequate demand, attractive package and competition. The inadequate demand and attractive package are the problems confronted by the schemes such as Surf/ Blue/ Phenoil, Sambar/Rasam Powder and Candle making. Transportation is the problem for the schemes of Petty Coats/ Tailoring, Fish Vending Carpets, Cut-Pieces selling and Vegetable/ Fruit Vending. The scheme of Woolen Works face problems due to inadequate demand and competition while inadequate demand and transport are the problems for Leaf Plate Making and lastly inadequate demand is the exclusive problem for Wire Baskets.

Comparative Analysis of Employment Generation

The main aim of DWCRA programme is to create employment to rural women to increase their earnings so as to improve the quality of life of poor rural women. Therefore, the success of the programme basically depend upon its ability to generate employment.

Scheme-wise Analysis of Employment Generation

The information in regard to Pre and Post-DWCRA employment assumes important as it indicates the success of the DWCRA programme in terms of creating employment. The relevant information is presented in Table-3.20.

Table-3.20 indicates the relationship between scheme and employment generation during pre and post DWCRA period. It can be observed that the average employment of the sample respondents in terms of number of days of employment per month was 15.17 during pre-DWCRA period. This has been

Table 3.20 : Scheme Wise Analysis Of Employment Generation During Pre & Post DWCRA Period In Khammam District

Trade	*Pre-DWCRA Employment*			*Post-DWCRA Employment*			*Difference of Avg. Employment*
	No. of Respondents	*Total Days*	*Avg. Emp (Days P.M)*	*No.of Respondents*	*Total Days*	*Avg.Emp (Days P.M)*	
Baniyans Making	19	290	15.26	20	553	27.65	12.39
Veg. Cultivation	17	305	17.94	17	457	26.88	8.94
Milch Animals	33	467	14.15	34	897	26.38	12.23
Pickles/Edible items	24	266	11.08	25	521	20.84	98.76
Surf/Blue/Phenoil	14	247	17.64	17	430	25.29	7.65
Sambar/Rasam Powders	5	45	9.00	14	243	17.35	8.35
Tailoring	25	314	12.56	28	620	22.14	9.58
Woolen works	6	110	18.33	10	163	16.30	-2.03
Fish Vending	7	140	20.00	7	210	30.00	10.00
Sheep Rearing	18	292	16.22	18	373	20.72	4.50
Candle Making	15	255	17.00	15	324	21.60	4.60
Carpets	12	190	15.83	12	280	23.33	7.50
Basket Making	22	375	17.04	22	508	23.09	6.05
Cut Pieces/Sarries Selling	10	142	14.20	10	233	23.30	9.10
Leaf Plate Making	15	188	12.53	18	398	22.11	9.58
Kiranam/Sale of Agri. products	15	260	17.33	17	390	26.00	8.67
Veg/ Fruit vending	2	30	15.00	2	45	22.50	7.50
Wire Baskets	5	75	15.00	5	121	24.20	9.20
Others	9	153	17.00	9	220	24.44	7.44
TOTAL	273	4144	15.17	300	6986	23.28	8.11

Source : Field Study.

increased to 23.28 days per month during post DWCRA period. Thus, rise in the employment due to the implementation of DWCRA is to the tune of 8.11 days of work per month. However, the scheme wise analysis indicates that the employment generation is not uniform in all the schemes and inter-scheme variation is noticed in this regard. The Pre-DWCRA employment in terms of number of days per month has varied between 9.00 in Sambar/ Rasam Powder and 20.00 in Fish Vending. During post-DWCRA period this has been in the range of 16.30 in Woolen Works and 30 in Fish Vending. It is interesting to note that the employment generation has exceeded 25 days per month during post-DWCRA period in the schemes of Baniyans Making, Vegetable Cultivation, Milch Animals, Surf/ Blue/ Phenoil Fish Vending and Kiranam and sale of Agricultural products. The difference in the employment generation during pre and post-DWCRA period is in the range of 4.50 in Sheep Rearing and 12.39 in Baniyans Making. Thus, on the whole there is a positive impact in all the schemes except in Woolen Works in terms of employment generation during post-DWCRA period. In this way, DWCRA programme is a success in Khammam district especially in fulfilling the objective of employment generation.

Relationship Between Caste and Employment Generation

The caste-wise analysis is also made to examine the success of DWCRA programme in terms of employment generation. The relevant information is presented in Table-3.21. The average employment during pre-DWCRA period is 15.17 per month. The average employment during pre-DWCRA period for Forward Caste and Backward Classes respondents is less than the average. However, the same for Scheduled Caste and Scheduled Tribe respondents is above the average. A close observation of the data further reveals that Scheduled Tribe respondents could stand first and Forward Caste respondents stand least in regard to pre-DWCRA employment. It is happy to note that post-DWCRA employment shows a rise for all the respondents irrespective of the caste but the rise is not uniform and inter-caste variation is noticed. Again Forward Caste respondents stand least and Scheduled Tribe

Table 3.21 : Caste-wise Analysis of Employment Generation During Pre & Post-DWCRA Period In Khammam District

Caste	*Pre-DWCRA Employment*			*Post-DWCRA Employment*			*Difference of Avg. Employment*
	No. of Respondents	*Total Days*	*Avg. Emp (Days P.M.)*	*No. of Respondents*	*Total Days*	*Avg. Emp (Days P.M.)*	
F C	60	818	13.63	75	1634	21.78	8.15
B C	146	2198	15.05	157	3690	23.50	8.45
S C	20	305	15.25	21	483	23.00	7.75
S T	47	823	17.51	47	1179	25.08	7.57
TOTAL	273	4144	15.17	300	6986	23.28	8.11

Source : Field Study.

respondents stand first in regard to post-DWCRA employment. Thus, Scheduled Tribe respondents could get employment to the tune of 25.08 days per month during post-DWCRA period.

Relationship Between Category & Employment Generation

The information in regard to the relationship between category and employment generation is shown in Table-3.22. The pre-DWCRA employment in terms of number of days of work per month has varied between 13.67 for Small Farmers and 19.73 for Others. However, this has increased for all the respondents irrespective of the category during post-DWCRA period. The employment generation during post-DWCRA period has varied between 21.41 for others and 25.05 days per month for Non-Agricultural Labourers. Therefore, the difference between Pre and Post DWCRA employment has varied between 1.68 for Others and 10.28 for Non-Agricultural Labourers.

Relationship Between Educational Qualifications and Employment Generation

The information in regard to the relationship between educational qualification and employment generation has been shown in Table-3.23. It can be noticed that the average employment in terms of number of days of employment per month is as high as 25.09 for illiterates and as the level of education increases the average employment has declined upto intermediate level. Interestingly, the employment generation has shown a rise for the respondents who could study upto degree level. Moreover, the difference between Pre and Post DWCRA employment is highest for the degree holders followed by illiterates. Thus, either no education or higher level education is resulting in the success of the scheme in terms of employment generation.

Relationship Between Age and Employment Generation

The information as to the relationship between age of the respondent and employment generation is presented in Table-

Table 3.22 : Category-wise Analysis of Employment Generation During Pre & Post-DWCRA Period in Khammam District

Category	*Pre-DWCRA Employment*			*Post-DWCRA Employment*			*Difference of Avg. Employment*
	No. of Respondents	*Total Days*	*Avg. Emp (Days P.M)*	*No. of Respondents*	*Total Days*	*Avg. Emp (Days P.M.)*	
Small Farmers	49	670	13.67	53	1235	23.30	9.63
Marginal Farmers	81	1223	15.09	87	2088	24.00	8.91
Agri. Labourers	38	565	14.86	41	932	22.73	7.87
Non-Agri. Labourers	18	266	14.77	19	476	25.05	10.28
Rural Artisans	61	907	14.86	61	1420	23.27	8.41
Others	26	513	19.73	39	835	21.41	1.68
TOTAL	273	4144	15.17	300	6986	23.28	8.11

Source : Field Study.

Table 3.23 : Educational Qualifications and Employment Generation During Pre & Post-DWCRA Period in Khammam District

Educational Qualifications	*Pre-DWCRA Employment*			*Post-DWCRA Employment*			*Difference of Avg. Employment*
	No. of Respondents	*Total Days*	*Avg. Emp (Days P.M)*	*No. of Respondents*	*Total Days*	*Avg. Emp (Days P.M.)*	
Illiterates	114	1792	15.71	116	2911	25.09	9.38
Primary	117	1742	14.88	129	2905	22.51	7.63
Secondary	34	465	13.67	42	898	21.38	7.71
Intermediate	6	120	20.00	11	226	20.54	0.54
Degree	2	25	12.50	2	46	23.00	10.50
TOTAL	273	4144	15.17	300	6986	23.28	8.11

Source : Field Study.

Table 3.24 : Relationship Between Age and Employment Generation During Pre & Post-DWCRA Period in Khammam District

Age	*Pre-DWCRA Employment*			*Post-DWCRA Employment*			*Difference of Avg. Employment*
	No. of Respondents	*Total Days*	*Avg. Emp (Days P.M)*	*No. of Respondents*	*Total Days*	*Avg. Emp (Days P.M.)*	
20 - 30	117	1866	15.94	130	3006	23.12	7.18
31 - 40	108	1575	14.58	121	2842	23.48	8.90
41 - 50	41	628	15.31	42	1004	23.90	8.59
Above 50	7	75	10.71	7	134	19.14	8.43
TOTAL	273	4144	15.17	300	6986	23.28	8.11

Source : Field Study.

3.24. It can be seen from the table-3.24 that the average employment has shown a small rise as age of the respondent increases from 20-30 years upto 50 years and a fall when the age of the respondent increases beyond 50 years. However, the difference between pre and post-DWCRA employment is highest for the age group of 31-40 years.

Employment Generation Exclusively From DWCRA

The information in regard to scheme wise analysis of employment generation is reported in Table-3.25.

It can be observed from Table-3.25 that 177 out of 300 respondents could get work less than 10 days per month and the remaining 123 are able to get employment to the extent of more than 11 days per month. Of them 23 are able to get work in the range of 16-20 days per month. Moreover, only 3 respondents are in a position to get more than 20 days employment per month. These 3 respondents belonged to the schemes of Baniyans Making, Surf/ Blue/ Phenoil and Sheep Rearing. Similarly, 23 respondents who get employment in the range of 16-20 days per month belonged to the schemes of Baniyans Making, Vegetable Cultivation, Milch Animals, Pickles/ Edible Items, Tailoring, Fish Vending, Sheep Rearing, Cut-Pieces and Sarees selling, Kiranam, sale of Agriculture products and Others. However, the scheme wise analysis did not reveal any specific relation between scheme and employment generation.

Consequential Employment Generation

The information in regard to scheme-wise generation of additional employment is presented in Table-3.26.The additional employment is generated in two ways, one for family members and two for others. In Khammam district the selected respondents could generate additional employment to 138 persons and out of them 88 are family members and 50 are others. The scheme-wise performance indicates that the additional employment generation is highest in Basket Making followed by Milch Animals.

Table 3.25 : Scheme Wise Analysis of Employment Generation From DWCRA in Khammam District

Trade	*Days Per Month*					*Total*
	Below 5	*6-10*	*11-15*	*16-20*	*Above 20*	
Baniyans Making	1	7	7	4	1	20
Veg. Cultivation	3	11	2	1	–	17
Milch Animals	2	6	22	4	–	34
Pickles/ Edible items	4	12	8	1	–	25
Surf/ Blue/ Phenoil	5	3	8	–	1	17
Sambar/ Rasam Powders	–	2	12	–	–	14
Tailoring	3	13	8	4	–	28
Woolen works	5	5	–	–	–	10
Fish Vending	3	–	2	2	–	7
Sheep Rearing	12	2	1	2	1	18
Candle Making	10	3	2	–	–	15
Carpets	1	9	2	–	–	12
Basket Making	11	7	4	–	–	22
Cut Pieces/Sarries Selling	2	4	3	1	–	10
Leaf Plate Making	–	7	11	–	–	18
Kiranam/Sale of Agri. products	8	4	3	2	–	17
Veg/ Fruit vending	1	1	–	–	–	2
Wire Baskets	1	2	2	–	–	5
Others	4	3	–	2	–	9
TOTAL	76 (25.3)	101 (33.7)	97 (32.3)	23 (7.7)	3 (1.0)	300 (100.0)

Source : Field Study.

Table 3.26 : Scheme-wise Analysis of Additional Employment Generation Under DWCRA in Khammam District

Trade	*Family Members*	*Other Members*	*Total*
Baniyans Making	4	2	6
Veg. Cultivation	17	—	17
Milch Animals	12	10	22
Pickles/ Edible items	5	6	11
Surf/ Blue/ Phenoil	1	3	4
Sambar/ Rasam Powders	2	3	5
Tailoring	11	5	16
Woolen works	1	—	1
Fish Vending	—	—	—
Sheep Rearing	4	8	12
Candle Making	—	—	—
Carpets	—	—	—
Basket Making	22	5	27
Cut Pieces/Sarries Selling	2	—	2
Leaf Plate Making	5	3	8
Kiranam/Sale of Agri. products	—	2	2
Veg/ Fruit vending	—	—	—
Wire Baskets	2	—	2
Others	—	3	3
TOTAL	88	50	138

Source : Field Study.

The data in regard to the relationship between caste and employment generation is shown in Table-3.27.

It can be observed that the Forward Caste respondents are seen in all the ranges of employment generation from more than 5 days to more than 20 days per month. However, 32 Forward Caste respondents could generate additional employment due to DWCRA between 11 to 15 days per month. The Backward Class and Scheduled Tribe respondents could not generate employment beyond 20 days per month and for Scheduled Caste respondents the upper limit is only 11 to 15 days per month.

Impact of DWCRA on Income Generation

As one of the main aims of the DWCRA programme is to increase the earnings of the rural poor, its success lies in its

Table 3.27 : Caste-wise Analysis of Employment Generation From DWCRA in Khammam Disirct

Caste	*Days Per Month*					*Total*
	Below 5	*6 - 10*	*11 - 15*	*16 - 20*	*Above 20*	
F C	12	24	32	4	3	75
B C	43	49	49	16	—	157
S C	2	13	6	—	—	21
S T	19	15	10	3	—	47
TOTAL	76 (25.3)	101 (33.7)	97 (32.3)	23 (7.7)	3 (1.0)	300 (100.0)

Source : Field Study.

ability to increase the income of the respondents. The impact of the DWCRA programme on the income of the respondents can be assessed in two ways. The additional income generated due to DWCRA to the respondents is one method to ascertain the success of the programme in terms of income generation. Another method is to examine the difference between pre and post DWCRA income levels of the respondents.

Income Generation Exclusively From DWCRA

In order to examine the impact of DWCRA on income of the beneficiaries, the data are elicited in regard to the additional earnings accrued to the respondents due to DWCRA and the relevant information is placed in Table-3.28.

It can be observed from Table-3.28 that the additional income earned by the respondents due to DWCRA is in the range of Rs. 501-750 for 101 beneficiaries out of 300 selected respondents and it is followed by 96 in the income range of Rs. 251-500. It is to be noted that 62 respondents could get an additional income to the tune of more than 751 per month and out of them, 37 could get an additional income in the highest range of Rs. 1001-1500 per month. However, 2.7 percent of the respondents could not get any additional income due to DWCRA. On the whole, it can be stated that 87.3 percent of the sample beneficiaries could get some amount of additional income positively due to DWCRA which itself clearly indicates the success of the programme.

Table 3.28 : Relationship Between Scheme and Income Generation in Khammam District

(Income in Rs.)

Trade	*Nil*	*Below 250*	*251-500*	*501-750*	*751-1000*	*Above 1000*	*Total*
Baniyans Making	–	–	1	15	–	4	20
Veg. Cultivation	–	1	9	6	1	–	17
Milch Animals	–	–	2	3	1	28	34
Pickles/ Edible items	1	5	2	9	4	4	25
Surf/ Blue/ Phenoil	–	–	1	16	–	–	17
Sambar/ Rasam Powders	–	–	2	10	2	–	14
Tailoring	–	2	16	6	4	–	28
Woolen works	5	2	3	–	–	–	10
Fish Vending	–	2	3	2	–	–	7
Sheep Rearing	–	–	5	8	5	–	18
Candle Making	1	13	1	–	–	–	15
Carpets	–	–	9	3	–	–	12
Basket Making	–	–	15	6	1	–	22
Cut Pieces/ Sarries Selling	–	–	4	4	1	1	10
Leaf Plate Making	–	–	9	7	2	–	18
Kiranam / Sale of Agri. products	1	4	7	3	2	–	17
Veg / Fruit vending	–	2	–	–	–	–	2
Wire Baskets	–	1	4	–	–	–	5
Others	–	1	3	3	2	–	9
TOTAL	8 (2.7)	33 (11.0)	96 (32.0)	101 (33.7)	25 (8.3)	37 (12.3)	300 (100.0)

Source : Field Study.

The scheme-wise analysis shows that the schemes of Baniyans Making, Milch Animals, Pickles/ Edible items and Cut-Pieces selling could generate additional income to the maximum extent of Rs. 1000-1500 per month. Interestingly, one respondent in the scheme of Pickles/ Edible items could not generate any additional income at all.

The data in regard to the relationship between caste and additional income generation are presented in Table-3.29. It can be seen from the Table 3.29 that 38.7 percent of Forward Caste respondents and 35 percent of Backward Classes respondents could earn on additional income in the range of Rs. 501-750 per month where as 76.2 percent of Scheduled Caste respondents could get an additional income to the tune of Rs. 251-500 per month. In the same range of income 46.8 percent of Scheduled Tribe respondents are found. Thus, majority of Forward Caste and Backward Class respondents are relatively in a better position in terms of additional earnings when compared to Scheduled Caste and Scheduled Tribe respondents. Similarly, 25.3 percent of Forward Caste respondents could get an additional earnings in the range of Rs. 1001-1500 per month and the percentage of Backward Class

Table 3.29 : Relationship Between Caste and Income Generation in Khammam District

(Income In Rs.)

Caste	*Nil*	*Below 250*	*251-500*	*501-750*	*751-1000*	*Above 1000*	*Total*
F C	2	5	11	29	9	19	75
	(2.7)	(6.7)	(14.7)	(38.7)	(12.0)	(25.3)	(100.0)
B C	6	17	47	55	15	17	157
	(3.8)	(10.8)	(29.9)	(35.0)	(9.6)	(10.8)	(100.0)
S C	–	1	16	3	–	1	21
		(4.8)	(76.2)	(14.3)		(4.8)	(100.0)
S T	–	10	22	14	1	–	47
		(21.3)	(46.8)	(29.8)	(2.1)		(100.0)
TOTAL	8	33	96	101	25	37	300
	(2.7)	(11.0)	(32.0)	(33.7)	(8.3)	(12.3)	(100.0)

Source : Field Study.

respondents in this range of income is only 10.8 while only 4.8 percent of Scheduled Caste respondents are found in this range of income but no Scheduled Tribe respondents is seen in this range. Contrastingly, out of 8 persons who could not get any additional income due to DWCRA 2 belongs to Forward Caste and 6 belonged to Backward Class and no Scheduled Caste and Scheduled Tribe respondent is found in this category. On the whole, it can be stated that Forward Caste and Backward Class respondents could get an additional earnings relatively in higher ranges of income when compared to Scheduled Caste and Scheduled Tribe respondents.

Comparative Analysis Pre and Post-DWCRA Income Generation

An analysis in regard to Pre and Post-DWCRA earnings reveals the impact of DWCRA on the income levels of respondents. A scheme-wise comparison is made as to Pre and Post-DWCRA earnings in Khammam district and relevant information is shown in Table-3.30.

It can be observed from Table-3.30 that the average income during Pre-DWCRA period is Rs. 364.06 per month and has been increased to Rs. 972.70 during Post-DWCRA period. The average income during Pre-DWCRA period has varied between Rs. 225 per month in Woolen works and Rs. 522.22 per month in Sambar/ Rasam powders. The average monthly income is below the total average in the eleven schemes of Baniyans Making, Vegetable Cultivation, Milch Animals Pickles/ Edible Items, Tailoring, Woolen Works, Fish Vending, Sheep Rearing, Candle Making, Veg/ Fruit Vending and Others. It is happy to notice that in all the selected schemes, the average monthly income has shown a rise during Post-DWCRA period except in woolen works. Keeping aside the only one scheme which is negatively affected, the average income per month during post DWCRA period has ranged between RS. 380/- in Candle Making and Rs. 1964.70 in Milch Animals. The average income per month during Post-DWCRA period has exceeded Rs. 1000/- in the schemes of Baniyans Making, Milch Animals, Pickles\ Edible Items, Sheep Rearing, Cut-Pieces & Sarees selling. The

Table 3.30 : Scheme-wise Analysis of Income Generation During Pre & Post-DWCRA Period in Khammam District

(Income In Rs)

Trade	*Pre-DWCRA Income*			*Post-DWCRA Income*			*Difference of Avg. Income*
	No. of Respondents	*Total Income*	*Avg. Income (P. M.)*	*No. of Respondents*	*Total Income*	*Avg. Income (P. M.)*	
Baniyans Making	15	5250	350.00	20	24150	1207.50	857.50
Veg. Cultivation	15	4450	296.66	17	13100	770.58	473.92
Milch Animals	22	7650	347.72	34	66800	1964.70	1616.98
Pickles/ Edible items	13	3450	265.38	25	25050	1002.00	736.62
Surf/ Blue/ Phenoil	13	5450	419.23	17	16460	968.23	549.00
Sambar/ Rasam Powders	9	4700	522.22	14	13600	971.42	449.20
Tailoring	21	6900	328.57	28	22550	805.36	476.79
Woolen works	4	900	225.00	10	-750	-75.00	-300.00
Fish Vending	7	2300	328.57	7	5300	757.14	428.57
Sheep Rearing	16	5150	321.87	18	20650	1147.22	825.35
Candle Making	10	3350	335.00	15	5700	380.00	45.00
Carpets	12	4900	408.33	12	10400	866.66	458.33
Basket Making	22	8950	406.81	22	20000	909.09	500.28
Cut Pieces/Sarries Selling	10	4100	410.00	10	10300	1030.00	620.00
Leaf Plate Making	11	4900	445.45	18	15150	841.66	396.21
Kiranam/Sale of Agri. products	12	4700	391.67	12	12050	708.82	317.15
Veg/ Fruit vending	2	700	350.00	2	1100	550.00	200.00
Wire Baskets	5	2550	510.00	5	4100	820.00	310.00
Others	5	1200	240.00	9	6100	677.77	437.77
TOTAL	224	81550	364.06	300	291810	972.70	608.66

Source : Field Study.

difference between Pre & Post-DWCRA earnings per month has ranged between Rs. 45 in Candle Making and Rs. 1616.98 in Milch Animals. Thus, the scheme of Milch Animals is highly successful in terms of generating income and it is followed by Baniyans Making.

Relationship Between Caste and Income Generation

The information in regard to caste-wise comparison of Pre and Post-DWCRA earnings in Khammam district is presented in Table-3.31. It can be noticed from Table-3.31 that Post-DWCRA earnings are higher when compared to Pre-DWCRA earnings for all the beneficiaries irrespective of the caste. However, inter-caste variation is noticed in regard to the amount of rise in income.

Table 3.31 : Caste - Wise Analysis of Income Generation During Pre & Post - DWCRA Period In Khammam District

(Income In Rs.)

Caste	*Pre-DWCRA Income*			*Post-DWCRA Income*			*Difference*
	No. of Respon-dents	*Total Income*	*Avg. Income (P. M.)*	*No. of Respon-dents*	*Total Income*	*Avg. Income (P. M.)*	*of Avg. Income*
F C	40	15500	387.50	75	88610	1181.46	793.96
B C	122	44050	361.50	157	149250	950.63	589.13
S C	20	8350	417.50	21	19050	907.14	489.64
S T	42	13650	325.00	47	34900	742.55	417.55
TOTAL	224	81550	364.06	300	291810	972.70	608.66

Source : Field Study.

The average monthly income during Pre-DWCRA period is highest for Scheduled Caste respondents at Rs. 417.50 followed by Forward Caste respondents at Rs. 387.50. Interestingly, this position is not maintained during Post-DWCRA period. The Forward Caste respondents stand first whose average income per month is Rs. 1181.46 during Post-DWCRA period followed by Backward Classes respondents who could secure Rs. 950.63 on an average and third place occupied by Scheduled Caste respondents while Scheduled

Tribe respondents took last place in this regard whose monthly earnings are only Rs. 742.55 on an average. Thus, the success of the programme in terms of generating income is related to the caste factor also.

Relationship Between Category and Income Generation

The data in regard to the category-wise comparison between Pre and Post-DWCRA earnings are presented in Table-3.32.

Table 3.32 : Category-Wise Analysis Of Income Generation During Pre & Post-DWCRA Period In Khammam District

(Income In Rs.)

Category	*Pre-DWCRA Income*			*Post-DWCRA Income*			*Difference*
	No. of Respon-dents	*Total Income*	*Avg. Income (P. M.)*	*No. of Respon-dents*	*Total Income*	*Avg. Income (P. M.)*	*of Avg. Income*
Small Farmers	28	10150	362.50	53	58710	1107.73	747.23
Marginal Farmers	68	22300	327.94	87	96100	1104.59	776.65
Agri. Labourers	37	12700	343.24	41	36300	885.36	542.12
Non-Agri. Labourers	18	8300	461.11	19	18700	984.21	523.10
Rural Artisans	55	19550	355.45	61	57750	946.72	591.27
Others	18	8550	475.00	39	24250	621.79	146.79
TOTAL	224	81550	364.06	300	291810	972.70	608.66

Source : Field Study.

It can be seen from Table-3.32 that the average income per month during Pre-DWCRA period has varied between Rs. 329.94 for Marginal Farmers and Rs. 475 for Others. The average income per month during Post-DWCRA period has increased for all the respondents irrespective of their economic category. However, the rise in income is not uniform during Post-DWCRA period and inter-category variation is noticed & their relative positions are also changed. The average income per month during Post-DWCRA period is Rs. 1107.73 for Small

Farmers followed by Rs. 1104.59 for Marginal Farmers and Non-Agricultural Labourers occupied third position and last position is taken by Others. Thus, the rise in income is least for 'Others'. Thus, Small Farmers and Marginal Farmers are relatively in a better position in terms of earnings per month during Post-DWCRA period. In this way, the success of the scheme is related to the economic category of the respondent.

Relationship Between Educational Qualifications & Income Generation

An analysis is made to examine the relationship between educational qualifications of the respondent and the success of the DWCRA in terms of income generation. The relevant information is presented in Table-3.33. It can be observed from the Table-3.33, that the average income per month during Pre-DWCRA period is in the range of Rs. 342.70 for illiterates and Rs. 528.57 for intermediate. However, the Pre-DWCRA income is nil for degree holders. It is interesting to note that the average income per month during Post-DWCRA period is on the rise for all the respondents irrespective of their educational qualifications but the rise in income is not uniform. The average income per month during Post-DWCRA period is Rs. 1375 for

Table 3.33 : Relationship Between Educational Qualifications and Income Generation During Pre & Post-DWCRA Period in Khammam District

(Income In Rs.)

Educational Qualification	*Pre-DWCRA Income*			*Post-DWCRA Income*			*Difference of Avg. Income*
	No. of Respondents	*Total Income*	*Avg. Income (P. M.)*	*No. of Respondents*	*Total Income*	*Avg. Income (P. M.)*	
Illiterate	96	32900	342.70	116	123500	1064.65	721.95
Primary	94	34450	366.48	129	115010	891.55	525.07
Secondary	27	10500	388.88	42	40800	971.42	582.54
Intermediate	7	3700	528.57	11	9750	886.36	357.79
Degree	–	–	–	2	2750	1375.00	1375.00
TOTAL	224	81550	364.06	300	291810	972.70	608.66

Source : Field Study.

degree holders followed by illiterates whose income is at Rs. 1064.65. Thus, either no education or higher level of education of the respondent is resulting in the success of DWCRA in terms of income generation.

Relationship Between Age and Income Generation

The information in regard to the age of the respondent and the success of the trade in terms of income generation is presented in Table-3.34.

Table 3.34 : Age-wise Analysis Of Income Generation During Pre & Post-DWCRA Period in Khammam District

(Income In Rs.)

Age	*Pre-DWCRA Income*			*Post-DWCRA Income*			*Difference*
	No. of Respon-dents	*Total Income*	*Avg. Income (P. M.)*	*No. of Respon-dents*	*Total Income*	*Avg. Income (P. M.)*	*of Avg. Income*
20 - 30	93	35350	380.10	130	112750	867.30	487.42
31 - 40	92	32000	347.82	121	124010	1024.87	677.05
41 - 50	34	12600	370.58	42	48800	1161.90	791.32
Above 50	5	1600	320.00	7	6250	892.85	572.85
TOTAL	224	81550	364.06	300	291810	972.70	608.66

Source : Field Study.

It can be observed from Table-3.34 that the Pre-DWCRA average income per month is in the range of Rs. 320 for the respondents who have above 50 years age and Rs.380.10 for the respondents of 20-30 years of age. It can also be noticed that the Post-DWCRA income per month has increased for all the age groups under study. However, the rise in the income is not uniform for all the age groups. The highest average income of Rs.1161.90 per month during Post-DWCRA period is secured by 41-50 years age group followed by Rs. 1024.87 by 31-40 years age group. The respondents who are in the age group of 20-30 years and above 50 years are relatively in a weak position in terms of average earnings per month during Post-DWCRA period. Thus, the success of DWCRA in terms of generating income is also related to the age of the respondent.

Impact on Living Conditions

The ultimate aim of DWCRA is to achieve an improvement in the quality of life of rural poor so as to increase their standard of living. The rise in income of rural poor naturally results in the rise in their level of consumption. Therefore, an analysis is also made to examine the impact of rise in income on various components of consumption. The rise in income also lead to rise in savings, repayment of debts, purchase of durable assets and expansion of trade to achieve further rise in income. The relevant information is presented in Table-3.35.

It can be noticed from Table-3.35, that the rise in income is resulted in rise in expenditure in terms of nutritious food, clothing, medical, education, purchase of assets, savings, debt repayment, expansion of trade and others. As high as 197 respondents out of 300 selected beneficiaries preferred to save their income and 183 respondents have given importance to education while 114 spent on medical expenses. However, 72 respondents tried to expand their trade.

The scheme wise analysis reveals that the majority of respondents in the schemes of Baniyans Making, Milch Animals, Pickles/ Edible Items, Tailoring, Woolen Works, Fish Vending, Candle Making, Vegetable and Fruit Vending and Others gave preference for the education of their children while the majority of respondents in Vegetable Cultivation, Milch Animals, Pickles/ Edible Items, Surf/ Blue/ Phenoil, Sambar/ Rasam Powders, Sheep Rearing, Carpets, Basket Making, Cut-Pieces and Sarees selling, Leaf Plate Making, Kiranam and Wire Baskets preferred to save part of their increased income. Thus, scheme-wise variation is noticed in regard to the impact of DWCRA on consumption levels.

Repayment

The regular repayment of loan is another indicator of the success of the programme. It is heartening to note that all the selected respondents in Khammam district are regular in repayment of loan irrespective of their scheme and caste.

Table 3.35 : Impact of DWCRA on Expenditure Pattern of the Selected Respondents in the Khammam District

Trade	*Nutritional Food*	*Clothing*	*Medical*	*Education*	*Assets*	*Savings*	*Debt Repayment*	*Exp. of the Trade*	*Any Other*
Baniyans Making	3	5	9	18	2	14	4	12	2
Veg. Cultivation	1	2	–	8	2	9	2	3	–
Milch Animals	18	8	21	26	7	26	12	18	5
Pickles/ Edible items	13	12	15	21	3	21	2	5	10
Surf/ Blue/ Phenoil	3	2	7	12	2	14	3	8	7
Sambar/ Rasam Powders	5	3	3	8	3	12	–	5	2
Tailoring	4	6	12	18	–	15	2	7	1
Woolen works	1	1	3	5	–	2	–	–	2
Fish Vending	–	–	2	3	–	3	–	2	1
Sheep Rearing	3	2	9	8	2	11	2	3	2
Candle Making	2	1	3	8	1	5	–	–	1
Carpets	–	–	2	3	–	8	–	–	2
Basket Making	–	–	7	13	–	16	–	–	3
Cut Pieces/Sarries Selling	–	2	2	4	1	6	–	6	2
Leaf Plate Making	2	1	5	8	–	11	3	2	5
Kiranam/Sale of Agri. products	6	2	10	11	1	16	2	1	5
Veg/ Fruit vending	1	–	2	2	–	2	–	–	–
Wire Baskets	–	–	–	2	–	3	–	–	1
Others	–	–	2	5	–	3	–	–	2
TOTAL	62	47	114	183	24	197	32	72	53

Source : Field Study.

SECTION - II

The economic impact of DWCRA in terms of generating employment, income, rise in consumption levels and repayment of loan is discussed in Section-I. Since DWCRA involves women, the economic success may or may not result in improvement in their status within the family as well as in the society owing to the prevalence of patriarchy. Therefore, this section is devoted exclusively to examine the impact of success of DWCRA on the status of rural women in Khammam district.

Section-I, clearly revealed that the programme is a success irrespective of the scheme & caste in terms of employment and income generation. In fact, the real success lies on the active participation of respondents in decision making related to decisions of the household in regard to short run consumption needs related to daily expenses, long-run consumption aspects of education of children, purchase of assets, arrangement of marriages to their children & expansion of trade. Thus, it is necessary to examine as to whether there is any change in the distributive rules of household in favour of women.

The participation of respondents in short-run decisions of the household related to daily expenditure may vary from caste to caste. The relevant information is presented in Table-3.36.

Table 3.36 : Participation of Respondents in Short Run Decision Making Related to Daily Expenditure Caste - Wise

Caste	*Own*	*Husband*	*Both*	*Others*	*Total*
F C	52	4	13	6	75
B C	94	21	31	11	157
S C	13	2	6	—	21
S T	26	10	7	4	47
TOTAL	185 (61.7)	37 (12.3)	57 (19.0)	21 (7.0)	300 (100.00)

Source : Field Study.

Table-3.36 indicates that on the whole 185 respondents out of 300 selected sample could take decision in regard to daily expenditure on their own while in the case of 57 both husband and wife together would take the decision. Thus, in the case of 80 percent of respondents either they themselves are in a position to take decision in regard to daily expenses or along with their husband they are able to take decision in this regard. The same trend is noticed in all the castes. Thus, active participation of women in decisions related to short-run expenditure of the household is observed in all the castes.

The participation of respondents in short-run decisions of the household may also related to their educational qualifications. The relevant information is shown in Table-3.37. It can be observed from Table-3.37 that the majority of selected women could take decisions of daily expenses of the household on their own in all the educational qualifications except in the case of degree holders. Similarly, the husband is the only decision maker in regard to daily expenses of the family in the case of 20 respondents who are illiterates 11 who have upto primary education and 6 who have upto secondary education. No respondent is found in this category when the respondent is having education to the level of Intermediate and beyond. Thus, the higher the level of education of women, their participation is active in short-run decision making of the household.

Table 3.37 : Education and Participation of Respondents in Short Run Decision Making related To Daily Expenditure

Educational Qualifications	*Own*	*Husband*	*Both*	*Others*	*Total*
Illiterate	72	20	14	10	116
Primary	88	11	24	6	129
Secondary	18	6	13	5	42
Intermediate	7	–	4	–	11
Degree	–	–	2	–	2
TOTAL	185 (61.7)	37 (12.3)	57 (19.0)	21 (7.0)	300 (100.00)

Source : Field Study.

Long-run Decision Making of the Family

The long-run decisions of the rural poor households mainly consist of purchase of consumer durables, expansion of trade, arrangement of marriages to their children, provision of education to the children, taking debt & making repayment.

Purchase of Consumer Durables

Table-3.38 indicates that out of 300 selected respondents, 140 could take decision on their own in regard to purchase of consumer durables while in 68 cases only husbands would take the decision and in the case of 74 both husband and wife together will take the decision. However, there is no any caste-wise variation in this regard. Similarly, the education level of the respondent did not play any role in regard to the purchase of consumer durables of the household (Table-3.39).

Table 3.38 : Caste & Decision Making of the Purchase of Consumer Durables

Caste	*Own*	*Husband*	*Both*	*Others*	*Total*
F C	38	17	18	2	75
B C	75	32	38	12	157
S C	10	4	7	–	21
S T	17	15	11	4	47
TOTAL	140 (46.7)	68 (22.7)	74 (24.7)	18 (6.0)	300 (100.0)

Source : Field Study.

Table 3.39 : Education and Decision Making of the Purchase of Consumer Durables

Educational Qualifacations	*Own*	*Husband*	*Both*	*Others*	*Total*
Illiterate	51	39	19	7	116
Primary	65	24	34	6	129
Secondary	21	4	15	2	42
Intermediate	3	1	4	3	11
Degree	–	–	2	–	2
TOTAL	140 (46.7)	68 (22.7)	74 (24.7)	18 (6.0)	300 (100.0)

Source : Field Study.

Decision Making in Regard to Expansion of Trade

As the trade belongs to the respondent, they themselves should be in a position to take decision in regard to the expansion of the trade. Owing to the prevalence of patriarchy, husband plays a dominant role even in this regard and interferes in the economic activity of the respondent.

Table-3.40 explains that out of selected 300 respondents, only 18 respondents are taking the decision in regard to the expansion of trade on their own while as high as in 176 cases, exclusively husbands are taking decision in this regard and both husband & wife together are taking decision in 83 cases where as in 23 cases other members of the family are taking decision. Same trend can be noticed in all the castes. Thus, no caste-wise variation is noticed. Similarly, Table-3.41 shows that out of 18 respondents who take decision on their own, 11 are illiterates,

Table 3.40 : Caste and Decision Making of Expansion of Trade

Caste	*Own*	*Husband*	*Both*	*Others*	*Total*
F C	5	45	23	2	75
B C	8	89	42	18	157
S C	3	11	7	–	21
S T	2	31	11	3	47
TOTAL	18 (6.0)	176 (58.7)	83 (27.7)	23 (7.7)	300 (100.0)

Source : Field Study.

Table 3.41 : Education and Decision Making of Expansion of Trade

Educational Qualifacations	*Own*	*Husband*	*Both*	*Others*	*Total*
Illiterate	11	78	21	6	116
Primary	3	80	34	6	129
Secondary	4	10	19	9	42
Intermediate	–	2	7	2	11
Degree	–	–	2	–	2
TOTAL	18 (6.0)	176 (58.7)	83 (27.7)	23 (7.7)	300 (100.0)

Source : Field Study.

3 have upto primary education and 4 have upto secondary education. The respondent who has education intermediate & beyond can not be seen in this. However, in the case of 7 out of 11 respondents, all the 2 who have upto degree level education both husband and wife together are taking decision in regard to the expansion of trade. Any how, it can be stated that the level of education of the respondent is not playing any significant role in this aspect.

Decision Making in Regard to the Arrangement of Marriages

Table-3.42, states that out of 300 selected respondents as high as in 156 cases, both husband and wife together are taking decision in regard to the arrangement of marriage to their children. In the case of 96, husband alone is taking decision in this regard. The domination of husband in taking decision in regard to marriage is relatively higher in Backward Classes and Scheduled Tribe respondents.

Table 3.42 : Caste and Decision Making in Regard to Marriages of the Children

Caste	*Own*	*Husband*	*Both*	*Others*	*Total*
F C	5	23	46	1	75
B C	26	49	77	5	157
S C	3	4	14	–	21
S T	5	20	19	3	47
TOTAL	39 (13.0)	96 (32.0)	156 (52.0)	9 (3.0)	300 (100.0)

Source : Field Study.

Table-3.43, indicates that out of 39 respondents who takes decision of marriages independently, 21 are illiterates and remaining 18 have upto intermediate level education. Out of 11 respondents who have education upto intermediate, in the case of 9 both wife & husband together are taking decision in this regard and all the 2 degree holders are also in similar position. Thus, the higher the level of education of the respondent the higher will be their participation in decision making as to the arrangement of marriages.

Table - 3.43 : Education and Decision Making in Regard to the Marriages of the Children

Educational Qualifacations	*Own*	*Husband*	*Both*	*Others*	*Total*
Illiterate	21	49	41	5	116
Primary	14	39	72	4	129
Secondary	3	7	32	—	42
Intermediate	1	1	9	—	11
Degree	—	—	2	—	2
TOTAL	39 (13.0)	96 (32.0)	156 (52.0)	9 (3.0)	300 (100.0)

Source : Field Study.

Decision Making in Regard to the Education of the Children

It can be noticed from Table-3.44 that out of 300 selected respondents in the case of 49 percent both husband and wife are participating in decision making in regard to the education

Table - 3.44 : Caste and Decision Making In regard to Education of the Children

Caste	*Own*	*Husband*	*Both*	*Others*	*Total*
F C	16	12	47	—	75
B C	36	44	72	5	157
S C	3	6	12	—	21
S T	8	20	16	3	47
TOTAL	63 (21.0)	82 (27.3)	147 (49.0)	8 (2.7)	300 (100.0)

Source : Field Study.

of the children and in the case of 21 percent the respondent is taking decision on her own. The respondents participation is nil in the case of 30 percent of the sample. No any significant caste-wise variation is noticed in this regard. Interestingly, participation of wife in decision making is on par with husband in the case of 9 out of 11 who have education upto intermediate and 2 degree holders (Table-3.45).

Table 3.45 : Education and Decision Making In regard to Education of the Children

Educational Qualifacations	*Own*	*Husband*	*Both*	*Others*	*Total*
Illiterate	26	45	42	3	116
Primary	26	31	70	2	129
Secondary	10	5	24	3	42
Intermediate	1	1	9	–	11
Degree	–	–	2	–	2
TOTAL	63 (21.0)	82 (27.3)	147 (49.0)	8 (2.7)	300 (100.0)

Source : Field Study.

Decision Making in Regard to Debt & Repayment

Table-3.46 indicates that in the case of 48.7 percent of the sample respondents, husbands alone take decision in regard to taking loans & its repayment. Only 9 percent of the sample respondents takes decision independently in this regard while in the case of 37.7 percent, both husband and wife together will take the decision. The caste-wise analysis in this regard states that in the case of Scheduled Caste respondents, out of 21, only in 8 cases husband domination is observed. In remaining castes, no significant deviation can be observed from the total average picture.

Table 3.46 : Caste and Decision Making Inregard to Debt and Repayment

Caste	*Own*	*Husband*	*Both*	*Others*	*Total*
F C	12	33	28	2	75
B C	8	76	64	9	157
S C	3	8	10	–	21
S T	4	29	11	3	47
TOTAL	27 (9.0)	146 (48.7)	113 (37.7)	14 (4.6)	300 (100.0)

Source : Field Study.

Table-3.47 states that the husband alone takes decision in regard to debt & repayment in more than 50 percent cases when wife's level of education is less than primary and later on wife's participation in the decision making is on the rise when wife's level of education is intermediate & beyond. Thus, education level of respondent plays a vital role in making the respondent active in decision making of the household in regard to debt & repayment.

Table 3.47 : Education and Decision Making In regard to Debt and Repayment

Educational Qualifacations	*Own*	*Husband*	*Both*	*Others*	*Total*
Illiterate	16	66	29	5	116
Primary	8	67	50	4	129
Secondary	3	12	23	4	42
Intermediate	–	1	9	1	11
Degree	–	–	2	–	2
TOTAL	27 (9.0)	146 (48.7)	113 (37.7)	14 (4.6)	300 (100.0)

Source : Field Study.

Ownership of Property

Though, women are earning on their own, usually property ownership is on the name of male members of the family. The ownership of property indicates control over property and which increases the status of any person. The lack of control over resources is identified as one of the serious causes of lower status of women. The prevalence of patriarchy manifests itself in this economic form. Therefore, the data elicited in regard to ownership of property of respondents and relevant data are shown as Table-3.48 and Table-3.49.

Table-3.48 indicates that out of 300 selected respondents as high as 277 persons do not have any ownership rights of the property. No any caste-wise variation is noticed in this regard Similarly, Table-3.49, states that the education level of the respondent also did not play any positive role in this regard.

Table 3.48 : Caste-wise Analysis of Ownership of Property by the Selected Respondent

Caste	*Yes*	*No*	*Total*
F C	9	66	75
B C	7	150	157
S C	1	20	21
S T	4	43	47
TOTAL	23 (7.7)	277 (92.3)	300 (100.0)

Source : Field Study.

Table 3.49 : Education and Ownership of Property by the Selected Respondent

Educational Qualifications	*Yes*	*No*	*Total*
Illiterate	6	110	116
Primary	15	114	129
Secondary	1	41	42
Intermediate	1	10	11
Degree	—	2	2
TOTAL	23 (7.7)	277 (92.3)	300 (100.0)

Source : Field Study.

Domestic Work

In patriarchal societies, the domestic work is the responsibility of women which will not yield any income but without which no family especially poor rural families can not survive. Inspite of its significance for the survival of the family i.e., in other words inspite of its enormous use value, as it does not possess any exchange value, it is not recognized either by the family or by the society.

Still, women should spend more time to perform domestic chores consist of cleaning house, utensils, washing cloths, cooking, bringing water from distant places, maintaining kitchen garden, looking after children and overall maintenance of the household.

The information in regard to number of hours spent on domestic work is presented in Table-3.50 and 3.51.

Table 3.50 : Caste-wise Analysis Number of Hours Spent on Domestic Work

Caste	*1 - 2*	*3 - 4*	*5 - 6*	*Above 6*	*Total*
F C	12	30	23	10	75
B C	15	56	69	17	157
S C	2	6	11	2	21
S T	3	14	21	9	47
TOTAL	32 (10.7)	106 (35.3)	124 (41.5)	38 (12.7)	300 (100.0)

Source : Field Study.

Table-3.50, reveals that out of 300 selected respondents, 41.5 percent of them spend 5-6 hours daily on domestic work while 35.3 percent in between 3-4 hours and 12.7 percent devote more than 6 hours per day to perform domestic work while 10.7 percent allot less than 2 hours per day. No caste-wise variation is noticed in this regard. The time spent on domestic work depends upon their economic status and not on the social status. It can be noticed from Table-3.51 that there is no any relationship between education level of the respondent and number of hours spent on domestic work. However, 2 degree holders spend 3-4 hours daily on domestic work.

Table 3.51 : Education and Number of Hours Spent on Domestic Work

Educational Qualifications	*1 - 2*	*3 - 4*	*5 - 6*	*Above 6*	*Total*
Illiterate	11	37	61	7	116
Primary	10	54	44	21	129
Secondary	8	9	15	10	42
Intermediate	3	4	4	–	11
Degree	–	2	–	–	2
TOTAL	32 (10.7)	106 (35.3)	124 (41.5)	38 (12.7)	300 (100.0)

Source : Field Study.

In performing domestic work, women may be assisted by family members. Relevant information is presented in Table-3.52 and 3.53.

Table 3.52 : Caste and Assistance Received in Performing Domestic Work

Caste	*Husband*	*Children*	*Others*	*Own*	*Total*
F C	32	15	7	21	75
B C	62	19	30	46	157
S C	5	3	7	6	21
S T	7	11	11	18	47
TOTAL	106 (35.3)	48 (16.0)	55 (18.3)	91 (30.4)	300 (100.0)

Source : Field Study.

Table-3.52, indicates that out of 300 selected respondents 106 are helped by husband in performing domestic chores. Out of them, 94 belonged to Forward and Backward Castes. In the case of 48 respondents, children are extending assistance and in 55 cases other members of the family are extending assistance. The husband's assistance in performing domestic work is relatively higher in Forward & Backward Castes.

Table-3.53, indicates that the husband's assistance in performing domestic work is on the rise as the education level of wife increases.

Table 3.53 : Education and Assistance Received in Performing Domestic Work

Educational Qualifications	*Husband*	*Children*	*Others*	*Own*	*Total*
Illiterate	44	19	20	33	116
Primary	42	17	20	50	129
Secondary	11	9	14	8	42
Intermediate	8	2	1	–	11
Degree	1	1	–	–	2
TOTAL	106 (35.3)	48 (16.0)	55 (18.3)	91 (30.4)	300 (100.0)

Source : Field Study.

Family Purchasing Priorities

Rise in the income leads to rise in consumption is a normal phenomenon. However, this phenomenon will not equally be applicable to all the members of the family. It has gender dimension too. Though the income of the family increases through the earnings of the women, the consumption priorities of the women are neglected. The details of family purchasing priorities are shown in Tables-3.54 and 3.55.

Table 3.54 : Caste-wise Analysis Family Purchasing Priorities

Caste	*Goods Used By Male Members of Family*	*Consumer Durables*	*Savings*	*Exp. of the Trade*	*Total*
F C	12	20	35	8	75
B C	42	39	45	31	157
S C	9	4	7	1	21
S T	14	11	14	8	47
TOTAL	77 (25.7)	74 (24.7)	101 (33.7)	48 (16.0)	300 (100.0)

Source : Field Study.

Table 3.55 : Education and Family Purchasing Priorities

Educational Qualifications	*Goods Used By Male Members of Family*	*Consumer Durables*	*Savings*	*Exp. of the Trade*	*Total*
Illiterate	45	25	30	16	116
Primary	27	21	59	22	129
Secondary	3	24	6	9	42
Intermediate	2	3	5	1	11
Degree	–	1	1	–	2
TOTAL	77 (25.7)	74 (24.7)	101 (33.7)	48 (16.0)	300 (100.0)

Source : Field Study.

Table-3.54 states that out of 300 selected respondents, 33.7 percent families give priority to save, 25.7 percent prefers to purchase goods exclusively consumed by male members of the family and 24.7 percent prefers to expansion of the trade. No any significant caste-wise variation is noticed. Similar trend can be seen even in relation to education level of the respondent (Table 3.55). Further, the field work has revealed that only 25 percent of the respondents could take decision as to spending of their earnings and as high as in 38.7 percent cases, husband alone takes decision as to how to spend the earnings of the wife.

Harassment

One of the serious problems that women has to confront is domestic violence which mainly consists of harassment by the family members. Table-3.56, shows that out of 300 selected sample, 66 are subjected to harassment by the family members. Of them, 12 belonged to Forward Caste, 31 to Backward Class, 9 to Schedule Castes and 14 to Scheduled Tribes. Table-3.57 states that out of 66 respondents who are subjected to harassment, 36 are illiterates, 25 have upto primary education, 4 have secondary education and only one is studied upto intermediate. Thus, lower the level of education of the wife, higher will be the harassment.

Table 3.56 : Caste and Harassment in the Family

Caste	*Yes*	*No*	*Total*
F C	12	63	75
B C	31	126	157
S C	9	12	21
S T	14	33	47
TOTAL	66 (22.0)	234 (78.0)	300 (100.0)

Source : Field Study.

The data as to who will harass are presented in Table-3.58 and 3.59.

Table-3.58 shows that in the case of 84.9 percent, husbands are harassing their wives followed by 12.1 percent by mother-in-law & lastly by sisters-in-law. The harassment by husband

Table 3.57 : Educational Level and Harassment in the Family

Educational Qualifications	*Yes*	*No*	*Total*
Illiterate	36	80	116
Primary	25	104	129
Secondary	4	38	42
Intermediate	1	10	11
Degree	–	2	2
TOTAL	66 (22.0)	234 (78.0)	300 (100.0)

Source : Field Study.

Table 3.58 : Caste-wise Analysis of Harassment From Whom

Caste	*Mother-In-law*	*Sister-In-law*	*Husband*	*Total*
F C	3	–	9	12
B C	4	2	25	31
S C	1	–	8	9
S T	–	–	14	14
TOTAL	8 (12.1)	2 (3.0)	56 (84.9)	66 (100.00)

Source : Field Study.

is relatively higher in Scheduled Caste and Scheduled Tribes. Similarly, it is relatively higher if wife is illiterate (Table-3.59).

Table 3.59 : Education-wise Analysis of Harassment From Whom

Educational Qualifications	*Mother-In-law*	*Sister-In-law*	*Husband*	*Total*
Illiterate	5	2	29	36
Primary	2	–	23	25
Secondary	1	–	3	4
Intermediate	–	–	1	1
Degree	–	–	–	–
TOTAL	8 (12.1)	2 (3.0)	56 (84.9)	66 (100.00)

Source : Field Study.

Table-3.60, states that out of 66 who are subjected to harassment, 35 suffer from wife beating 18 are subjected to dowry problem. No any caste-wise variation is noticed in this regard. However, the level of education of wife plays a positive role in this regard (Table-3.61).

Table 3.60 : Caste-wise Analysis Of Nature Of Harassment

Caste	*Dowry*	*Work*	*WifeBeating*	*Others*	*Total*
F C	4	2	6	–	12
B C	9	4	16	2	31
S C	1	2	5	1	9
S T	4	–	8	2	14
TOTAL	18 (27.3)	8 (12.1)	35 (53.0)	5 (7.6)	66 (100.0)

Source : Field Study.

Table 3.61 : Education and Nature of Harassment

Educational Qualifications	*Dowry*	*Work*	*WifeBeating*	*Others*	*Total*
Illiterate	10	7	15	4	36
Primary	7	1	16	1	25
Secondary	1	–	3	–	4
Intermediate	–	–	1	–	1
Degree	–	–	–	–	–
TOTAL	18 (27.3)	8 (12.1)	35 (53.0)	5 (7.6)	66 (100.0)

Source : Field Study.

Protest of Harassment

Since DWCRA consists of women groups, the respondents should be in a position to protest the harassment meted out to them either independently or as a group. Out of 66 who are subjected to harassment, only 33 have protested the harassment. Of them, 20 have informed the group members in regard to the harassment. Of them, the group members have initiated action in 16 cases. However, the problem is solved in 12 cases only.

Though the achievement appears to be little, the DWCRA has increased the confidence of the respondents. Now they are not isolated, they can discuss about the domestic violence in the group and find out solution also.

Social Awareness

DWCRA groups have to organise regular meeting of the members. Though they meet to discuss economic aspects of the programme, it invariably makes them to discuss their domestic problems also. At the same time, they start thinking about the society and prevalence of various problems in the society. The field study has revealed that out of 300 selected respondents, 73 are discussing about social problems also in their groups. Of them, 67 concentrates on local problems which is of their immediate need.

Social Activities of Respondents

The group activity of DWCRA results in their social awareness which invariably makes them to involve in social activities. This will not only increase their self-confidence but also improve their status.

The field study has revealed that the nature of social activities of the respondents consists of protesting atrocities on women, social evils, fighting against liquor consumption. Out of 300 selected respondents, 131 are involved in fighting against liquor consumption, 86 are fighting against social evils and 58 are protesting atrocities on women. No caste-wise variation is noticed in this regard.

The respondents are also actively involved in Janmabhoomi programme organised by the state government of Andhra Pradesh for providing better infrastructure in rural areas and for solving their problems in general. The participation of selected women is active in Janmabhoomi. As high as 205 respondents are participating in this activity. However, no caste-wise variation is noticed in this regard. The higher the level of education of the respondent lower was the participation in Janmabhoomi.

Political Awareness

The active participation of women in political decision making is a pre-condition for the attainment of women's empowerment. The political awareness begins with vote casting. The field study has revealed that as high as 296 out of 300 sample respondents are casting their vote. The personal qualities of the candidate who contest will be the basis for vote casting for 179 respondents while 121 gives preference on the basis of political party to which they belonged to.

Mere casting of vote will not determine the political awareness of women but to what extent they exercise their right independently assumes significance. Table-3.62 reveals that out of 300 selected respondents, 174 could take decision in regard to vote casting independently. However, 126 respondents are influenced either by husbands or by others in this regard. Any how, no significant caste-wise variation is noticed but level of education of women is playing a role and as the education level rises, women are in a position to take decision independently.

Table 3.62 : Caste-wise Analysis of Decision Making in Regard to Vote Casting

Caste	*Own*	*Husband*	*Others*	*Total*
F C	49	20	6	75
B C	91	56	10	157
S C	11	10	–	21
S T	23	20	4	47
TOTAL	174 (58.0)	106 (35.3)	20 (6.7)	300 (100.0)

Source : Field Study.

The active involvement in local politics by women is necessary for their empowerment. Though all the selected respondents cast their vote positively, only 63 are actively involved in local politics. Of them, 32 are involved in canvassing the candidate while 20 they themselves are contesting for a position.

Table 3.63 : Education and Decision Making in Regard to Vote Casting

Educational Qualifications	*Own*	*Husband*	*Others*	*Total*
Illiterate	52	56	8	116
Primary	90	36	3	129
Secondary	24	11	7	42
Intermediate	6	3	2	11
Degree	2	–	–	2
TOTAL	174 (58.0)	106 (35.3)	20 (6.7)	300 (100.0)

Source : Field Study.

Achievement of DWCRA

DWCRA is expected to increase the economic as well as social status of the rural women. The data are elicited as to the assessment of the programme made by the respondents themselves. Out of 300 selected, 131 opined that their economic along with social status has improved. While 98 felt that their economic status is improved whereas 40 experienced an improvement in their social status and 31 observes progress in their status within the family.

4

Employment, Income & Status of Rural Women–Part-II

This chapter is divided into two sections. As the main aim of DWCRA is to generate employment to increase their level of income so as to achieve an improvement in the quality of their lives, Section-I analyses the impact of DWCRA on rural women in Warangal district in terms of generating employment, income and improving their standard of living. Further, as DWCRA consists of rural women, their status determined not by mere economic factors owing to the prevalence of patriarchy. It restricts and controls their movement in domestic as well as social spheres. Therefore, unless and until their participation in decision making in domestic, social and political spheres improves, women's empowerment can not be achieved. The discussion in regard to this aspect is presented in Section-II.

SECTION-I

Prior to analyse the impact of DWCRA on rural women in terms of generating employment, income and improvement in the standard of living, it is essential to have an idea about the characteristics of the sample respondents in Warangal district.

Characteristics of Selected Respondents:

The village-wise distribution of trades, the caste-wise and category-wise distribution of selected respondents are discussed.

Village-wise Distribution of Selected Trades & Respondents

The information in regard to this aspect is presented in Table-4.1. It can be seen from Table-4.1 that 300 respondents are selected from 24 trades who are distributed in 20 villages. The selected trades consist of:

(i) Agriculture and allied activities like Milch Animals, Sheep Rearing, Piggery and growing Mushrooms.

(ii) Manufacturing activities consisting of Soft-toys, Candle making, Chalk pieces, Chappals making, Doop sticks, Beedi making & Weaving.

(iii) Artistic activities consisting of Embroidery work, Lace work and Thread work.

(iv) Food processing activities consisting of Pickles Making and various Masala Powders.

(v) Service activity like Tailoring, and

(vi) Business activities such as Cut pieces selling, Fish vending and Kiranam.

(vii) 'No trade' in which DWCRA groups utilise their finances as chits and profit will be distributed among themselves and loans taken by the respondents will be utilised for various purposes of the household.

The village-wise analysis reveals that the village Ghanpur (station) (which is also mandal headquarter) alone consists eight trades-Embroidery work, Soft-toys, Lace work, Candle making, Mushrooms, Chalk pieces, Piggery & Cut-pieces selling. Among them, Cut-pieces selling also can be seen in the village Narsampet. The trade Chappal Making can be found in Cheriyal and Gudibandal (Hnk). Similarly, the trade Milch Animals is found in Aagapet, Narmetta and Abdul Nagaram and Weaving is found in Kothawada (Wgl) and Kodakandla while Thread work is seen in Bheemaram only. The village Chinna Nagaram is having four trades viz., Fish vending, Tailoring, Kiranam and Others. The Nainala is having three trades-Veg/ Fruit Vending, Fish vending and Kiranam i.e., all the trades belonged to Business sector only. The village Kachikal

Table 4.1 : Village - Wise Distribution of Trades Under DWCRA In Warangal District

Trade	Embro-idary Work	Soft-Toys	Lace Work	Candle Making	Mush-Rooms	Chalk Pieces	Pig-gery	Cut-Pieces Selling	Chap-pals Mak-ing	Doop Sticks	Beedi Work	Pick-les	Sambar/ Rasam/ Pow-ders	Veg. Fruit Ven-ding	Woolen Work	Milch Ani-mals	Fish Vend-ing	Tailor-ing	Sheep Rear-ing	Kira-nam	Weav-ing	Thread Work	Others	No Trade	Total
Ghanpur (Station)	15	15	6	8	5	8	12	5	–	–	–	–	–	–	–	–	–	–	–	–	–	–	–	–	74 (24.7)
Cherial	–	–	–	–	–	–	–	–	14	–	–	–	–	–	–	–	–	–	–	–	–	–	–	–	14 (4.7)
Komaravelly	–	–	–	–	–	–	–	–	–	9	–	–	–	–	–	–	–	–	–	–	–	–	–	–	9 (3.0)
Kistam Pet	–	–	–	–	–	–	–	–	–	5	5	–	–	–	–	–	–	–	–	–	–	–	–	–	10 (3.3)
Saireddy Pally	–	–	–	–	–	–	–	–	–	–	–	12	10	–	–	–	–	–	–	–	–	–	–	–	22 (7.3)
Narsampet	–	–	–	–	–	–	–	10	–	–	–	–	–	7	6	–	–	–	–	–	–	–	–	–	23 (7.7)
Agapet	–	–	–	–	–	–	–	–	–	–	–	–	–	–	–	15	–	–	–	–	–	–	–	–	15 (5.0)
Narmetta	–	–	–	–	–	–	–	–	–	–	–	–	–	–	–	15	–	–	–	–	–	–	–	–	15 (5.0)
Abdul Nagaram	–	–	–	–	–	–	–	–	–	–	–	–	–	–	–	15	–	–	–	–	–	–	–	–	15 (5.0)
Chinna Nagaram	–	–	–	–	–	–	–	–	–	–	–	–	–	–	–	–	6	2	7	2	–	–	–	–	17 (5.7)
Nainala	–	–	–	–	–	–	–	–	–	–	–	–	–	4	–	–	3	–	–	–	–	–	1	–	8 (2.7)
Kachikal	–	–	–	–	–	–	–	–	–	–	–	–	–	–	–	–	–	3	–	–	–	–	2	3	8 (2.7)

Contd...

Table 4.1 : (Contd....)

Trade	Embro-idary Work	Soft-Toys	Lace Work	Candle Making	Mush-Rooms	Chalk Pieces	Pig-gery	Cut-Pieces Selling	Chap-pals Mak-ing	Doop Sticks	Beedi Work	Pick-les	Sambar/ Rasam/ Pow-ders	Veg. Fruit Ven-ding	Woolen Work	Milch Ani-mals	Fish Vend-ing	Tailor-ing	Sheep Rear-ing	Kira-nam	Weav-ing	Thread Work	Others	No Trade	Total
Rajulako-thapally	–	–	–	–	–	–	–	–	–	–	–	–	–	–	–	–	–	1	–	2	–	–	3	–	6 (2.0)
Pegadapally	–	–	–	–	–	–	–	–	–	–	–	–	–	–	–	–	–	–	–	–	–	–	–	10	10 (3.3)
Gudibandal (HNK)	–	–	–	–	–	–	–	–	12	–	–	–	–	–	–	–	–	–	–	–	–	–	–	–	12 (4.0)
Kothawada (WGL)	–	–	–	–	–	–	–	–	–	–	–	–	–	–	–	–	–	–	–	–	9	–	–	–	9 (3.0)
Kodakandla	–	–	–	–	–	–	–	–	–	–	–	–	–	–	–	–	–	–	–	–	5	–	–	–	5 (1.7)
Parvathagiri	–	–	–	–	–	–	–	–	–	–	–	–	–	5	–	–	–	–	–	2	–	–	1	–	8 (2.7)
Chowtapally	–	–	–	–	–	–	–	–	–	–	–	–	–	2	–	–	–	3	–	2	–	–	1	–	8 (2.7)
Bheemaram	–	–	–	–	–	–	–	–	–	–	–	–	–	–	–	–	–	–	–	–	–	12	–	–	12 (4.0)
TOTAL	15 (5.0)	15 (5.0)	6 (2.0)	8 (2.7)	5 (1.7)	8 (2.7)	12 (4.0)	15 (5.0)	26 (8.7)	14 (4.7)	5 (1.7)	12 (4.0)	10 (3.3)	18 (6.0)	6 (2.0)	45 (15.0)	9 (3.0)	9 (3.0)	7 (2.3)	8 (2.7)	14 (4.7)	12 (4.0)	8 (2.7)	13 (4.3)	300 (100.0)

Source : Field Study.

is having three trades i.e Tailoring, 'No trade' and Others while Rajulakotha Pally is having Tailoring, Kiranam and others and Parvathagiri consists of Veg/ Fruit vending, Kiranam and Others. The trade Doop sticks can be found in two villages - Komuravelli and Kistampet. However, the latter village is also having Beedi work. The village Saireddy Pally consists of Pickles Making and Sambar/ Rasam Powders making and the lastly, the village Pegadapally is having 'No trade'.

Caste-wise Distribution of Selected Respondents

Table-4.2 indicates that out of 300 selected respondents 207 (69 percent) belonged to Backward Classes followed by Scheduled Castes with 47 (15.7 percent) and 34 (11.1 percent) belonged to Forward Castes and lastly 12 (4 percent) belonged to Scheduled Tribes. It can be seen that out of 24 trades, in 20 trades Backward Class respondents can be found. They are not seen in Piggery, Chappals making, Pickles making and Thread work. Their percentage share in various trades varied between 0.5 percent in Sambar & Rasam Powders and 20.3 percent in Milch Animals. The Forward Caste respondents are found in 9 trades. However, as high as 35.3 percent of them are in the trade Pickles Making. The Scheduled Caste respondents are observed in 7 trades and 55.3 percent of them are in Chappals making followed by 25.5 percent in Thread work while Scheduled Tribe respondents are seen in only one trade i.e., Piggery. Thus, the distribution of Backward Classes among various trades is relatively wider when compared to other castes. Contrastingly, Scheduled Tribes are seen only in one trade.

Village and Caste-wise Distribution of Selected Sample

Table-4.3 reveals that the village-wise distribution of sample respondents varies between 24.7 percent in Ghanpur (Station) and 1.7 percent in Kodakandla. The data in regard to caste-wise distribution of sample respondents among 20 selected villages reveal that the distribution of Forward Caste respondents varied between 61.8 percent in Saireddy Pally and 2.9 percent each in Kistampet, Rajulakotha Pally, Parvathagiri and Chowtapally. Altogether, they appear in 9 out of selected 20 villages. The Backward Classes respondents can be seen in

Table 4.2 : Trade & Caste - Wise Distribution of Selected Respondents in Warangal District

Trade	*F C*	*B C*	*S C*	*S T*	*Total*
Embroidary Work	–	15 (7.2)	–	–	15 (5.0)
Soft-toys	–	15 (7.2)	–	–	15 (5.0)
Lace Work	–	6 (2.9)	–	–	6 (2.0)
Candle Making	–	8 (3.9)	–	–	8 (2.7)
Mushrooms	–	5 (2.4)	–	–	5 (1.7)
Chalk Pieces	–	8 (3.9)	–	–	8 (2.7)
Piggery	–	– (100.0)	–	12	12 (4.0)
Cut Pieces Selling	1 (2.9)	14 (6.8)	–	–	15 (5.0)
Chappals Making	–	--	26 (55.3)	–	26 (8.7)
Doop Sticks	–	14 (6.8)	–	–	14 (4.7)
Beedi Work	1 (2.9)	4 (1.9)	–	–	5 (1.7)
Pickles	12 (35.3)	–	–	–	12 (4.0)
Sambar/ Rasam Powders	9 (26.5)	1 (0.5)	–	–	10 (3.3)

Contd....

Table 4.2 : (Contd....)

Trade	*F C*	*B C*	*S C*	*S T*	*Total*
Veg/ Fruit Vending	1 (2.9)	12 (5.8)	5 (10.6)	–	18 (6.0)
Woolen Work	–	6 (2.9)	–	–	6 (2.0)
Milch Animals	3 (8.8)	42 (20.3)	–	–	45 (15.0)
Fish Vending	–	8 (3.9)	1 (2.1)	–	9 (3.0)
Tailoring	–	9 (4.3)	–	–	9 (3.0)
Sheep Rearing	–	6 (2.9)	1 (2.1)	–	7 (2.3)
Kiranam	2 (5.9)	5 (2.4)	1 (2.1)	–	8 (2.7)
Weaving	–	14 (6.8)	–	–	14 (4.7)
Thread Work	–	–	12 (25.5)	–	12 (4.0)
Others	1 (2.9)	6 (2.9)	1 (2.1)	–	8 (2.7)
No Trade	4 (11.8)	9 (4.3)	–	–	13 (4.3)
TOTAL	34 (11.3)	207 (69.0)	47 (15.7)	12 (4.0)	300 (100.0)

Source : Field Study.

Table 4.3 : Village & Caste - Wise Distribution of Selected Respondents in Warangal District

Village	*F C*	*B C*	*S C*	*S T*	*Total*
Ghanpur (Station)	–	62 (30.0)	–	12 (100.0)	74 (24.7)
Cheriyal	–	–	14 (29.8)	–	14 (4.7)
Komuravelly	–	9 (4.3)	–	–	9 (3.0)
Kistampet	1 (2.9)	9 (4.3)	–	–	10 (3.3)
Saireddy Pally	21 (61.8)	1 (0.5)	–	–	22 (7.3)
Narsampet	2 (5.9)	21 (10.1)	–	–	23 (7.7)
Agapet	3 (8.8)	12 (5.8)	–	–	15 (5.0)
Narmetta	–	15 (7.2)	–	–	15 (5.0)
Abdul Nagaram	–	15 (7.2)	–	–	15 (5.0)
Chinna Nagaram	–	14 (6.8)	3 (6.4)	–	17 (5.7)
Nainala	–	3 (1.4)	5 (10.6)	–	8 (2.7)

Contd...

Table 4.3 : (Contd....)

Village	*F C*	*B C*	*S C*	*S T*	*Total*
Kachikal	2 (5.9)	6 (2.9)	–	–	8 (2.7)
Rajulakotha Pally	1 (2.9)	5 (2.4)	–	–	6 (2.0)
Pegada Pally	2 (5.9)	8 (3.9)	–	–	10 (3.3)
Gudibandal (HNK)	–	–	12 (25.5)	–	12 (4.0)
Kothawada (WGL)	–	9 (4.3)	–	–	9 (3.0)
Kodakandla	–	5 (2.4)	–	–	5 (1.7)
Parvathagiri	1 (2.9)	6 (2.9)	1 (2.1)	–	8 (2.7)
Chowtapally	1 (2.9)	7 (3.4)	–	–	8 (2.7)
Bheemaram	–	–	12 (25.5)	–	12 (4.0)
TOTAL	34 (11.3)	207 (69.0)	47 (15.7)	12 (4.0)	300 (100.0)

Source : Field Study.

17 out of 20 villages and their percentage share in different villages ranged between 30 percent share in Ghanpur (Station) and 0.5 percent in Saireddy Pally. Further, the Scheduled Caste respondents can be seen in 6 villages and of them, 29.8 percent in Cheriyal, 25.5 percent each in Gudibandal (HNK) and Bheemaram and Parvathagiri stands last with 2.1 percent respondents. Interestingly, Scheduled Tribe respondents are seen in only one village Ghanpur (station). Thus, the data in regard to the village and caste-wise distribution of selected respondents clearly reveal that the Backward Classes respondents are distributed relatively in more villages followed by Forward Caste respondents and last position is for Scheduled Tribes in this regard.

Caste and Category-wise Distribution of Selected Sample

Table-4.4 indicates that 31.3 percent of the selected respondents are Marginal Farmers followed by 24.7 percent others and Non-Agricultural Labourers consists only 3.7 percent

Table 4.4 : Caste & Category - Wise Distribution of Selected Respondents In Warangal District

Category	*F C*	*B C*	*S C*	*S T*	*Total*
Small Farmers	12	39	2	–	53
	(35.3)	(18.8)	(4.3)		(17.7)
Marginal Farmers	15	71	8	–	94
	(44.1)	(34.3)	(17.0)		(31.3)
Agri. Labourers	1	9	2	–	12
	(2.9)	(4.3)	(4.3)		(4.0)
Non-Agri. Labourers	1	8	2	–	11
	(2.9)	(3.9)	(4.3)		(3.7)
Rural Artisans	–	30	26	–	56
		(14.5)	(55.3)		(18.7)
Others	5	50	7	12	74
	(14.7)	(24.2)	(14.9)	(100.0)	(24.7)
TOTAL	34	207	47	12	300
	(100.0)	(100.0)	(100.0)	(100.0)	(100.0)

Source : Field Study.

of the sample. The relationship between caste and category reveals that as high as 79.4 percent of Forward Caste respondents belonged either to the category of Marginal Farmers or to Small Farmers while 53.1 percent of Backward Class respondents can be seen in this category whereas only 21.3 percent Scheduled Caste respondents are found in this and finally no Scheduled Tribe respondent can be found in this category. All this clearly indicates that the land base continuously on the decline when one moves from Forward Caste to Scheduled Tribe. The majority of Scheduled Caste respondents are Rural Artisans and all the Scheduled Tribe respondents belonged to the category of others.

Trade and Category-wise Distribution of Selected Sample

Table-4.5 denotes that as many as 54.7 percent of the Small Farmers have selected the trade Milch Animals. Thus, though the category of Small Farmers could select 11 out of 24 trades selected, majority of them preferred Milch Animals owing to their land base. The Marginal Farmers can be found in 20 trades out of 24 selected and their percentage share varies between 10.6 percent each in Embroidery Work and Milch Animals and 1.1 percent in Mushrooms. The Agricultural labour can be seen in 7 trades and their percentage share varied between 33.3 percent in No trade and 8.3 percent each in Mushrooms, Sambar/ Rasam Powders, Milch Animals and Thread work. Non-Agricultural Labour can be found in 5 trades and 63.7 percent of them have preferred either Candle Making or Mushrooms while Rural Artisans are also found in 7 trades and 46.4 percent of them are in the trade Chappals Making. Finally, the category of 'Others' are found in 17 out of 24 trades. Thus, the distribution of Marginal Farmers and Others among various trades is relatively wider when compared to remaining category respondents.

Socio-Economic Background of the Selected Respondents In Warangal District

Table-4.6 indicates that 77.7 percent of the sample respondents are of less than 40 years old and of them, 39.66

Table 4.5 : Tradee and Category - Wise Distribution Of Selected Respondents In Warangal District

Trade	*S F*	*M F*	*A L*	*N A L*	*R A*	*Others*	*Total*
Embroidary Work	–	10 (10.6)	–	–	–	5 (6.8)	15 (5.0)
Soft-toys	–	2 (2.1)	–	–	6 (10.7)	7 (9.5)	15 (5.0)
Lace Work	–	4 (4.3)	–	–	–	2 (2.7)	6 (2.0)
Candle Making	–	4 (4.3)	–	4 (36.4)	–	–	8 (2.7)
Mushrooms	–	1 (1.1)	1 (8.3)	3 (27.3)	–	–	5 (1.7)
Chalk Pieces	1 (1.9)	6 (6.4)	–	–	–	1 (1.4)	8 (2.7)
Piggery	–	–	–	–	–	12 (16.2)	12 (4.0)
Cut Pieces Selling	–	5 (5.3)	–	–	–	10 (13.5)	15 (5.0)
Chappals Making	–	–	–	–	26 (46.4)	–	26 (8.7)
Doop Sticks	2 (3.8)	6 (6.4)	2 (16.7)	1 (9.1)	–	3 (4.1)	14 (4.7)
Beedi Work	–	4 (4.3)	–	–	–	1 (1.4)	5 (1.7)
Pickles	4 (7.5)	6 (6.4)	–	1 (9.1)	–	1 (1.4)	12 (4.0)
Sambar/ Rasam Powders	1 (1.9)	8 (8.5)	1 (8.3)	–	–	–	10 (3.3)

Contd....

Table 4.5 : (Contd....)

Trade	S F	M F	A L	N A L	R A	Others	Total
Veg/ Fruit Vending	4 (7.5)	6 (6.4)	–	–	–	8 (10.8)	18 (6.0)
Woolen Work	–	–	–	–	–	6 (8.1)	6 (2.0)
Milch Animals	29 (54.7)	10 (10.6)	1 (8.3)	–	4 (7.1)	1 (1.4)	45 (15.0)
Fish Vending	3 (5.7)	4 (4.3)	–	–	2 (3.6)	–	9 (3.0)
Tailoring	1 (1.9)	2 (2.1)	–	–	1 (1.8)	5 (6.8)	9 (3.0)
Sheep Rearing	–	4 (4.3)	–	–	3 (5.4)	–	7 (2.3)
Kiranam	2 (3.8)	2 (2.1)	–	–	–	4 (5.4)	8 (2.7)
Weaving	–	–	–	–	14 (25.0)	–	14 (4.7)
Thread Work	–	3 (3.2)	1 (8.3)	2 (18.2)	–	6 (8.1)	12 (4.0)
Others	2 (3.8)	3 (3.2)	2 (16.7)	–	–	1 (1.4)	8 (2.7)
No Trade	4 (7.5)	4 (4.3)	4 (33.3)	–	–	1 (1.4)	13 (4.3)
TOTAL	53 (100.0)	94 (100.0)	12 (100.0)	11 (100.0)	56 (100.0)	74 (100.0)	300 (100.0)

Source : Field Study.

Table 4.6 : Socio-economic Background of Selected Respondents In Warangal District

Age	*No. of Respondents*	*% To Total*
20 - 30	119 39.7	
31 - 40	114	38.0
41 - 50	47	15.7
Above 50	20	6.7
TOTAL	300	100.0
Caste	*No. of Respondents*	*% To Total*
F C	34	11.3
B C	207	69.0
S C	47	15.7
S T	12	4.0
TOTAL	300	100.0
Edn. Qua.	*No. of Respondents*	*% To Total*
Illiterate	153	51.0
Primary	86	28.7
Secondary	47	15.7
Intermediate	7	2.3
Degree	7	2.3
TOTAL	300	100.0

Contd....

Table 4.6 : (Contd....)

Marital Status	*No. of Respondents*	*% To Total*
Married	274	91.3
Un-Married	–	–
Divorced	3	1.0
Seperated	2	0.7
Widowed	21	7.0
TOTAL	300	100.0
Primay Occu.	*No. of Respondents*	*% To Total*
Agriculture	108	36.0
Agri. Labourers	30	10.0
Non-Agri. Labourers	38	12.7
Rural Artisans	61	20.3
Business	12	4.0
Tailoring	21	7.0
House Wives	20	6.7
Others	10	3.3
TOTAL	300	100.0

Contd....

Table 4.6 : (Contd....)

Sec. Occu.	*No. of Respondents*	*% To Total*
Agriculture	25	8.3
Agri. Labourers	86	28.7
Non-Agri. Labourers	46	15.3
Rural Artisans	52	17.3
Business	20	6.7
Tailoring	10	3.3
House Wives	51	17.0
Others	10	3.3
TOTAL	300	100.0

percent are in the age group of 20-30 years and only 6.66 respondents are of above 50 years age.

The caste-wise distribution of the sample in Warangal district shows that 69 percent belonged to Backward Classes followed by 15.7 percent to Scheduled Castes and 11.3 percent to Forward Castes and only 4 percent to Scheduled Tribes.

It can be denoted from the table that 51 percent of the sample respondents are illiterates. While 44.4 percent of the sample could have upto secondary education and among them 28.7 percent could have only primary level education. It is to be noted that only 4.6 percent of the sample could have opportunity to study upto Intermediate and beyond.

The data in regard to their marital status reveal that 91.3 percent of them are married.

The primary occupation of as many as 36 percent of the sample respondents is Agriculture followed by 20.3 percent in Rural Artisans and the last place occupied by 'Others'.

The information in regard to secondary occupation of the respondents indicates that it is Agricultural Labour for 28.7 percent of the sample followed by Rural Artisans in which 17.3 percent of the sample can be found.

Relationship Between Caste And Educational Qualifications

Table-4.7 indicates that out of 300 selected respondents as many as 153 are illiterates. However, Illiteracy is higher among Scheduled Tribe respondents in which 83.3 percent of the sample are found. It is followed by Backward Class respondents and third place goes to Scheduled Caste respondents and in Forward Castes 20.6 percent of the sample respondents. Thus, illiteracy is relatively lower in Forward Caste respondents. Similarly, the Backward Class and Forward Caste respondents could get the opportunity to have education upto Intermediate and beyond though their percentage is negligible.

Relationship Between Caste and Family Size

The size of the family is one of the indicators which shows the economic status of the family concerned. The higher the

Table 4.7 : Relationship Between Caste and Educational Qualifications of the Selected Respondents In Warangal District

Caste	*Illiterate*	*Primary*	*Secon-dary*	*Inter-Mediate*	*Degree*	*Total*
F C	7	14	10	3	–	34
	(20.6)	(41.2)	(29.4)	(8.9)		(100.0)
B C	114	53	29	4	7	207
	(55.0)	(25.7)	(14.0)	(1.9)	(3.4)	(100.0)
S C	22	17	8	–	–	47
	(46.8)	(36.2)	(17.0)			(100.0)
S T	10	2	–	–	–	12
	(83.3)	(16.7)				(100.0)
TOTAL	153	86	47	7	7	300
	(51.0)	(28.7)	(15.7)	(2.3)	(2.3)	(100.0)

Source : Field Study.

Table 4.8 : Relationship Between Caste and Family Size of the Selected Respondents in Warangal District

Caste	*1 - 2*	*3 - 4*	*5 - 6*	*Above 6*	*Total*
F C	4	23	7	–	34
	(11.8)	(67.6)	(20.6)		(100.0)
B C	17	86	80	24	207
	(8.2)	(41.5)	(38.6)	(11.6)	(100.0)
S C	3	14	25	5	47
	(6.4)	(29.8)	(53.2)	(10.6)	(100.0)
S T	–	4	2	6	12
	(33.3)	(16.7)	(50.0)		(100.0)
TOTAL	24	127	114	35	300
	(8.0)	(42.3)	(38.0)	(11.7)	(100.0)

Source : Field Study.

economic status lower will be the family size and vice versa. The family size is less than 4 for 50.3 percent of the respondents. The family size is relatively lesser in Forward Caste respondents followed by Backward Class respondents when compared to Scheduled Caste and Scheduled Tribe respondents. The family size is 7 and more persons in 50 percent of Scheduled Tribe respondents. This phenomenon can not be seen in Forward Caste respondents. Thus, the size of the family is also related to caste.

Relationship Between Caste and Economic Assets

The economic assets in the present study consists of house possession, other assets and savings.

Table-4.9 indicates that out of 300 selected sample 57.7 percent possessed Pucca houses, 17.3 percent RCC houses, 17 percent Kutcha houses and only 8 percent are residing in rented houses. The possession of Pucca houses is high among Backward Class respondents and Scheduled Tribes occupy last position in this regard. Similarly, 66.7 percent of Scheduled Tribes are residing in Kutcha houses. In the ownership of RCC houses, Forward Castes occupy first position followed by Scheduled Caste respondents. Thus, in the possession of house, Backward Class and Forward Castes are relatively in a better position when compared to Scheduled Caste and Scheduled Tribe respondents.

Table - 4.9 : Relationship Between Caste and House Possession of The Selected Respondents In Warangal District

Caste	*Kutcha*	*Pucca*	*R C C*	*Rented*	*Total*
F C	5	15	13	1	34
	(14.7)	(44.1)	(38.2)	(2.9)	(100.0)
B C	34	134	29	10	207
	(16.4)	(64.7)	(14.0)	(4.8)	(100.0)
S C	4	20	10	13	47
	(8.5)	(42.5)	(21.3)	(27.7)	(100.0)
S T	8	4	–	–	12
	(66.7)	(33.3)			(100.0)
TOTAL	51	173	52	24	300
	(17.0)	(57.7)	(17.3)	(8.0)	(100.0)

Source : Field Study.

Table-4.10 reveals that as high as 52 percent of the sample could get the possession of the house from their parents and 59.4 percent of Backward Class and 55.9 percent of Forward

Caste respondents can be seen in this regard. Similarly, 58.3 percent of Scheduled Tribe and 40.4 percent of Scheduled Caste respondents could get the house from Government.

Table 4.10 : Relationship Between Caste and Source of House Possession of the Selected Respondents In Warangal District

Caste	*Parents*	*Govt.*	*Own*	*Others*	*Total*
F C	19 (55.9)	5 (14.7)	9 (26.5)	1 (2.9)	34 (100.0)
B C	123 (59.4)	28 (13.5)	46 (22.2)	10 (4 8)	207 (100.0)
S C	12 (25.5)	19 (40.4)	3 (6.4)	13 (27.7)	47 (100.0)
S T	2 (16.7)	7 (58.3)	3 (25.0)	–	12 (100.0)
TOTAL	156 (52.0)	59 (19.7)	61 (20.3)	24 (8.0)	300 (100.0)

Source : Field Study.

Table-4.11 indicates that as high as 29.41 percent of Forward Caste respondents and 23.40 percent of Scheduled Caste respondents possessed assets in the range of above Rs. 15000.

Table 4.11 : Relationship Between Caste and Assets Position of the Selected Respondents In Warangal District

(Asset value in Rs.)

Caste	*Below 1000*	*1001-3000*	*3001-5000*	*5001-10000*	*10001-15000*	*Above 15000*	*Total*
F C	4 (11.8)	5 (14.7)	9 (26.5)	3 (8.8)	3 (8.8)	10 (29.4)	34 (100.0)
B C	28 (13.5)	53 (25.6)	43 (20.8)	13 (6.3)	34 (16.4)	36 (17.4)	207 (100.0)
S C	7 (14.9)	4 (8.5)	9 (19.1)	6 (12.8)	10 (21.3)	11 (23.4)	47 (100.0)
S T	–	4 (33.3)	6 (50.0)	2 (16.7)	–	–	12 (100.0)
TOTAL	39 (13.0)	66 (22.0)	67 (22.3)	24 (8.0)	47 (15.7)	57 (19.0)	300 (100.0)

Source : Field Study.

The Scheduled Tribe respondents can not be found in this range. The asset position did not vary much among Forward Caste, Backward Class and Scheduled Caste respondents. The Scheduled Tribe respondents are relatively weaker in this regard.

Table-4.12 denotes that 60.3 percent of the sample could save part of their income. The caste-wise analysis indicates that the percentage of respondents who could save is higher among Forward Castes followed by Scheduled Castes and Backward Classes respectively and Scheduled Tribes stand last in this regard.

Table 4.12 : Relationship Between Caste and Savings Position of the Selected Respondents In Warangal District

Caste	*Yes*	*No*	*Total*
F C	25	9	34
	(73.5)	(26.5)	(100.0)
B C	123	84	207
	(59.4)	(40.6)	(100.0)
S C	29	18	47
	(61.7)	(38.3)	(100.0)
S T	4	8	12
	(33.3)	(66.7)	(100.0)
TOTAL	181	119	300
	(60.3)	(39.7)	(100.0)

Source : Field Study.

It can be noticed from Table-4.13 that 41.43 percent of the respondents keep their savings in chits and 23 percent in post-office. Only 16.02 percent prefer to keep their savings in Banks. The percentage of respondents who prefer chits is relatively higher among Scheduled Tribes and Scheduled Castes. Similarly, the percentage of respondents who prefer banks is higher among Forward Castes and Scheduled Castes and Scheduled Tribes.

Table-4.14 explains that the amount of savings is in the range of Rs. 1000-3000 for 31.49 percent of the sample and Rs.

Table 4.13 : Caste and Savings in Various Institutions of the Selected Respondents in Warangal District

Caste	*Chits*	*L I C*	*Banks*	*Post-Office*	*Total*
F C	7 (28.0)	6 (24.0)	7 (28.0)	5 (20.0)	25 (100.0)
B C	49 (39.8)	26 (21.1)	13 (10.6)	35 (28.5)	123 (100.0)
S C	16 (55.2)	3 (10.3)	8 (27.6)	2 (6.9)	29 (100.0)
S T	3 (75.0)	–	1 (25.0)	–	4 (100.0)
TOTAL	75 (41.4)	35 (19.3)	29 (16.0)	42 (23.2)	181 (100.0)

Source : Field Study.

Table 4.14 : Caste and Amount Saved By Selected Respondents in Warangal District

(Savings in Rs.)

Caste	*Below 1000*	*1001-3000*	*3001-5000*	*5001-10000*	*10001-15000*	*Above 15000*	*Total*
F C	–	12 (48.0)	1 (4.0)	2 (8.0)	10 (40.0)	–	25 (100.0)
B C	13 (10.6)	38 (30.9)	34 (27.6)	7 (5.7)	27 (22.0)	4 (3.3)	123 (100.0)
S C	–	5 (17.2)	18 (62.1)	4 (13.8)	2 (6.9)	–	29 (100.0)
S T	2 (50.0)	2 (50.0)	–	–	–	–	4 (100.0)
TOTAL	15 (8.3)	57 (31.5)	53 (29.3)	13 (7.2)	39 (21.5)	4 (2.2)	181 (100.0)

Source : Field Study.

3001-5000 for 29.28 percent of the sample respondents. However, 4 persons could save more than Rs. 15000 and all of them belonged to Backward Class Community. However, 40 percent of Forward Caste and 21.75 percent of Backward Class respondents could save an amount in the range of Rs. 10000-15000 while the savings of Scheduled Tribe respondents did not exceed Rs. 3000.

Selection of Trade

Table-4.15 reveals that DRDA Officials played a role in the selection of trade for 95 respondents while 91 could select the trade on their own. The bank officials are behind the selection of trade in the schemes of Lace work, Piggery, Cut-pieces selling, Milch Animals and Sheep Rearing while VDO's are the source in the schemes of Soft-Toys, Veg/ Fruit Vending, Milch Animals, Fish Vending, Tailoring, Kiranam, Weaving and

Table 4.15 : Selection of the Trade by the Selected Respondents in Warangal District

Trade	*Own*	*VDO/ MPDO*	*DRDA Officials*	*Bank Officials*	*G.I/ Others*	*Total*
Embroidary Work	3	–	8	–	4	15
Soft-toys	–	5	1	6	3	15
Lace Work	–	–	6	–	–	6
Candle Making	–	–	6	–	2	8
Mushrooms	5	–	–	–	–	5
Chalk Pieces	–	–	7	–	1	8
Piggery	4	–	–	8	–	12
Cut Pieces Selling	–	–	10	5	–	15
Chappals Making	13	–	8	–	5	26
Doop Sticks	–	–	14	–	–	14
Beedi Work	2	–	3	–	–	5
Pickles	8	–	4	–	–	12
Sambar/ Rasam Powders	8	–	2	–	–	10
Veg/ Fruit Vending	10	2	4	–	2	18
Woolen Work	–	–	6	–	–	6
Milch Animals	7	3	8	23	4	45
Fish Vending	3	5	–	–	1	9
Tailoring	6	3	–	–	–	9
Sheep Rearing	–	–	–	7	–	7
Kiranam	5	2	–	–	1	8
Weaving	3	2	7	–	2	14
Thread Work	–	–	–	–	12	12
Others	1	5	1	–	1	8
No Trade	13	–	–	–	–	13
TOTAL	91 (30.3)	27 (9.0)	95 (31.7)	49 (16.3)	38 (12.7)	300 (100.0)

Source: Field Study.

Others. However, every scheme is encouraged by different agencies.

Problems of Trade

The problems confronted by the respondents in running the scheme mainly consist of procurement of raw-material and marketing of the product.

It is heartening to note from the Table-4.16 that out of 300 selected respondents as many as 224 did not face any problems in regard to the procurement of raw-materials. Out of 76

Table 4.16 : Problems in the Procurement of Raw-material by the Selected Respondents in Warangal District

Trade	*Yes*	*No.*	*Total*
Embroidary Work	3	12	15
Soft-toys	9	6	15
Lace Work	–	6	6
Candle Making	8	–	8
Mushrooms	5	–	5
Chalk Pieces	1	7	8
Piggery	4	8	12
Cut Pieces Selling	–	15	15
Chappals Making	5	21	26
Doop Sticks	4	10	14
Beedi Work	–	5	5
Pickles	–	12	12
Sambar/ Rasam Powders	–	10	10
Veg./ Fruit Vending	4	14	18
Woolen Work	–	6	6
Milch Animals	11	34	45
Fish Vending	2	7	9
Tailoring	–	9	9
Sheep Rearing	–	7	7
Kiranam	2	6	8
Weaving	11	3	14
Thread Work	–	12	12
Others	7	1	8
No Trade	–	13	13
TOTAL	76 (25.3)	224 (74.7)	300 (100.0)

Source : Field Study.

respondents who face problems in this regard consist of Embroidery Work, Soft-Toys, Candle Making, Mushrooms, Chalk-Pieces, Chappals Making, Veg/ Fruit Vending, Milch Animals, Fish Vending, Kiranam, Weaving and Others.

Marketing of the Product

Table-4.17 indicates that 192 respondents could market their product on their own while 50 are exclusively depend upon DWCRA Bazars and 58 could sell the product through both the channels. The respondents who depend exclusively on

Table - 4.17 : Marketing of the Product by the Selected Respondents in Warangal District

Trade	*DWCRA Bazar*	*Own*	*Both*	*Total*
Embroidary Work	5	2	8	15
Soft-toys	9	—	6	15
Lace Work	—	6	—	6
Candle Making	8	—	—	8
Mushrooms	—	5	—	5
Chalk Pieces	—	8	—	8
Piggery	—	12	—	12
Cut Pieces Selling	—	5	10	15
Chappals Making	—	9	17	26
Doop Sticks	—	4	10	14
Beedi Work	—	5	—	5
Pickles	12	—	—	12
Sambar/ Rasam Powders	10	—	—	10
Veg/ Fruit Vending	—	18	—	18
Woolen Work	6	—	—	6
Milch Animals	—	45	—	45
Fish Vending	—	9	—	9
Tailoring	—	7	2	9
Sheep Rearing	—	7	—	7
Kiranam	—	8	—	8
Weaving	—	9	5	14
Thread Work	--	12	—	12
Others	--	8	—	8
No Trade	—	13	—	13
TOTAL	50 (16.7)	192 (64.0)	58 (19.3)	300 (100.0)

Source : Field Study.

DWCRA Bazars for sale consist of 5 respondents in Embroidery work, 9 in Soft-toys and all the respondents in Candle Making, Pickles, Sambar/ Rasam Powder and Woolen Work. The respondents who sell their product through both the channels consist of 8 in Embroidery work, 6 in Soft-Toys, 10 in Cut-Pieces selling 17 in Chappals Making 10 in Doop sticks, 2 in Tailoring and 5 in Weaving.

Table-4.18 denotes that as many as 226 respondents out of 300 selected did not face any marketing problems. Out of 84

Table 4.18 : Marketing Problems of the Selected Respondents in Warangal District

Trade	*Yes*	*No*	*Total*
Embroidary Work	3	12	15
Soft-toys	—	15	15
Lace Work	—	6	6
Candle Making	8	—	8
Mushrooms	5	—	5
Chalk Pieces	8	—	8
Piggery	3	9	12
Cut Pieces Selling	5	10	15
Chappals Making	6	20	26
Doop Sticks	6	8	14
Beedi Work	5	—	5
Pickles	—	12	12
Sambar/ Rasam Powders	7	3	10
Veg/ Fruit Vending	12	6	18
Woolen Work	6	—	6
Milch Animals	—	45	45
Fish Vending	2	7	9
Tailoring	—	9	9
Sheep Rearing	—	7	7
Kiranam	—	8	8
Weaving	2	12	14
Thread Work	—	12	12
Others	6	2	8
No Trade	—	13	13
TOTAL	84 (28.0)	216 (72.0)	300 (100.0)

Source : Field Study.

respondents who face marketing problem, Table-4.19 explains that inadequate demand for 37, Transport is for 23, competition is for 17 and 7 face problem due to low quality. The trades which do not have any marketing problems are Soft-Toys, Lace work, Pickles, Milch Animals, Tailoring, Sheep Rearing, Kiranam, Thread work and No Trade.

Table 4.19 : Nature of the Marketing Problems of the Selected Respondents in Warangal District

Trade	*Inadequate Demand*	*Trans-port*	*Quality/ Packing*	*Compe-tition*	*Total*
Embroidary Work	2	–	1	–	3
Soft-toys	–	–	–	–	–
Lace Work	–	–	–	–	–
Candle Making	6	–	–	2	8
Mushrooms	5	–	–	–	5
Chalk Pieces	7	–	–	1	8
Piggery	–	3	–	–	3
Cut Pieces Selling	1	3	–	1	5
Chappals Making	–	1	2	3	6
Doop Sticks	2	–	1	3	6
Beedi Work	–	4	1	–	5
Pickles	–	–	–	–	–
Sambar/ Rasam Powders	5	–	2	–	7
Veg./ Fruit Vending	–	8	–	4	12
Woolen Work	6	–	–	–	6
Milch Animals	–	–	–	–	–
Fish Vending	–	2	–	–	2
Tailoring	–	–	–	–	–
Sheep Rearing	–	–	–	–	–
Kiranam	–	–	–	–	–
Weaving	–	–	–	2	2
Thread Work	–	–	–	–	–
Others	3	2	–	1	6
No Trade	–	–	–	–	–
TOTAL	37 (44.04)	23 (27.38)	7 (8.33)	17 (2.23)	84 (100.0)

Source : Field Study.

Comparative Analysis of Employment Generation

As one of the main aims of DWCRA is to generate employment, a detailed analysis is made in this regard. The employment generation can be assessed by making a comparison between Pre and Post-DWCRA employment. The generation of employment may depend upon scheme, caste and category of the respondent, educational qualifications and finally of their age.

Scheme-wise Analysis of Employment Generation

Table-4.20 denotes the generation of employment during Pre and Post-DWCRA period in Warangal district. It can be noticed that the average employment in terms of days per month is 16.34 during Pre-DWCRA period and it has been increased to 24.23 during Post-DWCRA period. This clearly denotes a positive impact of DWCRA on employment generation. Moreover, the number of respondents who are employed is only 287 during Pre-DWCRA period and it has been increased to 300 during Post-DWCRA period i.e., an addition of 13 respondents is made to total who are employed.

The scheme-wise analysis reveals that the employment generated in terms of number of days per month is increased in all the schemes though the rise may vary from scheme to scheme. During Pre-DWCRA period, the average employment is 16.34 days per month and 12 out of 24 scheme have the average employment above the total average. They are Embroidery work, Soft-toys, Lace work, Mushrooms, Chappals making, Pickles, Sambar/ Rasam powders, Veg/ Fruit vending, Kiranam, No Trade, Weaving and Thread work. During Post-DWCRA period, the average employment per month is 24.23 days and 10 schemes show the employment above total average. However, the highest employment in terms of days per month can be seen in Kiranam with 29.37 days and Piggery stands lowest with 15.50 days. Therefore, the difference between Pre and Post-DWCRA employment vary between 15.83 in Tailoring and 0.07 in No Trade. Except in 4 trades viz. Chalk Pieces, Piggery, Doop sticks and Others, in all the remaining 20 trades the employment is more than 20 days per month.

Table 4.20 : Scheme-Wise Analysis of Employment Generation During Pre & Post-DWCRA Period in Warangal District

Trade	*Pre-DWCRA Employment*			*Post-DWCRA Employment*			*Difference of Avg. Emplo-ment*
	No. of Respon-dents	*Total Days*	*Avg.Emp Days (P. M.)*	*No. of Respon-dents*	*Total Days*	*Avg.Emp Days (P. M.)*	
Embroidary Work	15	255	17.00	15	360	24.00	7.00
Soft-toys	15	287	19.13	15	381	25.40	6.27
Lace Work	6	104	17.33	6	137	22.83	5.50
CandleMaking	8	129	16.12	8	162	20.25	4.13
Mushrooms	5	95	19.00	5	120	24.00	5.00
Chalk Pieces	8	127	15.87	8	148	18.50	2.63
Piggery	12	154	12.83	12	186	15.50	2.67
Cut Pieces Selling	13	193	14.84	15	373	24.86	10.02
Chappals Making	26	437	16.80	26	682	26.23	9.43
Doop Sticks	14	197	14.07	14	302	21.57	7.50
Beedi Work	5	63	12.60	5	85	17.00	4.40
Pickles	11	181	16.45	12	289	24.08	7.63
Sambar/Rasam Powders	10	176	17.60	10	224	22.40	4.80
Veg./ Fruit Vending	18	375	20.83	18	530	29.44	8.61
Woolen Work	6	82	13.66	6	141	23.50	9.84
Milch Animals	45	669	14.86	45	1149	25.53	10.67
Fish Vending	9	107	11.88	9	243	27.00	15.12
Tailoring	8	100	12.50	9	255	28.33	15.83
Sheep Rearing	7	105	15.00	7	160	22.85	7.85
Kiranam	7	135	19.28	8	235	29.37	10.09
Weaving	14	270	19.28	14	391	27.92	8.64
Thread Work	6	102	17.00	12	320	26.66	9.66
Others	6	87	14.50	8	137	17.12	2.62
No Trade	13	260	20.00	13	261	20.07	0.07
TOTAL	287	4690	16.34	300	7271	24.23	7.89

Source : Field Study.

Relationship Between Caste and Employment Generation

It can be noticed from Table-4.21 that the average employment in terms of number of days of employment per month during Post-DWCRA period is higher in all the castes. However, the employment per month is higher for Scheduled Caste respondents with 26.63 and Scheduled Tribe respondents stand last place with 15.50 days. Therefore, the difference between Pre and Post-DWCRA employment vary from 9.98 for Scheduled Caste respondents and 2.67 for Scheduled Tribe respondents.

Table 4.21 Caste-Wise Analysis Of Employment Generation During Pre and Post-DWCRA Period in Warangal District

Caste	*Pre-DWCRA Employment*			*Post-DWCRA Employment*			*Difference of Avg. Emplo-ment*
	No. of Respon-dents	*Total Days*	*Avg.Emp Days (P. M.)*	*No. of Respon-dents*	*Total Days*	*Avg.Emp Days (P. M.)*	
F C	33	497	15.06	34	693	20.38	5.32
B C	202	3373	16.69	207	5140	24.83	8.14
S C	40	666	16.65	47	1252	26.63	9.98
S T	12	154	12.83	12	186	15.50	2.67
TOTAL	287	4690	16.34	300	7271	24.23	7.89

Source : Field Study.

Relationship Between Category and Employment Generation

Table-4.22 indicates the relationship between category and employment generation and the employment generated in terms of days per month has increased for all the respondents irrespective of their economic category. The average employment in days per month during Pre-DWCRA period has varied between 19.09 days for Agricultural Labour and 13.15 days for Small Farmers. However, these positions are not retained during Post-DWCRA period in which the average employment has varied between 26 days for Rural Artisans and 21.72 days for Non-Agricultural Labourers. The difference between Pre and Post-DWCRA average employment is in the range of 10.00 days in Small Farmers and 3.82 days in Agricultural Labour. However, DWCRA has shown a positive impact on all the respondents irrespective of their economic category.

Table 4.22 : Category-Wise Analysis of Employment Generation During Pre & Post-DWCRA Period in Warangal District

Trade	*Pre-DWCRA Employment*			*Post-DWCRA Employment*			*Difference of Avg. Employment*
	No. of Respondents	*Total Days*	*Avg.Emp Days (P. M.)*	*No. of Respondents*	*Total Days*	*Avg.Emp Days (P. M.)*	
Small Farmers	52	684	13.15	53	1227	23.5	10.00
Marginal Farmers	92	1562	16.97	94	2262	24.06	7.09
Agri. Labourers	11	210	19.09	12	275	22.91	3.82
Non-Agri. Labourers	10	155	15.50	11	239	21.72	6.22
Rural Artisans	56	954	17.03	56	1456	26.00	8.97
Others	66	1125	17.04	74	1812	24.48	7.44
TOTAL	287	4690	16.34	300	7271	24.23	7.89

Source : Field Study.

Relationship Between Educational Qualifications of the Respondents and Employment Generation

Table-4.23 depicts that the average employment during Pre-DWCRA period is almost same with minor variation for all the respondents irrespective of their educational qualifications. Moreover, the average employment has increased for all the respondents too. However, it is relatively higher for Degree holders followed by the respondents who have upto primary education. Interestingly, the average employment is least during Post-DWCRA period for the respondents who could study upto Intermediate. Therefore, the difference between Pre and Post-DWCRA employment has varied between 5.26 days for Intermediate and 11.19 days for Degree holders. Thus, there is no any exact relationship between educational qualification of the respondent and employment generation.

Table 4.23 : Educational Qualifications and Employment Generation During Pre and Post-DWCRA Period In Warangal District

Educational Qualifications	*Pre-DWCRA Employment*			*Post-DWCRA Employment*			*Difference of Avg. Emplo-ment*
	No. of Respon-dents	*Total Days*	*Avg.Emp Days (P. M.)*	*No. of Respon-dents*	*Total Days*	*Avg.Emp Days (P. M.)*	
Illiterate	151	2473	16.37	153	3714	24.27	7.90
Primary	82	1359	16.57	86	2176	25.30	8.73
Secondary	42	673	16.02	47	1050	22.34	6.32
Intermediate	6	85	14.16	7	136	19.42	5.26
Degree	6	100	16.66	7 .	195	27.85	11.19
TOTAL	287	4690	16.34	300	7271	24.23	7.89

Source : Field Study.

Relationship Between Age of the Respondent and Employment Generation

It can be observed from Table-4.24 that the average employment during Pre-DWCRA period is almost uniform for all the age groups except the respondents who are in the age group of above 50 years. However, the average employment during Post-DWCRA period is on the rise for all the respondents irrespective of their age group and it has been in the smaller

Table 4.24 : Relationship between Age and Employment Generation During Pre and Post-DWCRA Period in Warangal District

Age	*Pre-DWCRA Employment*			*Post-DWCRA Employment*			*Difference of Avg. Emplo-ment*
	No. of Respon-dents	*Total Days*	*Avg.Emp Days (P. M.)*	*No. of Respon-dents*	*Total Days*	*Avg.Emp Days (P. M.)*	
20 - 30	112	1865	16.65	119	2901	24.37	7.72
31 - 40	110	1790	16.27	114	2720	23.85	7.58
41 - 50	46	780	16.95	47	1154	24.55	7.60
Above 50	19	255	13.42	20	496	24.80	11.38
TOTAL	287	4690	16.34	300	7271	24.23	7.89

Source : Field Study.

range of 23.85 days for 31-40 years age group and 24.80 days for the 50 years age group. Though the difference between Pre and Post-DWCRA average employment vary from age group to age group, the average employment during Post-DWCRA period is almost same with negligible variation.

Employment Generation Exclusively From DWCRA

As all the respondents belonged to rural poor families, they do whatever the work available and try to earn for the sustenance of the family even prior to the implementation of DWCRA. Therefore, in order to ascertain the success of the programme in terms of employment generation, it is desired to note the number of days of additional employment created by DWCRA. The relevant information is presented in Table-4.25. Additional days of employment per month generated by DWCRA is less than 5 days for 104 respondents, 6-10 days for 93 respondents, 11-15 for 61, 16-20 days for 26 while the generation of additional employment is more than 20 days per month for 16 respondents and 9 trades can be found in this viz. Embroidery work, Soft-toys, Cut-pieces selling, Chappals making, Pickles, Veg/ Fruit Vending, Tailoring, Kiranam and Others. Interestingly, the additional employment generation in these schemes vary from less than 5 days per month to more than 20 days per month depending upon other variables that determines the success of trade that has already been discussed in preceding analysis.

The relationship between caste and employment exclusively created by DWCRA has been shown in Table-4.26. It can be observed that for as many as 20 out of 34 Forward Caste respondents, the additional employment generation by DWCRA is less than 5 days per month. Similar position can be seen even in the case of Backward Class respondents. However, 65 of them out of 207 selected, the additional employment generation from DWCRA is in between 6-10 days per month. In this range same majority of Scheduled Caste respondents can also be observed. It is to be noted that the additional employment generation is less than 15 days per month for all the Scheduled Tribe respondents.

Table 4.25 : Sceme-Wise Analysis of Employment Generation From DWCRA in Warangal District

Trade	*Days Per Month*					*Total*
	Below 5	*6 - 10*	*11 - 15*	*16 - 20*	*Above 20*	
Embroidary Work	3	4	4	1	3	15
Soft-toys	4	6	3	–	2	15
Lace Work	2	4	–	–	–	6
Candle Making	6	2	–	–	–	8
Mushrooms	4	1	–	–	–	5
Chalk Pieces	6	2	–	–	–	8
Piggery	6	3	3	–	–	12
Cut Pieces Selling	1	6	4	2	2	15
Chappals Making	2	13	6	2	3	26
Doop Sticks	6	8	–	–	–	14
Beedi Work	5	–	–	–	–	5
Pickles	2	5	2	1	2	12
Sambar/ Rasam Powders	7	1	1	1	–	10
Veg./ Fruit Vending	9	3	2	3	1	18
Woolen Work	–	5	1	–	–	6
Milch Animals	10	13	16	6	–	45
Fish Vending	–	2	4	3	–	9
Tailoring	–	1	6	1	1	9
Sheep Rearing	4	1	1	1	–	7
Kiranam	3	1	–	3	1	8
Weaving	5	7	2	–	–	14
Thread Work	–	4	6	2	–	12
Others	6	1	–	–	1	8
No Trade	13	–	–	–	–	13
TOTAL	104 (34.7)	93 (31.0)	61 (20.3)	26 (8.7)	16 (5.3)	300 (100.0)

Source : Field Study.

TAble 4.26 : Caste-Wise Analysis of Employment Generation From DWCRA in Warangal District

Caste	*Days Per Month*					*Total*
	Below 5	*6 - 10*	*11 - 15*	*16 - 20*	*Above 20*	
F C	20	7	3	2	2	34
B C	69	65	47	15	11	207
S C	9	18	8	9	3	47
S T	6	3	3	–	–	12
TOTAL	104 (34.7)	93 (31.0)	61 (20.3)	26 (8.7)	16 (5.3)	300 (100.0)

Source : Field Study.

Additional Employment Generation

The functioning of various trades under DWCRA generates employment not only to the respondents but also to others. In this, some times they may involve their own family members or others. Table-4.27 indicates scheme-wise additional employment generation which denotes that on the whole additionally 154 persons got employment and of them, 121 are family members and 33 are others. The scheme-wise analysis

Table 4.27 : Scheme-wise Analysis of Additional Employment Generation Under DWCRA in Warangal District

Trade	*Family Members*	*Other Members*	*Total*
Embroidary Work	4	1	5
Soft-toys	2	5	7
Lace Work	—	—	—
Candle Making	—	—	—
Mushrooms	—	—	—
Chalk Pieces	1	2	3
Piggery	7	—	7
Cut Pieces Selling	5	3	8
Chappals Making	26	5	31
Doop Sticks	6	—	6
Beedi Work	1	—	1
Pickles	4	3	7
Sambar/ Rasam Powders	—	—	—
Veg/ Fruit Vending	4	—	4
Woolen Work	—	—	—
Milch Animals	39	6	45
Fish Vending	—	—	—
Tailoring	4	1	5
Sheep Rearing	—	7	7
Kiranam	2	—	2
Weaving	9	—	9
Thread Work	4	—	4
Others	3	—	3
No Trade	—	—	—
TOTAL	121	33	154

Source : Field Study.

states that the trades of Lace work, Candle making, Mushrooms, Woolen work, Fish vending and No Trade (6) did not generate any additional employment while Piggery, Doop Sticks, Beedi work, Veg/ Fruit vending, Kiranam, Others, Weaving and Thread work could involve their family members to run the trade. The highest additional employment is generated in Milch Animals with 45 persons followed by Chappals Making with 31 persons. Nearly 50 percent additional employment generation is only from these two schemes. This clearly denotes the scope of additional employment generation of these schemes.

Impact of DWCRA on Income Generation

The main aim of the DWCRA is to create employment so as to raise the income levels of the rural poor. Therefore, the success of the programme will be assessed on the basis of its ability to generate income. The performance of DWCRA in terms of income generation will be ascertained in two ways (i) The additional income generated by DWCRA i.e., the income generation exclusively from DWCRA (ii) The difference between Pre and Post-DWCRA income.

Scheme-wise Income Generation From DWCRA

Table-4.28 indicates that the income generated exclusively from DWCRA has varied between nil and Rs. 1001-1500 per month. The DWCRA has generated additional income in the range of Rs. 251-500 per month to as many as 109 respondents out of 300 selected. However, the income generation has exceeded Rs. 500 per month to 134 respondents and of them, 37 could get an additional income in the range of Rs. 1001-1500. It is to be noticed that 10 respondents could not get any additional income. They belonged to the trades of Candle making, Mushrooms, Chalk-pieces and Milch Animals. Except Mushrooms in the remaining 3 trades, the remaining respondents earn some additional income positively from DWCRA. The trades that generate income in excess of Rs. 751 per month are Embroidery work, Soft-toys, Cut-pieces selling, Chappals making, Pickles, Sambar/ Rasam powder, Veg/ Fruit

Vending, Milch Animals, Fish vending, Tailoring, Sheep Rearing, Weaving and Thread work, i.e., 13 out of 24 trades selected.

Table 4.28 : Relationship Between Scheme and Income Generation in Warangal Disttrict

(Income In Rs.)

Trade	*Nil*	*Below 250*	*251-500*	*501-750*	*751-1000*	*Above 1000*	*Total*
Embroidary Work	—	—	1	3	9	2	15
Soft-toys	—	—	4	4	3	4	15
Lace Work	—	1	5	—	—	—	6
Candle Making	1	5	2	—	—	—	8
Mushrooms	5	—	—	—	—	—	5
Chalk Pieces	1	5	2	—	—	—	8
Piggery	—	2	9	1	—	—	12
Cut Pieces Selling	—	—	4	2	1	8	15
Chappals Making	—	1	12	5	4	4	26
Doop Sticks	—	5	5	4	—	—	14
Beedi Work	—	4	1	—	—	—	5
Pickles	—	—	8	1	1	2	12
Sambar/Rasam Powders	—	1	6	2	—	1	10
Veg/ Fruit Vending	—	1	3	5	8	1	18
Woolen Work	—	2	4	—	—	—	6
Milch Animals	3	4	14	8	10	6	45
Fish Vending	—	—	3	2	2	2	9
Tailoring	—	1	4	1	2	1	9
Sheep Rearing	—	—	2	2	1	2	7
Kiranam	—	—	2	3	3	—	8
Weaving	—	—	8	2	2	2	14
Thread Work	—	—	4	3	3	2	12
Others	—	3	5	—	—	—	8
No Trade	—	12	1	—	—	—	13
TOTAL	10 (3.3)	47 (15.7)	109 (36.3)	48 (16.0)	49 (16.3)	37 (12.3)	300 (100.0)

Source : Field Study.

Caste-wise Analysis of Income Generation Exclusively From DWCRA

Table-4.29 indicates that the income generated exclusively from DWCRA is nil for 10 respondents and of them one belonged to Forward Caste and 9 belonged to Backward Classes. However, irrespective of the caste, majority of respondents can be found in the income range of Rs. 251-500 per month. The Backward Class respondents alone can be seen in all the ranges of income varying from zero to Rs. 1001 and above per month. The range is relatively narrower for Scheduled Tribe respondents where no Scheduled Tribe respondent can be seen beyond the income range of Rs. 501-750 per month. Contrastingly, no Scheduled Caste respondent can be observed below Rs. 250 per month.

Table 4.29 : Relationship Between Caste and Income Generation in Warangal Disttrict

(Income In Rs.)

Caste	*Nil*	*Below 250*	*251-500*	*501-750*	*751-1000*	*Above 1000*	*Total*
F C	1	7	22	1	–	3	34
B C	9	38	61	35	40	24	207
S C	–	–	17	11	9	10	47
S T	–	2	9	1	–	–	12
TOTAL	10 (3.3)	47 (15.7)	109 (36.3)	48 (16.0)	49 (16.3)	37 (12.3)	300 (100.0)

Source : Field Study.

Comparative Analysis of Pre and Post-DWCRA Income Generation

Income generation will depend upon the scheme, caste, category, educational qualifications and age of the respondents. The data in regard to pre and post-DWCRA income in relation to scheme are shown in Table-4.30.

Table 4.30 : Scheme-Wise Analysis of Income Generation During Pre and Post-DWCRA Period in Warangal District

(Income In Rs.)

Trade	*Pre-DWCRA Income*			*Post-DWCRA Income*			*Difference*
	No. of Respon-dents	*Total Income*	*Avg. Income (P. M.)*	*No. of Respon-dents*	*Total Income*	*Avg. Income (P. M.)*	*of Avg. Income*
Embroidary Work	13	6800	523.07	15	21100	1406.66	883.59
Soft-toys	15	11800	786.66	15	22550	1503.33	716.67
Lace Work	6	4000	666.66	6	8700	1450.00	783.34
Candle Making	8	4600	575.00	8	6100	762.50	187.50
Mushrooms	5	4900	980.00	5	3450	690.00	-290.00
Chalk Pieces	8	2950	368.75	8	4550	568.75	200.00
Piggery	12	3500	291.66	12	7500	625.00	333.34
Cut Pieces Selling	13	6350	488.46	15	21500	1433.33	944.87
Chappals Making	26	18950	728.84	26	40150	1544.23	815.39
Doop Sticks	11	4850	440.90	14	10300	735.71	294.81
Beedi Work	5	1350	270.00	5	2500	500.00	230.00
Pickles	5	4050	810.00	12	9850	820.83	10.83
Sambar/Rasam Powders	7	3150	450.00	10	7150	715.0	265.00
Veg/Fruit Vending	17	9150	538.23	18	24720	1373.33	835.10
Woolen Work	6	4700	783.33	6	6500	1083.33	300.00
Milch Animals	31	9650	311.29	45	24300	540.00	228.71
Fish Vending	6	1950	325.00	9	10500	1166.66	841.66
Tailoring	8	3050	381.25	9	8700	966.66	585.41
Sheep Rearing	7	2250	321.42	7	8300	1185.71	864.29
Kiranam	5	2250	450.00	8	10200	1275.00	825.00
Weaving	14	13400	957.14	14	22200	1585.71	628.57
Thread Work	6	2950	491.66	12	11800	983.33	491.67
Others	5	2350	470.00	8	4750	593.75	123.75
No Trade	10	6250	625.00	13	8350	642.30	17.30
TOTAL	249	135200	542.97	300	298820	996.06	453.09

Source : Field Study.

Scheme-wise Comparision of Pre and Post-DWCRA Income

It can be observed from Table-4.30 that out of 300 selected respondents only 249 are employed during Pre-DWCRA period and their average earnings per month is Rs. 542.97/-. The average income per month during Post-DWCRA period has increased to Rs. 996.06/-. It is to be noticed that the average income has increased for all the respondents irrespective of the scheme that they have chosen except Mushrooms. However, the rise in the income during Post-DWCRA period is not uniform and it has varied from scheme to scheme. Therefore, the difference between Pre and Post-DWCRA average income is in the range of Rs. 290 in Mushrooms and Rs. 944.87 in Cut-pieces selling. A close examination of table further reveals that the rise in the average income per month during Post-DWCRA period is above Rs. 500/- in 11 out of 24 schemes selected. They are Embroidery work, Soft-toys, Lace work, Cut-pieces selling, Chappals making, Veg/ Fruit vending, Fish vending, Tailoring, Sheep rearing, Kiranam and Weaving. Keeping aside Mushrooms, the average income per month during Post-DWCRA period has varied between Rs. 485.71 in Sheep rearing and Rs. 1544.23 in Chappals making. Moreover, the average income per month has exceeded Rs. 1400 in 6 schemes - Embroidery Work, Soft-Toys, Lace work, Cut-pieces selling, Chappals making and Weaving. On the whole, it can be stated that the DWCRA is the success in terms of attaining rise in the income.

Caste-wise Comparision of Pre and Post-DWCRA Income

The data in regard to Pre and Post-DWCRA average income in relation to caste has been shown in Table-4.31. The average income per month during Pre-DWCRA period has varied between Rs. 291.66 for Scheduled Tribe respondents and Rs. 623.07 for Scheduled Caste respondents. Thus, first position in this regard is occupied by Scheduled Caste respondents followed by Backward Classes respondents. Moreover, their relative positions are retained even during Post-DWCRA period but the change in the average income is negative for Forward Caste respondents. Thus, the DWCRA has shown a positive impact in terms of income generation for Backward Class, Schedule Caste and Scheduled Tribe respondents but it is negative for Forward Caste respondents.

Table 4.31 : Caste-Wise Analysis of Income Generation During Pre & Post-DWCRA Period in Warangal District

(Income In Rs.)

Caste	Pre-DWCRA Income			Post-DWCRA Income			Difference of Avg. Income
	No. of Respondents	Total Income	Avg. Income (P. M.)	No. of Respondents	Total Income	Avg. Income (P. M.)	
F C	16	8600	537.50	34	16550	486.76	- 50.74
B C	182	98800	542.85	207	213400	1030.91	488.06
S C	39	24300	623.07	47	61370	1305.74	682.67
S T	12	3500	291.66	12	7500	625.00	333.34
TOTAL	249	135200	542.97	300	298820	996.06	453.09

Source : Field Study.

Category-wise Comparision of Pre and Post-DWCRA Income

The information as to the comparison of Pre and Post-DWCRA average income in relation to economic category of the respondents is presented in Table-4.32.

Table - 4.32 : Category - Wise Analysis of Income Generation During Pre and Post-DWCRA Period In Warangal District

(Income In Rs.)

Category	Pre-DWCRA Income			Post-DWCRA Income			Difference of Avg. Income
	No. of Respondents	Total Income	Avg. Income (P. M.)	No. of Respondents	Total Income	Avg. Income (P. M.)	
Small Farmers	26	7500	288.46	53	28200	532.07	243.61
Marginal Farmers	82	32650	398.17	94	80720	858.72	460.55
Agri.Labourers	11	6700	609.09	12	8100	675.00	65.91
Non-Agri. Labourers	10	8100	810.00	11	7200	654.54	- 155.46
Rural Artisans	55	37300	678.18	56	80500	1437.50	759.32
Others	65	42950	660.76	74	94100	1271.62	610.86
TOTAL	249	135200	542.97	300	298820	996.06	453.09

Source : Field Study.

The average income per month during Pre-DWCRA period has varied between Rs. 288.46 for Small Farmers and Rs. 810/- for Non-Agricultural Labourers. The average income has increased during Post-DWCRA period for all the categories except Non-Agricultural Labourers. However, the range of average income during Post-DWCRA period is on the rise when compared to Pre-DWCRA period. Thus, it has varied in between Rs. 654.54/-for Non-Agricultural Labourers and Rs. 1437.50/- for Rural Artisans. Thus, the rise in the income is as high as Rs. 759.32/- for Rural Artisans. On the whole, the average income per month during Post-DWCRA period has exceeded Rs. 532/ - for all the respondents irrespective of their category.

Relationship Between Educational Qualifications and Pre and Post-DWCRA Income

The material in regard to Pre and Post-DWCRA income in relation to educational qualifications of respondents is depicted in Table-4.33. The Pre-DWCRA average income per month has varied between Rs. 627.27 for secondary education and Rs. 1266.66 for intermediate. It is to be noted that the average income per month during Post-DWCRA period has increased for all the respondents except for the women who have studied

Table 4.33 : Relationship Between Educational Qualification and Income Generation During Pre and Post-DWCRA Period in Warangal District

(Income In Rs.)

Educational Qualifications	*Pre-DWCRA Income*			*Post-DWCRA Income*			*Difference of Avg. Income*
	No. of Respondents	*Total Income*	*Avg. Income (P. M.)*	*No. of Respondents*	*Total Income*	*Avg. Income (P. M.)*	
Illiterate	136	60450	444.48	153	144920	947.18	502.70
Primary	71	45150	635.91	86	92450	1075.00	439.09
Secondary	33	20700	627.27	47	46250	984.04	356.77
Intermediate	3	3800	1266.66	7	1100	157.14	-1109.52
Degree	6	5100	850.00	7	14100	2014.28	1164.28
TOTAL	249	135200	542.97	300	298820	996.06	453.09

Source : Field Study.

upto Intermediate level. It is happy to note that the degree holders could get average income to the tune of Rs. 2014.28 during Post-DWCRA period which is followed by Rs. 1075/- for the respondents who could studied upto primary level. Thus, DWCRA has shown a negative effect in terms of income generation on the respondents who have studied upto Intermediate level. Moreover, either primary or degree level education has been yielding more income.

Relaltionship Between Age and Pre and Post-DWCRA Income

The study has also examined the relationship between the income generation from DWCRA and the age of the respondents and the relevant information is shown in Table-4.34.

Table 4.34 : Age-Wise Analysis Of Income Generation During Pre and Post-DWCRA Period In Warangal District

(Income In Rs.)

Age	*Pre-DWCRA Income*			*Post-DWCRA Income*			*Difference*
	No. of Respon-dents	*Total Income*	*Avg. Income (P. M.)*	*No. of Respon-dents*	*Total Income*	*Avg. Income (P. M.)*	*of Avg. Income*
20 - 30	98	62650	639.28	119	130050	1092.85	453.57
31 - 40	98	48700	496.93	114	108770	954.12	457.19
41 - 50	37	17600	475.67	47	39750	845.74	370.07
Above 50	16	6250	390.62	20	20250	1012.50	621.88
TOTAL	249	135200	542.97	300	298820	996.06	453.09

Source : Field Study.

It is interesting to note from the table that the average income per month has increased for all the respondents during Post-DWCRA period irrespective of the age of the respondent. The average income during Pre-DWCRA period has varied between Rs. 390.62 for the respondents who are above 50 years old and Rs. 639.28 for the respondents who are in the age group of 20-30 years. The average income during Post-DWCRA period is as high as Rs. 1092.85 for 20-30 years age group followed by Rs. 1012.50 for the respondents who are of above 50 years. Thus, the rise in the average income is not uniform for all the respondents. Therefore, the difference between Pre and Post-DWCRA average income has varied between Rs. 370.07 for the respondents who are in the age group of 41-51 years and Rs. 621.88 for who are above 50 years. Thus, the DWCRA is relatively a success in terms of income generation for the age group of 20-30 years and above 50 years.

Impact on Living Conditions

As already discussed in the preceding chapter that the ultimate aim of the DWCRA programme is to attain an improvement in the living conditions of rural poor. The preceding analysis has revealed that the implementation of DWCRA has resulted in the rise in the income of the respondents. This naturally raises their quality of life. Therefore, an analysis is made in regard to the impact of DWCRA on various components of consumption and the relevant information is presented in Table-4.35. The components consist of nutritional food, clothing, medical, educational qualifications, purchase of assets, savings, debt and repayment, expansion of trade and others.

Table-4.35 indicates that 218 out of 300 respondents preferred to keep their rise in the income in the form of savings followed by preference for education by 181 and third place goes to medical. However, the rise in the income has resulted in approaching nutritious food for 98 respondents. It is disheartening to note that though they get benefit out of trade, only 58 out of 300 respondents have utilised the rise in the income for the purpose of expansion of trade and they belonged to 15 out of 24 selected trades. No any specific relationship is observed between impact on living conditions and trade selected.

Repayment

The regular repayment of loan, however, will be an indicator of the success of any programme. The field work has revealed that all the selected respondents in Warangal district are regular in repayment irrespective of the scheme and caste.

Table 4.35 : Impact on Expenditure Pattern of the Selected Respondents in the Warangal District

Trade	*Nutritional Food*	*Clothing*	*Medical*	*Education*	*Assets*	*Savings Rapayment*	*Debt Trade*	*Exp. of Other*	*Any*
Embroidary Work	8	3	6	8	2	12	5	5	3
Soft-toys	8	2	7	8	2	12	5	3	2
Lace Work	2	—	3	5	—	3	2	—	—
Candle Making	3	3	4	4	1	5	1	—	—
Mushrooms	2	2	3	3	1	5	—	—	—
Chalk Pieces	2	4	3	5	5	7	2	—	—
Piggery	3	2	6	5	10	10	4	4	2
Cut Pieces Selling	—	6	9	8	6	12	8	3	2
Chappals Making	12	6	10	10	2	16	6	9	3
Doop Sticks	9	—	5	6	—	10	4	2	1
Beedi Work	4	1	1	—	—	3	—	1	2
Pickles	6	2	3	14	2	18	3	6	7
Sambar/ Rasam Powders	5	1	10	10	4	10	2	—	6
Veg/ Fruit Vending	8	—	4	8	6	8	8	3	1
Woolen Work	2	2	4	4	—	6	—	—	—
Milch Animals	12	3	11	35	8	27	9	12	6
Fish Vending	—	—	3	6	1	5	—	—	—

Contd.....

Table 4.35 : (Contd....)

Trade	*Nutritional Food*	*Clothing*	*Medical*	*Education*	*Assets*	*Savings Rapayment*	*Debt Trade*	*Exp. of Other*	*Any*
Tailoring	2	2	3	5	–	4	–	1	1
Sheep Rearing	2	2	2	3	2	5	1	2	3
Kiranam	3	–	1	2	–	4	1	1	2
Weaving	1	1	–	6	1	8	2	4	4
Thread Work	3	2	8	15	3	10	4	2	1
Others	1	1	3	6	–	10	2	–	–
No Trade	–	–	3	5	–	8	–	–	–
TOTAL	98	45	112	181	56	218	69	58	46

Source : Field Study.

SECTION - II

The preceding section clearly explained that the DWCRA is a success in terms of generating employment and income and this has ultimately resulted in the improvement in their living conditions. Thus, as far as economic aspects are concerned, the scheme is a success. The specific feature of the programme is its involvement of women. It is a known fact that owing to the prevalence of patriarchy, status of woman not only depends upon economic factors but also on man-woman relations determined by patriarchy. Therefore, this present section is devoted to discuss the impact of DWCRA on the status of women with in the family and society as well as in political decision-making.

The real success of the programme lies in its ability to make the women active in participating in decision-making related to the family. The consumption decisions can be divided into short-run and long-run. The short-run consumption aspects of the household mainly consists of purchase daily needs while the long-run consumption consists of education of children, purchase of assets, arrangement of marriages to their children and expansion of trade. Therefore, an examination of participation of women in decision-making related to the household assumes importance because it determines the change in the distributive rules of the household in favour of women.

Short-run Decision Making of the Households

The short-run decision making of the household mainly consists of purchase of daily needs and the information in regard to who takes decision in this regard is presented in Tables-4.36 and 4.37.

Table-4.36 reveals that out of selected 300 respondents as many as 206 would take decision on their own and in the case of 34 respondents, husbands alone take decision while both wife and husband together take decision in the case of 42 respondents. No caste-wise variation is noticed in this regard. It is to be noticed from Table-4.37 that the domination of husband in this regard decreases as the education level of respondent increases. Therefore, when the respondent could study to the level of Intermediate and beyond, then they take decision either on their own or along with husband. However, the active participation of respondents in the short-run decision making of the household is noticed irrespective of the caste and education.

Table 4.36 : Participation of Respondents in Short Run Decision Making Related to Daily Expenditure Caste-Wise

Caste	*Own*	*Husband*	*Both*	*Others*	*Total*
F C	27	2	5	–	34
B C	149	19	27	12	207
S C	22	11	9	5	47
S T	8	2	1	1	12
TOTAL	206 (68.7)	34 (11.3)	42 (14.0)	18 (6.0)	300 (100.0)

Source : Field Study.

Table 4.37 : Education and Participation of Respondents Short Run Decision Making Related to Daily Expenditure

Educational Qualifications	*Own*	*Husband*	*Both*	*Others*	*Total*
Illiterate	104	21	14	14	153
Primary	58	8	16	4	86
Secondary	35	5	7	–	47
Intermediate	4	–	3	–	7
Degree	5	–	2	–	7
TOTAL	206 (68.7)	34 (11.3)	42 (14.0)	18 (6.0)	300 (100.0)

Source : Field Study.

Long-run Decision Making of the Family

The long-run decision making of the household mainly consists of purchase of consumer durables, expansion of trade, arrangement of marriages to their children, provision of education to the children, taking loan and making repayment.

Purchase of Consumer Durables

Table-4.38 indicates that the husband alone takes decision in regard to the purchase of consumer durables in the case of 16.7 percent of selected respondents. As many as 161 out of 300 respondents could take decision independently in this regard while in 22 cases both wife and husband together take decision. A close examination of table reveals that the domination of husband in the purchase of consumer durables is least in Forward Castes and high in Scheduled Castes. Similarly, Table-4.39 denotes that the education level of the respondent determines their active participation in decision making. Therefore, when the respondent could study upto Intermediate and beyond, then the domination of husband is nil.

Table 4.38 : Caste and Decision Making of the Purchase of Consumer Durables

Caste	*Own*	*Husband*	*Both*	*Others*	*Total*
F C	21	1	11	1	34
B C	114	31	46	16	207
S C	20	16	6	5	47
S T	6	2	3	1	12
TOTAL	161 (53.7)	50 (16.7)	66 (22.0)	23 (7.6)	300 (100.0)

Source : Field Study.

Table 4.39 : Education and Decision Making of the Purchase of Consumer Durables

Educational Qualifications	*Own*	*Husband*	*Both*	*Others*	*Total*
Illiterate	78	39	28	8	153
Primary	43	10	24	9	86
Secondary	32	1	8	6	47
Intermediate	4	–	3	–	7
Degree	4	–	3	–	7
TOTAL	161 (53.7)	50 (16.7)	66 (22.0)	23 (7.6)	300 (100.0)

Source : Field Study.

Decision-making in Regard to Expansion of Trade

Table-4.40 indicates that only 30 respondents out of 300 selected could take decision independently as to the expansion of trade. The husband is the decision maker in the case of 121 respondents. However, 99 respondents are taking decision together with the husband. Interestingly, though the active participation of wife is seen in regard to the purchase of daily needs and consumer durables, their participation is less active in regard to expansion of trade where the trade belongs to the respondents is a contradiction. Though the wife is the owner of the trade, decision-making lies with the husband. No caste-wise variation is noticed. However, the domination of husband is relatively lesser in the case where wife could study upto Intermediate and beyond (Table-4.41).

Table 4.40 : Caste and Decision Making of Expansion of Trade

Caste	*Own*	*Husband*	*Both*	*Others*	*Total*
F C	4	6	18	6	34
B C	21	90	64	32	207
S C	3	23	12	9	47
S T	2	2	5	3	12
TOTAL	30 (10.0)	121 (40.3)	99 (33.0)	50 (16.7)	300 (100.0)

Source : Field Study.

Table 4.41 : Education and Decision Making of Expansion of Trade

Educational Qualifications	*Own*	*Husband*	*Both*	*Others*	*Total*
Illiterate	13	81	45	14	153
Primary	8	22	30	26	86
Secondary	7	18	15	7	47
Intermediate	1	–	5	1	7
Degree	1	–	4	2	7
TOTAL	30 (10.0)	121 (40.3)	99 (33.0)	50 (16.7)	300 (100.0)

Source : Field Study.

Decision Making in Regard to the Arrangement of Marriages

Table-4.42 clearly states that the participation of respondent is negligible in decision making related to the arrangement of marriages to their children. However, respondents are consulted by their husbands in the case of 222 out of 300 selected. It is disheartening to notice that in the case of 10 percent of respondents, neither wife nor husband have any role to play in the decision-making and other elders are the decision-makers. Independent decision-making can not be seen in Scheduled Tribes. However, level of education of the respondent is a determining factor for their active participation in decision making. Therefore, all the 7 degree holders are involved in making decision in regard to arrangement of marriages to their children (Table-4.43).

Table 4.42 : Caste and Decision Making in Regard to Marriages of the Children

Caste	*Own*	*Husband*	*Both*	*Others*	*Total*
F C	4	3	21	6	34
B C	7	21	165	14	207
S C	2	8	29	8	47
S T	–	3	7	2	12
TOTAL	13 (4.3)	35 (11.7)	222 (74.0)	30 (10.0)	300 (100.0)

Source : Field Study.

Table 4.43 : Education and Decision Making in Regard to Marriages of the Children

Educational Qualifications	*Own*	*Husband*	*Both*	*Others*	*Total*
Illiterate	6	20	109	18	153
Primary	3	9	71	3	86
Secondary	3	5	30	9	47
Intermediate	1	1	5	–	7
Degree	–	–	7	–	7
TOTAL	13 (4.3)	35 (11.7)	222 (74.0)	30 (10.0)	300 (100.0)

Source : Field Study.

Decision Making in Regard to Education of Children

Table-4.44 states that out of 300 selected respondents, as many as in 189 cases both husband and wife together are taking decision in regard to education of their children but in 61 cases husbands alone are taking decision in this regard. However, the domination of other members of the family can not be found in Forward Castes and while wife's independent decision can not be seen in Scheduled Tribes. Apart from this, no any major caste-wise variation is noticed. Further, husband's domination in this regard is nil in the case of degree holders. Thus, the level of education of the respondent plays a positive role in making them active in decision making related to household (Table-4.45).

Table 4.44 : Caste and Decision Making in Regard to Education of the Children

Caste	*Own*	*Husband*	*Both*	*Others*	*Total*
F C	9	2	23	–	34
B C	24	42	131	10	207
S C	4	8	33	2	47
S T	–	9	2	1	12
TOTAL	37 (12.3)	61 (20.3)	189 (63.0)	13 (4.4)	300 (100.0)

Source : Field Study.

Table 4.45 : Education and Decision Making in Regard to Education of the Children

Educational Qualifications	*Own*	*Husband*	*Both*	*Others*	*Total*
Illiterate	8	42	91	12	153
Primary	15	13	57	1	86
Secondary	13	5	29	–	47
Intermediate	1	1	5	–	7
Degree	–	–	7	–	7
TOTAL	37 (12.3)	61 (20.3)	189 (63.0)	13 (4.4)	300 (100.0)

Source : Field Study.

Decision Making in Regard to Debt and Re-payment

Table-4.46 explains that the husband alone takes decision in the case of 109 out of 300 selected respondents in regard to the decisions related to debt and repayment. While wife and husband together takes decision in this regard in the case of 141 respondents. Moreover, husband's domination is high among Scheduled Caste respondents where 20 out of 47, husband's domination is prevalent. Even in regard to decisions related to debt and repayment, wife's active participation is noticed when they are educated. Therefore, out of 14 respondents who could study upto Intermediate and beyond, 2 are taking decision independently and in the case of remaining 12, both wife and husband together are taking decision. Contrast to this, out of 153 illiterates, in 80 cases, husband alone is the decision maker in regard to debt and repayment (Table-4.47). Thus the education level of respondent makes her active in decision making related to the Debt and Repayment.

Table 4.46 : Caste and Decision Making in Regard to Debt and Repayment

Caste	*Own*	*Husband*	*Both*	*Others*	*Total*
F C	4	3	23	4	34
B C	19	84	91	13	207
S C	5	20	19	3	47
S T	2	2	8	–	12
TOTAL	30 (10.0)	109 (36.3)	141 (47.0)	20 (6.7)	300 (100.0)

Source : Field Study.

Table 4.47: Education and Decision Making in Regard to Debt and Repayment

Educational Qualifications	*Own*	*Husband*	*Both*	*Others*	*Total*
Illiterate	21	80	38	14	153
Primary	3	17	65	1	86
Secondary	4	12	26	5	47
Intermediate	1	–	6	–	7
Degree	1	–	6	–	7
TOTAL	30 (10.0)	109 (36.3)	141 (47.0)	20 (6.7)	300 (100.0)

Source : Field Study.

Ownership of Property

The ownership of property and control over resources go together. This is one of the variables which determines the status of any person. Owing to the prevalence of patriarchy, the women, though they earn, they have neither ownership of property nor control over resources which results in their subordination and weakens their status. The information as to the ownership of property is presented in Tables-4.48 and 4.49.

Table 4.48 : Caste-wise Analysis of Onwership of Property by the Selected Respondent

Caste	*Yes*	*No*	*Total*
F C	12	22	34
B C	20	187	207
S C	2	45	47
S T	–	12	12
TOTAL	34 (11.3)	266 (88.7)	300 (100.0)

Source : Field Study.

Table 4.49 : Education and Onwership of Property by the Selected Respondents

Educational Qualifications	*Yes*	*No*	*Total*
Illiterate	15	138	153
Primary	8	78	86
Secondary	7	40	47
Intermediate	3	4	7
Degree	1	6	7
TOTAL	34 (11.3)	266 (88.7)	300 (100.0)

Source : Field Study.

Table-4.48 indicates that out of 300 selected respondents, as many as 266 do not have any ownership rights and 34 respondents possess ownership rights and of them 12 belong to Forward Castes, 20 to Backward Classes and 2 to Scheduled Castes and nil in Scheduled Tribes. Thus, relatively more number of women own property in Forward Castes which is followed by Backward Class respondents. Interestingly, there is no any relation between ownership of property by women and their education level. Thus, women lack control over resources irrespective of the caste and education.

Domestic Work

No household particularly rural poor households can survive without the domestic work performed by women. Inspite of its enormous use value, as it does not possess any exchange value, it is not recognised. However, women have to spend time to perform domestic work consists of cleaning house, vessels, washing cloths, cooking, bringing water from distant places, maintaining kitchen garden, looking after children, bringing fire wood and overall maintenance of the house. The extent of domestic work may vary from household to household depending upon their social and economic status. The information pertaining to the number of hours spent on domestic work by the selected respondents is presented in Tables-4.50 and 4.51.

Table 4.50 : Caste-wise Analysis of Number of Hours Spent on Domestic Work

Caste	*1 - 2*	*3 - 4*	*5 - 6*	*Above 6*	*Total*
F C	8	14	7	5	34
B C	22	100	80	5	207
S C	6	18	21	2	47
S T	4	1	5	2	12
TOTAL	40 (13.3)	133 (44.3)	113 (37.7)	14 (4.7)	300 (100.0)

Source : Field Study.

Table 4.51 : Education and Number of Hours Spent on Domestic Work

Educational Qualifications	*1 - 2*	*3 - 4*	*5 - 6*	*Above 6*	*Total*
Illiterate	23	74	49	7	153
Primary	5	36	43	2	86
Secondary	7	20	15	5	47
Intermediate	2	2	3	–	7
Degree	3	1	3	–	7
TOTAL	40 (13.3)	133 (44.3)	113 (37.7)	14 (4.7)	300 (100.0)

Source : Field Study.

It can be noticed from Table-4.50 that out of 300 selected respondents as many as 133 spend 3-4 hours to perform domestic work while 113 spend 5-6 hours per day on domestic chores and 14 respondents are compelled to spend beyond 6 hours per day on this. It can also be observed that the percentage of Forward Caste respondents who devote 1-2 hours per day on domestic work is relatively higher when compared to other castes. Contrast to this, Scheduled Tribes spend relatively more number of hours when compared to other respondents. Thus, inter-caste variation is seen in this aspect. Table-4.51 states that the burden of domestic work is terms of number of hours is less on degree holders when compared to others.

The field study has revealed that all the respondents irrespective of their caste and educational qualifications, would perform cleaning of house, vessels and cooking, 20 respondents bear the burden of fire wood collection, 45 are to bring water from distant places while 21 maintains kitchen garden.

Table-4.52 indicates the information as to who will assist in domestic work. It can be seen that 58 out of 300 selected respondents did not get any assistance from any one while 91 are assisted by husbands, 90 are by children and finally 61 are by others. The majority of respondents who belonged to Forward Caste and Backward Classes are able to get assistance from husband in performing domestic chores. This phenomenon is least in Scheduled Caste respondents.

Table 4.52 : Caste and Assistance Received In Performing Domestic Work

Caste	*Husband*	*Children*	*Others*	*Own*	*Total*
F C	15	12	4	3	34
B C	71	63	41	32	207
S C	1	13	12	21	47
S T	4	2	4	2	12
TOTAL	91 (30.3)	90 (30.0)	61 (20.3)	58 (19.3)	300 (100.0)

Source : Field Study.

Table-4.53 denotes that the majority of illiterates get assistance from their children in performing domestic work. While majority of literates could get assistance from their husband and it is on the rise as the education level of respondent increases.

Table 4.53 : Education and Assistence Received in Performing Domestic Work

Educational Qualifications	*Husband*	*Children*	*Others*	*Own*	*Total*
Illiterate	23	59	34	37	153
Primary	33	21	18	14	86
Secondary	24	8	9	6	47
Intermediate	5	2	—	—	7
Degree	6	—	—	1	7
TOTAL	91 (30.3)	90 (30.0)	61 (20.3)	58 (19.3)	300 (100.0)

Source : Field Study.

Family Purchasing Priorities

According to consumption function, rise in the income leads to rise in the consumption and however, the extent of change in consumption is determined by other variables like assets, past consumption, life-cycle etc. All the studies have ignored one important determinant i.e., gender dimension of consumption function. Though the rise in the family's income results in rise in the family's consumption, the priorities and preferences of women are either ignored or neglected.

DWCRA has increased earning capacity of rural women and this has resulted in the rise in the family's income. Consequently, family's expenditure on consumption increases but whether this 'rise' includes the priorities of women assumes important. Therefore, the data in regard to family purchasing priorities are elicited and presented as Table-4.54 and 4.55.

Table 4.54 : Caste-wise Analysis of Family Purchasing Priorities

Caste	*Goods Used by Male Members of the Family*	*Consumer Durables*	*Savings*	*Exp. of the trade*	*Total*
F C	1	17	12	4	34
B C	35	76	76	20	207
S C	3	16	21	7	47
S T	2	4	6	–	12
TOTAL	41 (13.7)	113 (37.7)	115 (38.3)	31 (10.3)	300 (100.0)

Source : Field Study.

Table 4.55 : Education And Family Purchasing Priorities

Educational Qualifications	*Goods Used by Male Members of the Family*	*Consumer Durables*	*Savings*	*Exp. of the trade*	*Total*
Illiterate	26	48	62	17	153
Primary	10	33	34	9	86
Secondary	4	23	16	4	47
Intermediate	1	3	2	1	7
Degree	–	6	1	–	7
TOTAL	41 (13.7)	113 (37.7)	115 (38.3)	31 (10.3)	300 (100.0)

Source : Field Study.

It is to be noted that in the case of 41 respondents, the rise in consumption due to DWCRA earnings mainly consists of the goods exclusively used by the male members of the family. This clearly explains as to how the women who earn income independently also marginalised within the family while 113 respondents preferred to purchase consumer durables and 115 respondents preferred to keep their rise in the income in the form of savings. It is disheartening to note that only 10.3 percent of the respondents could utilise the rise in their earnings for the purpose of expansion of trade. Thus, the priorities of women as well as the trade which is the cause for their improved earnings are equally neglected by the family. The exclusive purchase of goods consumed by male members of the family is relatively higher among Backward Class respondents while expansion of trade is totally neglected by Scheduled Tribe respondents.

Similarly, Table-4.55 states that majority of illiterates preferred to keep their additional income in the form of savings, while in remaining respondents who could study Primary to Degree level, the majority of them preferred to purchase consumer durables. This clearly states the spread of consumerism in rural areas. Further, the field study has revealed that 44 percent of the selected respondents could exercise control over their earnings to some extent.

Harassment

Till today, harassment by the family members is a serious problem confronted by women. In other words, domestic violence is a serious problem which critically suffers women. The relevant data are elicited and placed as Table-4.56 and Table-4.57.

Table - 4.56 : Caste and Harrassment in the Family

Caste	*Yes*	*No*	*Total*
F C	8	26	34
B C	56	151	207
S C	9	38	47
S T	4	8	12
TOTAL	77 (25.7)	223 (74.3)	300 (100.0)

Source : Field Study.

Table 4.57 : Educational Level and Harrassment in the Family

Educational Qualifications	*Yes*	*No*	*Total*
Illiterate	46	107	153
Primary	19	67	86
Secondary	11	36	47
Intermediate	–	7	7
Degree	1	6	7
TOTAL	77 (25.7)	223 (74.3)	300 (100.0)

Source : Field Study.

Table-4.56 states that as many as 77 out of 300 selected are subjected to harassment by the family members. Of them, 8 are Forward Castes 56 Backward Classes 9 Scheduled Castes and 4 belonged to Scheduled Tribes. Thus, no any significant caste-wise variation is noticed. Table-4.57 indicates that among the respondents who are subjected to harassment, majority are illiterates. As the level of education of the respondent increases, the harassment meted out to number of women decreases. Thus, out of 14 respondents who could study upto Intermediate and beyond, only one respondent is subjected to harassment. This clearly states that the level of education of the respondent plays a positive role in lessening the problem of harassment.

The present study is also elicited information as to who will harass the respondent? The relevant information is presented in Tables-4.58 and 4.59. It can be noticed from Table-4.58 that out of 77 who are subjected to harassment, 48, i.e., 62.3 percent are harassed by their husbands only. This is followed by 18 i.e., 23.4 percent by Mother-in-law and 11 i.e., 14.3 percent by their sisters-in-law. The majority of respondents irrespective of the caste are subjected to harassment by the husbands. Thus, 5 out 8 in Forward Castes, 32 out of 56 in Backward Classes, 7 out of 9 in Scheduled Castes and all the 4 Scheduled Tribes are harassed by huband. Moreover, irrespective of the education level of the respondent, majority of them are harassed by husbands (Table-4.59).

Table 4.58 : Caste-wise Analysis of Harassment From Whom

Caste	*Mother-in-law*	*Sister-in-law*	*Husband*	*Total*
F C	2	1	5	8
B C	15	9	32	56
S C	1	1	7	9
S T	–	–	4	4
TOTAL	18 (23.4)	11 (14.3)	48 (62.3)	77 (100.0)

Source : Field Study.

Table 4.59 : Education and Analysis of Harrassment From Whom

Educational Qualifications	*Mother-in-law*	*Sister-in-law*	*Husband*	*Total*
Illiterate	9	10	27	46
Primary	6	–	13	19
Secondary	3	1	7	11
Intermediate	–	–	–	–
Degree	–	–	1	1
TOTAL	18 (23.4)	11 (14.3)	48 (62.3)	77 (100.0)

Source : Field Study.

The information in regard to nature of harassment is shown in Tables-4.60 and 4.61. It is disheartening to notice from Table-4.60 that 36 out of 77 are subjected to wife-beating and 24 are for dowry. In all the castes, wife beating is a major problem followed by dowry. However, the latter problem is not seen in Scheduled Tribes. The nature of harassment did not vary according to the level of education of the respondent as shown in Table-4.61. Thus, no any relationship is observed between the nature of harassment and education level of the respondent.

Protest of Harassment

The respondents belonged to DWCRA group and all of them are economically independent i.e., income earners. Therefore, the respondents can protest the harassment meted out to them either as an individual or as a group.

The field study has revealed that 49 out of 77 have protested the harassment meted out to them. No caste-wise variation is

Table 4.60 : Caste-wise Analysis of Nature of Harrassment

Caste	*Dowry*	*Work*	*Wife Beating*	*Other*	*Total*
F C	4	1	3	–	8
B C	18	9	24	5	56
S C	2	1	5	1	9
S T	–	–	4	–	4
TOTAL	24 (31.2)	11 (14.3)	36 (46.7)	6 (7.8)	77 (100.0)

Source : Field Study.

Table 4.61 : Educational Level and Nature of Harrassment

Educational Qualifications	*Dowry*	*Work*	*Wife Beating*	*Other*	*Total*
Illiterate	14	6	22	4	46
Primary	8	2	8	1	19
Secondary	2	3	5	1	11
Intermediate	–	–	–	–	–
Degree0	–	–	1	–	1
TOTAL	24 (31.2)	11 (14.3)	36 (46.7)	6 (7.8)	77 (100.0)

Source : Field Study.

noticed in this regard. However, 52 out of 77 have informed about the problem to the DWCRA group. The group discussed about the problem of harassment faced by its members and took action in 29 cases but problem has been solved only in 18 cases. Though the success is insignificant, the 'group' has raised the confidence of rural women and now they no longer think that the problem of harassment is personal. Therefore, they came forward to discuss about it in the group. They also feel that they are not isolated and they are part of the DWCRA group. Therefore, they could face the problem of domestic violence as a group.

Social Awareness

Under DWCRA, rural women are formed as groups. They organise regular meetings of the members to discuss about economic aspects of the programme. The discussion as to domestic as well as social problems becomes indispensable in the meetings. The field study has revealed that 87 out of 300 selected respondents discuss about the social problems too in their meetings. Usually, they discuss about the specific social problem which is prevalent in that region. It is their immediate need too to discuss and take measures to challenge it.

Social Activities of the Respondents

The team work and group activity and consequent discussion about social problems naturally results in the rise in their social awareness. Then, it becomes indispensable for them to involve in social activities. The rise in the social awareness and consequent involvement in social activity raises the self-confidence of the rural poor women. This also improves their status in the family as well as in the society.

The field study has revealed that almost all the selected respondents are involved in social activities. They fought against social evils, liquor consumption and protested attrocities. However, the majority of Backward Class and Scheduled Caste respondents are involved in fighting against liquor consumption. of course, the majority of selected respondents are involved in fighting against social evils irrespective of their level of education.

'Janmabhoomi' is a social activity introduced by the government of Andhra Pradesh on various socio-economic issues. Out of 300 selected respondents, 197 have participated in 'Janmabhoomi' activity. The field study has also revealed that 24 out of 34 Forward Castes, 150 out of 207 Backward Classes, 13 out of 47 Scheduled Castes and 10 out of 12 Scheduled Tribe respondents have participated in this activity. The education level of respondent did not play any role.

Political Awareness

Human Development Report rightly recognises the significance of political awareness and active political participation of women for their empowerment. The political awareness starts with vote casting which is considered as a fundamental political right because the success of democracy depends upon proper exercise of right to vote.

The field study has revealed that out of 300 selected respondents, 298 are casting their vote irrespective of their caste and level of education. However, of them, 151 gives priority to the person while 147 gives importance to party to which the contestant belonged to while exercising their right to vote. It is to be noted that the majority of illiterates give importance to party while literates give priority to the person.

The vote casting by the respondent should be associated with independent decision-making in this regard. Therefore, the relevant information is elicited and presented in Table-4.62 and 4.63.

Table 4.62 : Caste-wise Analysis of Decision Making in Regard to Vote Casting

Caste	*Own*	*Husband*	*Others*	*Total*
F C	19	10	5	34
B C	86	77	44	207
S C	16	22	9	47
S T	3	4	5	12
TOTAL	124 (41.3)	113 (37.9)	63 (21.2)	300 (100.0)

Source : Field Study.

Table 4.63 : Educational Level and Decision Making in Regard to Vote Casting

Educational Qualifications	*Own*	*Husband*	*Others*	*Total*
Illiterate	50	76	27	153
Primary	39	27	20	86
Secondary	24	9	14	47
Intermediate	4	1	2	7
Degree	7	–	–	7
TOTAL	124 (41.3)	113 (37.9)	63 (21.2)	300 (100.0)

Source : Field Study.

Table-4.62 states that out of 300 selected respondents as many as 124 are taking decision in regard to vote casting independently and of them, 85 belonged to Backward Classes, 19 to Forward Castes, 16 to Scheduled Castes and 3 to Scheduled Tribes. However, 113 respondents are influenced by their husbands and 63 respondents are by others. The caste-wise analysis states that the majority of Forward Caste and Backward Class respondents are taking decision on their own, while majority of Scheduled Caste respondents are influenced by husbands and majority of Scheduled Tribe respondents are influenced by others.

Table-4.63 examines the relationship between independent decision-making in regard to vote casting and educational qualifications of the respondent. It is interesting to note that the majority of illiterates are influenced by husbands in political decision-making as to vote-casting while the majority of literates could take decision on their own in this regard. Moreover, all the 7 degree holders could take decision on their own. This clearly indicates that there is a positive relationship between educational qualifications of the respondent and ability to take independent decision in vote casting.

Participation in Political Decisions:

Human Development Report 1995 identifies the significance of active involvement of women in political decision-making for their empowerment. AS far as vote casting is concerned, 100 percent participation is noticed. Moreover, 62 out of 300 selected respondents are actively involved in local politics. However, the participation in local politics is relatively higher among Forward Caste and Scheduled Caste respondents when compared to Backward Class and Scheduled Tribe respondents. Interestingly, degree holders did not involve in local politics. The participation in local politics is relatively higher in illiterates and the respondents who could have primary level education.

The field study has revealed that out of 57 respondents who actively involved in local politics 21 are involved in canvassing about the contesting candidate, 17 used to give encouragement while 19 they themselves are involved in local politics. However, self-participation is relatively higher among Forward Caste and Scheduled Caste respondents. Out of 57 respondents who actively involved in local politics, 20 are illiterates and 50 percent of them involved in canvassing, 24 are studied upto primary level education and of them, self-participation can be noticed for 40 percent 11 are studied upto secondary education and of them, 8 are actively involved either in giving encouragement or in canvassing and lastly 2 are studied upto Intermediate and both of them are in self-participation.

Achievements of DWCRA

The present study has elicited the information as to the achievement of DWCRA in the opinion of respondents themselves.

Out of 300 selected respondents, 122 have opined that they feel improvement in their economic status which however, indicates the success of DWCRA in terms of achieving an improvement in income which lead to attain better quality of life. It is to be noted that 84 respondents feel an improvement both in economic as well as social status. This indicates the inter-dependence between economic and social status while 48 feel an improvement in social status only and finally 41 are of the opinion that their status within the family has improved. An achievement of an improvement in economic status in the opinion of respondents themselves is relatively higher and no any inter-caste variation is noticed in this regard. However, social status has also improved along with the economic status in many cases when the respondent is educated. Thus, the education level of the respondent plays a significant role in attaining over all improvement in their status.

5

Employment, Income & Status of Rural Women–Part-III

The present chapter has been divided into two sections for the purpose of convenience. Section-I is devoted exclusively to discuss about the performance of DWCRA in economic terms. In other words, the impact of DWCRA on employment, income and living conditions of the rural poor women, while Section-II is devoted to examine the impact of DWCRA on the status of rural women in Karimnagar District.

SECTION-I

The main aim of DWCRA is to generate employment in order to raise the earnings of the rural poor women so as to attain improvement in their living conditions. Prior to examine all these aspects, the characteristics of the sample are analysed.

Village and Trade-wise Distribution of Sample Respondents

The total sample respondents 220 are distributed in 18 villages consisting of 19 trades.

(i) *Agriculture and allied activities:* Two schemes - Vegetable cultivation, Milch Animals belonged to this category.

(ii) *Manufacturing Activity :* Leather work, Soft-toys, Basket making, Greeting Cards, Petty coats, Leaf Plate making, Nawar making, Surf/ Blue/ Phenol, Lace work, Ready-Made Dresses and Embroidery Work i.e., 11 trades belonged to this activity.

(iii) *Business :* Sale of cosmetics, Veg./ Fruit vending would come into the business sector.

(iv) *Services :* Tailoring, Others and 'No Trade' belonged to service sector. The term 'No Trade' is used that it does not take up any productive activity but the mobilised funds are used like the Chits, among themselves.

The village-wise distribution of trades in Karimnagar district reveals that in the village Pathipaka 5 trades - Leather work, Soft-toys, Basket making, Greeting Cards and Petty coats - can be seen. However, the trade Soft-Toys can also be observed in Mankamma Thota while Basket making in Huzurabad, Petty coats in Kothapally and Veldi. The village Peddapapaiah Pally consists of two trades - Thread work and Sale of cosmetic goods and in Rangapoor, the trades of Nawar making and Veg/ Fruit vending. While Bommakal is having Tailoring and Embroidery Works and Others. In remaining selected villages one trade each can be noticed viz., Surf/ Blue/ Phenol in Nusthalapur, Lace work in Reddyramayya pally, Ready-made Dress in Manakondur, Vegetable cultivation in Gollapally, Milch Animals in Annaram, Devampally and Srinivasanagar while Others in Mulkanoor and 'No Trade' in Kothapally (Table 5.1).

Caste-wise Distribution of Selected Trades and Respondents

Table-5.2 denotes that out of selected 220 respondents, 128 (58.2 percent) belonged to Backward Classes followed by 65 (29.5 percent) to Scheduled Castes, 17 (7.7 percent) to Forward Castes and 10 (4.5 percent) to Scheduled Tribes. It is to be noted that the Backward Classes respondents are seen in all the selected trades except in Thread work and in Veg/ Fruit Vending while Scheduled Caste respondents are seen in 8 trades -Leather works, Soft-toys, Petty coats, Thread work, Veg./ Fruit vending, Vegetable cultivation, Milch Animals and Embroidery work. The respondents belonged to Forward Castes are seen in 7 trades-Leather works, Soft-toys, Greeting Cards, Petty Coats, Leaf Plate Making, Others and 'No Trade' but Scheduled Tribe respondents are seen in only two trades - Basket making and Lace work. Thus, the scope of selection of trades is relatively

Table 5.1 : Village - Wise Distribution of Trades Under DWCRA in Karim nagar District

Village	*Leather Works*	*Soft-Toys*	*Basket Making*	*Greet-ing Cards*	*Petty Coats*	*Leaf Plating Making*	*Thread Work*	*Saleof Cosmo-Tics*	*Navar Making*	*Veg. Fruit Vending*	*Surf/ Blue/ Phenoil*	*Lace Work*	*Ready-Made Dresses*	*Veg. Culti-Vation*	*Milch Animals*	*Tailo-ring*	*Embro-Idary Work*	*others*	*NoTrade*	*Total*
Pathipaka	12	6	8	4	6	–	–	–	–	–	–	–	–	–	–	–	–	–	–	36 (16.4)
Bommareddy Pally	–	–	–	–	–	8	–	–	–	–	–	–	–	–	–	–	–	–	–	8 (3.6)
Padapapayya Pally	–	–	–	–	–	–	6	2	–	–	–	–	–	–	–	–	–	–	–	8 (3.6)
Huzurabad	–	–	10	–	–	–	–	–	–	–	–	–	–	–	–	–	–	–	–	10 (4.5)
Rangapur	–	–	–	–	–	–	–	–	4	8	–	–	–	–	–	–	–	–	–	12 (5.5)
Nustalapur	–	–	–	–	–	–	–	–	–	–	10	–	–	–	–	–	–	–	–	10 (4.5)
Kothapally (KRMR)	–	–	–	–	7	–	–	–	–	–	–	–	–	–	–	–	–	–	–	7 (3.2)
Reddyramayya Pally	–	–	–	–	–	–	–	–	–	–	–	7	–	–	–	–	–	–	–	7 (3.2)
Manakondur	–	–	–	–	–	–	–	–	–	–	–	–	7	–	–	–	–	–	–	7 (3.2)
Veldhi	–	–	–	–	10	–	–	–	–	–	–	–	–	–	–	–	–	–	–	10 (4.5)
Gollapally	–	–	–	–	–	–	–	–	–	–	–	–	–	10	–	–	–	–	–	10 (4.5)
Annaram	–	–	–	–	–	–	–	–	–	–	–	–	–	–	15	–	–	–	–	15 (6.8)

Contd....

Table 5.1 : (Contd....)

Village	Leather Works	Soft-Toys	Basket Making	Greet-ing Cards	Petty Coats	Leaf Plating Making	Thread Work	Saleof Cosmo-Tics	Nawar Making	Veg. Fruit Vending	Surf/ Blue/ Phenoil	Lace Work	Ready-Made Dresses	Veg. Culti-Vation	Milch Animals	Tailo-ring	Embro-Idary Work	others	NoTrade	Total
Devampally	–	–	–	–	–	–	–	–	–	–	–	–	–	–	40	–	–	–	–	40 (18.2)
Srinivasa Nagar	–	–	–	–	–	–	–	–	–	–	–	–	–	–	15	–	–	–	–	15 (6.8)
Bommakal	–	–	–	–	–	–	–	–	–	–	–	–	–	–	–	2	1	2	–	5 (2.3)
Mankamma Thota	–	6	–	–	–	–	–	–	–	–	–	–	–	–	–	–	–	–	–	6 (2.7)
Mulkanoor	–	–	–	–	–	–	–	–	–	–	–	–	–	–	–	–	4	–	–	4 (1.8)
Kothapally (Mulkanoor)	–	–	–	–	–	–	–	–	–	–	–	–	–	–	–	–	–	–	10	10 (4.5)
TOTAL	12 (5.5)	12 (5.5)	18 (8.2)	4 (1.8)	23 (10.5)	8 (3.6)	6 (2.7)	2 (0.9)	4 (1.8)	8 (3.6)	10 (4.5)	7 (3.2)	7 (3.2)	10 (4.5)	70 (31.8)	2 (0.9)	5 (2.3)	2 (0.9)	10 (4.5)	220 (100.0)

Source : Field Study.

Table 5.2 : Trade and Caste-wise Distribuiton of Selected Respondents in Karimnagar District

Trade	*F C*	*B C*	*S C*	*S T*	*Total*
Leather Works	5 (29.4)	5 (3.9)	2 (3.1)	–	12 (5.5)
Soft-Toys	1 (5.9)	10 (7.8)	1 (1.5)	–	12 (5.5)
Basket Making	–	10 (7.8)	–	8 (80.0)	18 (8.2)
Greeting Cards	2 (11.8)	2 (1.6)	–	–	4 (1.8)
Petty Coats	1 (5.9)	13 (10.2)	9 (13.8)	–	23 (10.5)
Leaf Plate Making	6 (35.3)	2 (1.6)	–		8 (3.6)
Thread Work	–	–	6 (9.2)	–	6 (2.7)
Cosmetic Sales	–	2 (1.6)	–	–	2 (0.9)
Nawar Making	–	4 (3.1)	–	–	4 (1.8)
Veg./ Fruit Vending	–	–	8 (12.3)	–	8 (3.6)
Surf/ Blue/ Phenoil	–	10 (7.8)	–	–	10 (4.5)
Lace Work	–	5 (3.9)	–	2 (20.0)	7 (3.2)
Readymade Dresses	–	7 (5.5)	–	–	7 (3.2)
Veg. Cultivation	–	2 (1.6)	8 (12.3)	–	10 (4.5)
Milch Animals	–	40 (31.3)	30 (46.2)	–	70 (31.8)
Tailoring	–	2 (1.6)	–	–	2 (0.9)
Embroidary Work	–	4 (3.1)	1 (1.5)	–	5 (2.3)
Others	1 (5.9)	1 (0.8)	–	–	2 (0.9)
No Trade	1 (5.9)	9 (7.0)	–	–	10 (4.5)
TOTAL	17 (7.7)	128 (58.2)	65 (29.5)	10 (4.5)	220 (100.0)

Source : Field Study.

more for Backward Classes followed by Scheduled castes while Scheduled Tribes stand last in this regard.

Village and Caste-wise Distribution of Selected Respondents

Table-5.3 denotes that the village-wise distribution of sample is in the range of 40 respondents in Devampally and 4 respondents in Mulkanoor. It can be noticed from the table that the respondents belonged to Backward Classes can be observed in 17 out of 18 villages selected. They are not found only in Annaram village. The Scheduled Caste respondents are found in 8 villages while Forward Caste respondents are seen in 6 villages and Scheduled Tribe respondents are seen only in two villages-Pathipaka and Reddyramayya Pally. However, the respondents belonged to all the castes can be seen only in Pathipaka while in Bommakal all the castes except Scheduled Tribes can be found.

Caste and Category wise Distribution of Selected Sample

Table-5.4 indicates that the relationship between caste and category of the selected respondents. It can be observed from the table that as many as 58 out of 220 selected respondents are Agricultural Labourers and this is followed by 51 Marginal Farmers while third place goes to Rural Artisans. The place of Non-Agricultural Labourers is last in this sample. A close examination of caste and category reveals that the majority of Forward Caste respondents are either Small Farmers or Marginal Farmers while the majority i.e., 28.9 percent of the Backward Class respondents are Rural Artisans and this is followed by 21.1 percent Small Farmers. In the case of Scheduled Caste respondents 58.5 percent of them are Agricultural Labourers and 30.8 percent are Marginal Farmers while 70 percent of Scheduled Tribe respondents are Rural Artisans. Thus, there is a close relationship between caste and category. Therefore, land is the basis for the sustenance for the majority of Forward Caste respondents while the majority of Backward Classes and Scheduled Tribe respondents are Rural Artisans and it is to be noted that the majority of Scheduled Caste respondents are Agricultural Labourers.

Table - 5.3 : Village and Caste - Wise Distribution of Selected Respondents In Karimnagar District

Village	*F C*	*B C*	*S C*	*S T*	*Total*
Pathipaka	8 (47.1)	17 (13.3)	3 (4.6)	8 (80.0)	36 (16.4)
Bommareddy Pally	6 (35.3)	2 (1.6)	–	–	8 (3.6)
Peddapapayya Pally	–	2 (1.6)	6 (9.2)	–	8 (3.6)
Huzurabad	–	10 (7.8)	–	–	10 (4.5)
Rangapur	–	4 (3.1)	8 (12.3)	–	12 (5.5)
Musthalapur	–	10 (7.8)	–	–	10 (4.5)
Kothapally (KRMR) (R)	–	7 (5.5)	–	–	7 (3.2)
Reddyramayya Pally	–	5 (3.9)	–	2 (20.0)	7 (3.2)
Manakondur	–	7 (5.5)	–	–	7 (3.2)
Veldhi	–	1 (0.8)	9 (13.8)	–	10 (4.5)
Gollapally	–	2 (1.6)	8 (12.3)	–	10 (4.5)
Annaram	–	–	15 (23.1)	–	15 (6.8)
Devampally	–	25 (19.5)	15 (23.1)	–	40 (18.2)
Sreenivasa Nagar	–	15 (11.7)	–	–	15 (6.8)
Bommakal	1 (5.9)	3 (2.3)	1 (1.5)	–	5 (2.3)
Mankammathota (KRMR)	1 (5.9)	5 (3.9)	–	–	6 (2.7)
Mulkanoor	–	4 (3.1)	–	–	4 (1.8)
Kothapally (Mulkanoor)	1 (5.9)	9 (7.0)	–	–	10 (4.5)
TOTAL	17 (7.7)	128 (58.2)	65 (29.5)	10 (4.5)	220 (100.0)

Source : Field Study.

Table - 5.4 : Caste and Category Wise Distribution of Selected Respondents In Karimnagar District

Category	*F C*	*B C*	*S C*	*S T*	*Total*
Small Farmers	7 (41.2)	27 (21.1)	2 (3.1)	1 (10.0)	37 (16.8)
Marginal Farmers	56 (36.3)	23 (18.0)	20 (30.8)	2 (20.0)	51 (23.2)
Agri. Labourers	–	20 (15.6)	38 (58.5)	–	58 (26.4)
Non-Agri. Labourers	–	6 (4.7)	3 (4.6)	–	9 (4.1)
Rural Artisans.	1 (5.9)	37 (28.9)	1 (1.5)	7 (70.0)	46 (20.9)
Others	3 (17.6)	15 (11.7)	1 (1.5)	–	19 (8.6)
TOTAL	17 (100.0)	128 (100.0)	65 (100.0)	10 (100.0)	220 (100.0)

Source : Field Study.

Trade and Category Wise Distribution of Selected Samples

Table-5.5 indicates that Marginal Farmers can be seen in 16 out of 19 trades selected while Small Farmers and others can be found in 12 trades. It is to be noticed that Rural Artisans are distributed in 11 trades and Agricultural Labourers are seen in 10 trades. However, Non-Agricultural Labourers are distributed in less number of trades when compared to others. Thus, the scope of selecting trades is relatively wider for Marginal Farmers and it is least for Non-Agricultural Labourers.

Socio-Economic Background of the Selected Respondents

Table-5.6 explains the socio-economic background of the selected respondents consists of age, caste, educational qualifications, marital status as well as their economic status inclusive of their primary and secondary occupation.

The data is regard to age group of the respondents denote that 169 out of 220 selected (76.8 percent) are of below 40 years

Table 5.5 : Trade and Category-Wise Distribution of Selected Respondents in Karimnagar District

Trade	*SF*	*M F*	*A L*	*N A L*	*R A*	*Others*	*Total*
Leather Works	4 (10.8)	4 (7.8)	2 (3.4)	—	—	2 (10.5)	12 (5.5)
Soft-Toys	3 (8.1)	2 (3.9)	2 (3.4)	—	1 (2.2)	4 (21.1)	12 (5.5)
Basket Making	1 (2.7)	2 (3.9)	—	—	15 (32.6)	—	18 (8.2)
Greeting Cards	1 (2.7)	1 (2.0)	—	—	1 (2.2)	1 (5.3)	4 (1.8)
Petty Coats	2 (5.4)	7 (13.7)	8 (13.8)	—	5 (10.9)	1 (5.3)	23 (0.5)
Leaf Plate Making	5 (13.6)	—	1 (1.7)	—	1 (2.2)	1 (5.3)	8 (3.6)
Thread Work	1 (2.7)	2 (3.9)	3 (5.2)	—	—	—	6 (2.7)
Cosmetic Sales	—	1 (2.0)	—	—	—	1 (5.3)	2 (0.9)
Nawar Making	—	1 (2.0)	—	—	3 (6.5)	—	4 (1.8)
Veg./ Fruit Vending	—	1 (2.0)	6 (10.3)	1 (11.1)	—	—	8 (3.6)
Surf/ Blue/ Phenoil	4 (10.8)	3 (5.9)	1 (1.7)	1 (11.1)	—	1 (5.3)	10 (4.5)
Lace Work	—	—	1 (1.7)	3 (33.3)	2 (4.3)	1 (5.3)	7 (3.2)
Readymade Dresses	—	—	—	1 (11.1)	6 (13.0)	—	7 (3.2)
Veg. Cultivation	1 (2.7)	3 (5.9)	5 (8.6)	1 (11.1)	—	—	10 (4.5)
Milch Animals	12 (32.4)	20 (39.2)	29 (50.0)	2 (22.2)	5 (10.9)	2 (10.5)	70 (31.8)
Tailoring	1 (2.7)	1 (2.0)	—	—	—	—	2 (0.9)
Embroidary Work	—	1 (2.0)	—	—	3 (6.5)	1 (5.3)	5 (2.3)
Others	—	1 (2.0)	—	—	—	1 (5.3)	2 (0.9)
No Trade	2 (5.4)	1 (2.0)	—	—	4 (8.7)	3 (15.8)	10 (4.5)
TOTAL	37 (16.8)	51 (23.2)	58 (26.4)	9 (4.1)	46 (2.9)	19 (8.6)	220 (100.0)

Source : Field Study.

Table 5.6 : Socio-Economic Background Of Selected Respondents in Karimnagar District

Age	*No. of Respondents*	*% to Total*
20 - 30	79	35.9
31 - 40	90	40.9
41 - 50	46	20.9
Above 50	5	2.3
TOTAL	220	100.0
Caste	*No. of Respondents*	*% to Total*
F C	17	7.7
B C	128	58.2
S C	65	29.5
S T	10	4.5
TOTAL	220	100.0
Edn. Quali.	*No. of Respondents*	*% to Total*
Illiterate	95	43.2
Primary	66	30.0
Secondary	48	21.8
Intermediate	9	4.1
Degree	2	0.9
TOTAL	220	100.0

Contd....

Table 5.6 : (Contd....)

Marital Status	*No.of Respondents*	*% to Total*
Married	187	85.0
Un-Married	7	3.2
Divorced	1	0.5
Seperated	4	1.8
Widowed	21	9.5
TOTAL	220	100.0
Primary Occu.	*No. of Respondents*	*% to Total*
Agriculture	56	25.5
Agri. Labourers	50	22.7
Non-Agri. Labourers	10	4.5
Rural Artisans	29	13.2
Business	4	1.8
Tailoring	18	8.2
House Wives	26	11.8
Others	27	12.3
TOTAL	220	100.0

Contd....

Table 5.6 : (Contd....)

Sec. Occu.	*No. of Respondents*	*% to Total*
Agriculture	17	7.7
Agri. Labourers	89	40.5
Non-Agri. Labourers	14	6.4
Rural Artisans	24	10.9
Business	6	2.7
Tailoring	24	10.9
House Wives	20	9.1
Others	26	11.8
TOTAL	220	100.0

and of them 79 are in the age group of 20-30 years. The respondents are also seen in the age group of above 50 years but their percentage is only 2.3.

The caste-wise information states that 58.2 percent of the respondents belonged to Backward Classes and it is followed by 29.5 percent of Scheduled Caste respondents. However, the percentage share of Scheduled Tribes is least.

It is disheartening to note that 95 out of 220 selected respondents (43.2 percent) are illiterates and which is followed by 66 (30 percent) respondents who could study upto primary level and only 2 respondents are degree holders while 9 could study upto intermediate level.

The information in regard to the Marital status of the respondents explains that 187 out of 220 selected respondents (85 percent) are married and only one respondent is divorced.

The economic status of the respondents in terms of their Primary Occupation indicates that the Agriculture is the Primary Occupation for 56 respondents while 50 are Agricultural Labourers and "Business" stands last in this regard where in which only 4 respondents are found.

The information in regard to Secondary occupation shows that "Agricultural Labour" occupies first position while 24 each can be seen in Rural Artisans and Tailoring. Since majority of the respondents are Marginal Farmers, their land position will not provide work throughout the year. Therefore, the information in regard to their secondary occupation shows that as many as 89 out of 220 selected respondents are Agricultural Labourers.

Relationship Between Caste and Educational Qualifications

Table-5.7 reveals that the majority i.e., 35.3 percent among Forward Caste respondents could study upto Primary level. However, 23.5 percent of them could study upto Intermediate. The Backward Class respondents can be found in all the levels of education i.e., from Illiteracy to Degree level. Of course, as many as 48 out of 128. Backward Class respondents are

Table 5.7 : Relationship Between Caste and Educational Qualifications of the Selected Respondents in Karimnagar District

Caste	*Illiterate*	*Primary*	*Secon-dary*	*Inter-Mediate*	*Degree*	*Total*
F C	4	6	3	4	–	17
	(23.5)	(35.3)	(17.6)	(23.5)		(100.0)
B C	48	40	33	5	2	128
	(37.5)	(31.3)	(25.8)	(3.9)	(1.6)	(100.0)
S C	35	19	11	–	–	65
	(53.8)	(29.2)	(16.9)			(100.0)
S T	8	1	1	–	–	10
	(80.0)	(10.0)	(10.0)			(100.0)
TOTAL	95	66	48	9	2	220
	(43.2)	(30.0)	(21.8)	(4.1)	(0.9)	(100.0)

Source : Field Study.

illiterates. Contrarily, all the 2 degree holders belonged to Backward Classes. As high as 53.8 percent of Scheduled Caste respondents and 80 percent of Scheduled Tribe respondents are Illiterates. Thus, the illiteracy has increased as one moves from Forward Caste to Scheduled Tribe. Moreover, some of the Forward Caste and Backward Class respondents could study upto Intermediate and beyond and 2 Backward Class respondents could study upto Degree level. In this way, there is a close relationship between caste and educational qualifications.

Relationship Between Caste and Family Size of the Respondents

Table-5.8 explains that the size of the family is in the range of 3-4 for 108 out of 220 selected respondents while it is in the range of 5-6 for 73 respondents. Moreover, the size of the family is more than 7 for 13 respondents. The caste-wise analysis reveals that the size of the family is in the range of 3-4 for 64.7 percent of Forward Caste respondents. Similar trend can be noticed for Backward Class, Scheduled Caste and Scheduled Tribe respondents. The size of the family is relatively higher among Scheduled Tribe respondents when compared to other castes.

Table 5.8 : Relationship Between Caste and Family Size of the Selected Respondents in Karimnagar District

Caste	*1 - 2*	*3 - 4*	*5 - 6*	*Above 7*	*Total*
F C	–	11	5	1	17
		(64.7)	(29.4)	(5.9)	(100.0)
B C	16	62	43	7	128
	(12.5)	(48.3)	(33.6)	(5.5)	(100.0)
S C	10	31	21	3	65
	(15.4)	(47.7)	(32.3)	(4.6)	(100.0)
S T	–	4	4	2	10
		(40.0)	(40.0)	(20.0)	(100.0)
TOTAL	26	108	73	13	220
	(11.8)	(49.1)	(33.2)	(5.9)	(100.0)

Source : Field Study.

Relationship Between Caste and Economic Assets

The assets are divided into house, other assets and savings. Table-5.9 denotes the type of house in which the selected respondents are residing. Out of 220 selected respondents 126

Table 5.9 : Relationship Between Caste and House Possession of the Selected Respondents in Karimnagar District

Caste	*Kutcha*	*Pucca*	*R C C*	*Rented*	*Others*
F C	1	10	6	–	17
	(5.9)	(58.9)	(35.3)		(100.0)
B C	13	79	21	15	128
	(10.2)	(61.7)	(16.4)	(11.7)	(100.0)
S C	16	32	14	3	65
	(24.6)	(49.2)	(21.5)	(4.6)	(100.0)
S T	5	5	–	–	10
	(50.0)	(50.0)			(100.0)
TOTAL	35	126	41	18	220
	(15.9)	(57.3)	(18.6)	(8.2)	(100.0)

Source : Field Study.

are residing in Pucca houses and 41 are in RCC houses while 35 are in Kutcha houses. However, 18 respondents do not possess own houses and therefore, they live in rented houses. The caste-wise analysis states that the majority of Forward Caste, Backward Class and Scheduled Caste respondents reside in "Pucca" house. While in the case of Scheduled Tribes 50 percent of them, reside in Pucca houses and remaining 50 percent live in `Kutcha' house.

It is to be noticed that as one moves from Forward Caste to Scheduled Tribe the percentage of respondents who reside in "Kutcha" houses increases. Similarly, no Scheduled Tribe respondents could afford to live in RCC house. The percentage of respondents who reside in RCC house is relatively higher among Forward Castes when compared to Backward Class, Scheduled Caste and Scheduled Tribe respondents. Further, no Forward Caste and Scheduled Tribe respondents can be found in Rented houses.

Table-5.10 denotes the source of house possession and its relation to caste. Out of 220 selected respondents, 88 have inherited the house from their parents while 84 could construct the house on their own and government finance is the source for 31 respondents to construct own house. The caste-wise

Table 5.10 : Relationship Between Caste and Source of House Possession of the Selected Respondents in Karimnagar District

Caste	*Parents*	*Govt.*	*Own*	*Others*	*Total*
F C	11	3	3	–	17
	(64.7)	(17.6)	(17.6)		(100.0)
B C	15	55	5	14	128
	(11.7)	(43.0)	(3.9)	(10.9)	(100.0)
S C	21	21	20	3	65
	(32.3)	(32.3)	(30.8)	(4.6)	(100.0)
S T	1	2	7	–	10
	(10.0)	(20.0)	(70.0)		(100.0)
TOTAL	48	81	35	17	220
	(21.8)	(36.8)	(16.0)	(7.7)	(100.0)

Source : Field Study.

analysis explains that 64.7 percent of Forward Caste respondents could inherit the house from their parents while 43 percent of Backward Class respondents could get finance from the government to own the house whereas they are 32.3 percent among Scheduled Caste respondents. As much as 70 percent of Scheduled Tribe respondents could construct houses on their own.

Table-5.11 explains the relationship between caste and assets. It can be observed from the table that 60 out of 220 selected respondents could possess assets worth in the range of Rs. 3001-5000 while 55 could possess in the range of Rs. 1001-3000. It is to be noted that 57 respondents could possess the assets worth beyond Rs. 10,001 and among them, 38 could possess assets in excess of Rs. 15000. However, in this range, no Scheduled Caste and Scheduled Tribe respondents can be seen. The caste-wise analysis reveals that the majority of Forward Caste respondents could possess assets in the range of Rs. 5001-10,000. Interestingly, 27.3 percent of Backward Class respondents could possess assets more than Rs. 15,000. Similarly, 41.5 percent of Scheduled Caste respondents possess assets worth Rs. 1001-3000 whereas 40 percent of Scheduled Tribe respondents could have assets in the range of Rs. 3001-

Table - 5.11 : Relationship Between Caste and Assets Position of the Selected Respondents in Karimnagar District

(Asset value in Rs.)

Caste	*Below 1000*	*1001-3000*	*3001-5000*	*5001-10000*	*10001-15000*	*Above 15000*	*Total*
F C	–	1	5	6	2	3	17
		(5.9)	(29.4)	(35.3)	(11.8)	(17.6)	(100.0)
B C	2	24	32	25	10	35	128
	(1.6)	(18.8)	(25.0)	(19.5)	(7.8)	(27.3)	(100.0)
S C	5	27	19	8	6	–	65
	(7.7)	(41.5)	(29.2)	(12.3)	(9.2)		(100.0)
S T	2	3	4	–	1	–	10
	(20.0)	(30.0)	(40.0)		(10.0)		(100.0)
TOTAL	9	55	60	39	19	38	220
	(4.1)	(25.0)	(27.3)	(17.7)	(8.6)	(17.3)	(100.0)

Source : Field Study.

5000. Thus, the economic status of Backward Class respondents in terms of assets is relatively in a better position while it is relatively weaker for Scheduled Caste respondents.

Table-5.12 states the ability of the respondents to save part of their income. Out of 220 selected respondents, 84 are capable of saving part of their income. The caste-wise information reveals that the percentage of respondents who could save declines as one moves from Forward Caste to Scheduled Tribe. Therefore, 52.9 percent of Forward Caste respondents are able to save while it is nil in the case of Scheduled Tribe respondents.

Table 5.12 : Relationship Between Caste and Savings Position of the Selected Respondents in Karimnagar District

Caste	*Yes*	*No*	*Total*
F C	9	8	17
	(52.9)	(47.1)	(100.0)
B C	59	69	128
	(46.1)	(53.9)	(100.0)
S C	16	49	65
	(24.6)	(75.4)	(100.0)
S T	–	10	10
		(100.0)	(100.0)
TOTAL	84	136	220
	(38.2)	(61.8)	(100.0)

Source : Field Study.

Table-5.13 indicates that out 84 respondents who could save, 34 prefers to keep their savings in Chits, 24 prefer LIC, 18 prefer Post-office and Banks occupy last position in this regard. The caste-wise analysis reveals that the majority (44.4 percent) of Forward Caste respondents prefer to keep their savings in Post-office while it is chits which is preferred by the majority of Backward Class and Scheduled Caste respondents.

Table-5.14 indicates the amount saved by the selected respondents. The amount saved has varied between Rs. 1,000 and Rs. 20,000. However, the Backward Class respondents alone can be found in the amount of saving which is in excess of Rs. 10,000 and beyond.

Table 5.13 : Caste and Savings in Various Institutions of the Selected Respondents in Karimnagar District

Caste	*Chits*	*L I C*	*Banks*	*Post-office*	*Total*
F C	2	2	1	4	9
	(22.2)	(22.2)	(1.1)	(44.4)	(100.0)
B C	21	19	7	12	59
	(35.6)	(32.2)	(11.9)	(20.3)	(100.0)
S C	11	3	–	2	16
	(68.8)	(18.8)		(12.5)	(100.0)
S T	–	–	–	–	–
TOTAL	34	24	8	18	84
	(40.5)	(28.6)	(9.5)	(21.4)	(100.0)

Source : Field Study.

Table 5.14 : Caste and Amount Saved by the Selected Respondents in Karimnagar District

(Savings in Rs.)

Caste	*Below 1000*	*1001-3000*	*3001-5000*	*5001-10000*	*10001-15000*	*Above 15000*	*Total*
F C	–	–	3	5	–	1	9
			(33.3)	(55.5)		(11.1)	(100.0)
B C	–	–	25	25	7	2	59
			(42.4)	(42.4)	(11.9)	(3.4)	(100.0)
S C	–	2	11	3	–	–	16
		(12.5)	(68.8)	(18.7)			(100.0)
S T	–	–	–	–	–	–	–
TOTAL	–	2	39	33	7	3	84
		(2.4)	(46.4)	(39.3)	(8.3)	(3.6)	(100.0)

Source : Field Study.

Selection of Trade

The selection of trade by the respondents will be determined (i) on their own (ii) VDO or MPDO (iii) DRDA officials (iv) Bank officials and (v) Others. Table-5.15 indicates relevant information.

It can be observed that 74 out of 220 have selected the trade on the advice of DRDA Officials while 54 could select the trade on their own where as 38 are influenced by VDO, MPDO and

Table 5.15 : Selection of the Trade by the Selected Respondents in Karimnagar District

Trade	*Own*	*VDO/ MDO*	*Drda Offi-cials*	*Bank Offi-cials*	*Group Leader/ Others*	*Total*
Leather Works	1	–	7	–	4	12
Soft-Toys	–	–	10	–	2	12
Basket Making	10	5	–	–	3	18
Greeting Cards	–	–	4	–	–	4
Petty Coats	10	3	10	–	–	23
Leaf Plate Making	–	–	8	–	–	8
Thread Work	–	1	1	–	4	6
Cosmetic Sales	–	–	2	–	–	2
Nawar Making	4	–	–	–	–	4
Veg/ Fruit Vending	5	2	1	–	–	8
Surf/ Blue/ Phenoil	–	–	10		–	10
Lace Work	–	–	5	–	2	7
Readymade Dresses	1	4	2	–	–	7
Veg. Cultivation	–	5	3	–	2	10
Milch Animals	5	18	10	37	–	70
Tailoring	2	–	–	–	–	2
Embroidary Work	4	–	1	–	–	5
Others	2	–	–	–	–	2
No Trade	10	–	–	–	–	10
TOTAL	54 (24.5)	38 (17.3)	74 (33.6)	37 (16.9)	17 (7.7)	220 (100.0)

Source : Field Study.

37 are influenced by Bank Officials. Thus, the majority of respondents could not take decision in regard to the selection of trade on their own. Trade-wise analysis reveals that own decision can be found in 11 trades while in the selection of 14 trades DRDA officials played significant role where as Bank Officials could influence in only one case i.e., Milch Animals. However, as the many of the respondents are illiterates or with lower level education, they could not take decision as to the selection of trade on their own. Therefore, they depend upon various officials in selecting the trade.

Problems of Trade

The problems of selected respondents in running the trade are usually related to the procurement of raw-material and marketing.

Table-5.16 denotes that out of 220 selected respondents as many as 161 (73.2 percent) did not face any problem in regard to the procurement of raw-material. The scheme-wise analysis explains that 9 out of 19 selected trades have the problems in this regard. They are-Leather Work, Soft-Toys, Basket Making, Greeting Cards, Leaf Plate Making, Nawar Making, Veg/ Fruit Vending, Surf/ Blue/ Phenol and Milch Animals. However, some of the respondents in the same trade did not face any problem in this regard.

Table 5.16 : Problems in the Procurment of Raw-material by the Selected Respondents in Karimnagar District

Trade	*Yes*	*No*	*Total*
Leather Works	4	8	12
Soft-Toys	2	10	12
Basket Making	4	14	18
Greeting Cards	4	—	4
Petty Coats	—	23	23
Leaf Plate Making	5	3	8
Thread Work	—	6	6
Cosmetic Sales	—	2	2
Nawar Making	1	3	4
Veg./ Fruit Vending	6	2	8
Surf/ Blue/ Phenoil	8	2	10
Lace Work	—	7	7
Readymade Dresses	—	7	7
Veg. Cultivation	—	10	10
Milch Animals	25	45	70
Tailoring	—	2	2
Embroidary Work	—	5	5
Others	—	2	2
No Trade	—	10	10
TOTAL	59 (26.8)	161 (73.2)	220 (100.0)

Source : Field Study.

Marketing of The Product

The respondents will sell the product in either through own channel, or exclusively through DWCRA Bazars or utilise both the channels. Table-5.17 indicates relevant material.

Table-5.17 indicates that as many as 137 out of 220 selected respondents used to sell the product only through 'own' channel. It is to be noticed that 49 could sell the product only through DWCRA bazars which are organised by DRDA. However, 34 respondents could utilise both the channels of sales. The own channel is the only source for marketing of the product in 15 trades while exclusive utilisation of DWCRA bazars for selling the product can be found in 10 trades where as 7 trades could utilise both the channels viz own as well as DWCRA bazars to sell the product.

Table 5.17 : Marketing of the Product by the Selected Respondents in Karimnagar District

Trade	*DWCRA Bazar*	*Own*	*Both*	*Total*
Leather Works	4	1	7	12
Soft-Toys	6	2	4	12
Basket Making	2	16	–	18
Greeting Cards	4	–	–	4
Petty Coats	8	4	11	23
Leaf Plate Making	2	1	5	8
Thread Work	6	–	–	6
Cosmetic Sales	–	2	–	2
Nawar Making	–	3	1	4
Veg./ Fruit Vending	–	8	–	8
Surf/ Blue/ Phenoil	8	–	2	10
Lace Work	7	–	–	7
Readymade Dresses	2	1	4	7
Veg. Cultivation	–	10	–	10
Milch Animals	–	70	–	70
Tailoring	–	2	–	2
Embroidary Work	–	5	–	5
Others	–	2	–	2
No Trade	–	10	–	10
TOTAL	49 (22.3)	137 (62.3)	34 (15.5)	220 (100.0)

Source : Field Study.

Table-5.18 states that 141 out of 220 selected respondents did not face any problem in connection with the marketing of the product. It can be noticed that 79 respondents belonged to

Table 5.18 : Marketing Problems of the Selected Respondents in Karimnagar District

Trade	*Yes*	*No*	*Total*
Leather Works	3	9	12
Soft-Toys	8	4	12
Basket Making	12	6	18
Greeting Cards	4	–	4
Petty Coats	15	8	23
Leaf Plate Making	6	2	8
Thread Work	6	–	6
Cosmetic Sales	2	–	2
Nawar Making	4	–	4
Veg./ Fruit Vending	–	8	8
Surf/ Blue/ Phenoil	8	2	10
Lace Work	6	1	7
Readymade Dresses	5	2	7
Veg. Cultivation	–	10	10
Milch Animals	–	70	70
Tailoring	–	2	2
Embroidary Work	–	5	5
Others	–	2	2
No Trade	–	10	10
TOTAL	79 (35.9)	141 (64.1)	220 (100.0)

Source : Field Study.

12 trades are facing marketing problem. Table-5.19 denotes that out of these 79 who face marketing problem, as many as 38 are from inadequate demand while competition is the problem for 27 respondents where as quality of the product is a problem for 8 respondents and transportation problem confronted by 6 respondents. The problem of inadequate demand is confronted by Leather Works, Soft-Toys, Basket Making, Leaf Plate Making, Thread Work, Nawar Making, Surf/ Blue/ Phenol and Lace

Work. However, transport is the problem for Petty Coats, Cosmetic products and Nawar Making. It can be observed that 5 trades are suffering from the problem of quality of the product and 5 trades are from competition.

Table 5.19 : Nature of Marketing Problems of the Selected Respondents in Karimnagar District

Trade	*Inadequate Demand*	*Trans-port*	*Quality/ Packing*	*Compe-tition*	*Total*
Leather Works	1	–	2	–	3
Soft-Toys	6	1	1	–	8
Basket Making	4	–	–	8	12
Greeting Cards	1	–	2	1	4
Petty Coats	–	2	–	13	15
Leaf Plate Making	6	–	–	–	6
Thread Work	6	–	–	–	6
Cosmetic Sales	–	2	–	–	2
Nawar Making	3	1	–	–	4
Veg./ Fruit Vending	–	–	–	–	–
Surf/ Blue/ Phenoil	6	–	2	–	8
Lace Work	5	–	–	1	6
Readymade Dresses	–	–	1	4	5
Veg. Cultivation	–	–	–	–	–
Milch Animals	–	–	–	–	–
Tailoring	–	–	–	–	–
Embroidary Work	–	–	–	–	–
Others	–	–	–	–	–
No Trade	–	–	–	–	–
TOTAL	38 (48.1)	6 (7.6)	8 (10.1)	27 (34.2)	79 (100.0)

Source : Field Study.

Employment Generation

The main objective of DWCRA is to generate employment to rural women. Therefore, the success of the programme is determined on the basis of its ability to generate employment. This can be assessed in two ways - (i) The Pre and Post-DWCRA employment of the respondents will be examined to ascertain the impact of DWCRA in this regard. (ii) The employment in terms of days per month exclusively created by DWCRA is to be studied.

Comparative Analysis of Employment Generation

A comparison is made between Pre and Post-DWCRA employment in relation to Scheme, Caste, Category, Educational Qualification and Age of the respondent.

Relationship Between Scheme and Pre and Post-DWCRA Employment Generation:

Table-5.20 indicates that the average employment in terms of days per month during Pre-DWCRA period is 15.01 and out of 220 selected respondents, only 184 are earning members during Pre-DWCRA period. An examination of the table further reveals that all the 220 respondents are employed during Post-DWCRA period and moreover, the average employment has increased to 20.61 days in this period. Thus, an increase can be noticed in terms of number of respondents employed as well as average employment created in terms of days per month.

However, the rise in the average employment is not uniform in all the schemes. Therefore, the difference between Pre and Post-DWCRA employment is positive in 15 out of 19 schemes selected and has varied between 2 days in Embroidery Work and 10.88 days in Veg./ Fruit Vending. The difference is zero in the case of 'Others' and negative in schemes of Soft-Toys, Greeting Cards and 'No Trade'.

The average employment during Pre-DWCRA period has varied between 10 days in Greeting Cards and 26.60 days in 'No Trade'. However, it is in the range of 8 days in Greeting cards and 25.80 days in 'Vegetable cultivation'.

Thus, it is interesting to note that though there is a rise in the average employment during Post-DWCRA period, the lower and upper limit in average employment has declined during Post-DWCRA period when compared to Pre-DWCRA period. A close examination of the table further explains that in the three schemes - Soft Toys, Greeting Cards and No Trade

Table 5.20 : Scheme-Wise Analysis of Employment Generation During Pre and Post-DWCRA Period in Karimnagar District

Trade	*Pre-DWCRA Employment*			*Post-DWCRA Employment*			*Difference of Avg.*
	No. of Respon-dents	*Total Days*	*Avg.Emp Days (P. M.)*	*No. of Respon-dents*	*Total Days*	*Avg.Emp Days (P. M.)*	*Emplo-ment*
Leather Works	12	141	11.75	12	259	21.58	9.83
Soft-Toys	7	125	17.85	12	182	15.16	-2.69
Basket Making	18	277	15.38	18	394	21.88	6.50
Greeting Cards	1	10	10.00	4	32	8.00	-2.00
Petty Coats	23	336	14.60	23	488	21.21	6.61
Leaf Plate Making	5	90	18.00	8	200	25.00	7.00
Thread Work	6	90	15.00	6	115	19.16	4.16
Cosmetic Sales	1	15	15.00	2	45	22.50	7.50
Nawar Making	4	54	13.50	4	87	21.75	8.25
Veg./Fruit Vending	8	101	12.62	8	188	23.50	10.88
Surf/Blue/ Phenoil	8	120	15.00	10	177	17.70	2.70
Lace Work	7	143	20.42	7	171	24.42	4.00
Readymade Dresses	5	75	15.00	7	126	18.00	3.00
Veg.Cultivation	10	153	15.30	10	258	25.80	10.50
Milch Animals	56	733	13.08	70	1454	20.77	7.69
Tailoring	2	45	22.50	2 50	2	5.00	2.50
Embroidary Work	3	45	15.00	5	85	17.00	2.00
Others	2	50	25.00	2	50	25.00	0.00
No Trade	6	160	26.60	10	175	17.50	-9.1
TOTAL	184	2763	15.01	220	4536	20.61	5.60

Source : Field Study.

-in which the impact of DWCRA in terms of average employment generated is negative of course, one can observe a rise in the number of persons employed in all these three schemes. In Soft-toys, the number of persons employed is 7 during Pre-DWCRA period and it has been increased to 12 days during Post-DWCRA period. While in Greeting Cards, it is from 1 to 4 persons and finally in No Trade it is from 6 persons to 10 persons. Therefore, total days of employment generated in all these three trades show a rise. Only in one trade i.e., 'others' the employment generated in terms of number of persons as well as average employment reveals no change. However, it can be stated that the total days of employment generated has increased from 2763 days during Pre-DWCRA period to 4536 days during Post-DWCRA period. On the whole, the scheme is a success in terms of employment generation.

Relationship Between Caste and Employment Generation During Pre and Post-DWCRA Period

It can be observed from Table-5.21 that total days of employment as well as average employment has increased during Post-DWCRA period when compared to Pre-DWCRA period for all the respondents irrespective of their caste. However, the rise is not uniform and inter-caste variation can be noticed. Therefore, the difference between Pre and Post-DWCRA average employment has varied between 0.15 days Forward Caste respondents and 7.99 days for Scheduled Caste respondents.

Table 5.21 : Caste-wise Analysis of Employment Generation During Pre and Post-DWCRA Period in Karimnagar District

Caste	*Pre-DWCRA Employment*			*Post-DWCRA Employment*			*Difference of Avg. Emplo-ment*
	No. of Respon-dents	*Total Days*	*Avg.Emp Days (P. M.)*	*No. of Respon-dents*	*Total Days*	*Avg.Emp Days (P. M.)*	
F C	11	186	16.90	17	290	17.05	0.15
B C	102	1585	15.53	128	2611	20.39	4.86
S C	61	849	13.91	65	1424	21.90	7.99
S T	10	143	14.30	10	211	21.10	6.80
TOTAL	184	2763	15.01	220	4536	20.61	5.60

Source : Field Study.

The average employment during Pre-DWCRA period has ranged between 13.91 days for Scheduled Caste respondents and 16.90 for Forward Caste respondents. A radical change in their relative positions can be noticed during Post-DWCRA period. Thus, the Scheduled Caste respondents who were last in terms of average employment during Pre-DWCRA period comes to first position in this regard during Post-DWCRA period. In a similar way, Forward Caste respondents who were first in terms of average employment during Pre-DWCRA period have gone down to last position during Post-DWCRA period in this regard.

Thus, though the DWCRA is a success in terms of employment generation in all the castes, it is relatively more successful in Schedule Caste respondents.

Relationship Between Category and Employment Generation During Pre and Post-DWCRA Period

Table-5.22 indicates that the average employment in terms of days per month has increased for all the respondents

Table - 5.22 : Category-wise Analysis of Employment Generation During Pre and Post-DWCRA Period in Karimnagar District

Category	*Pre-DWCRA Employment*			*Post-DWCRA Employment*			*Difference of Avg. Employment*
	No. of Respondents	*Total Days*	*Avg.Emp Days (P. M.)*	*No. of Respondents*	*Total Days*	*Avg.Emp Days (P. M.)*	
Small Farmers	28	332	11.85	37	684	18.48	6.63
Marginal Farmers	45	719	15.97	51	1142	22.39	6.42
Agri. Labourers	55	718	13.05	58	1215	20.94	7.89
Non-Agri. Labourers	9	173	19.22	9	240	26.66	7.44
Rural Artisans	40	673	16.77	46	984	21.39	4.62
Others	7	150	21.42	19	271	14.26	-7.16
TOTAL	184	2763	15.01	220	4536	20.61	5.60

Source : Field Study.

irrespective of their category except for Others during Post-DWCRA period when compared to Pre-DWCRA period. However, in the category of others, number of persons employed has increased from 7 in Pre-DWCRA period to 19 in Post-DWCRA period. Therefore, though the average employment in this category shows a decline, total days of employment created for this category has shown a rise from 150 days in Pre-DWCRA to 271 days during Post-DWCRA period. Moreover, total days of employment has increased from 2763 during Pre-DWCRA period to 4536 during Post-DWCRA period.

The category-wise analysis reveals that the average employment during Pre-DWCRA period has varied between 11.85 days for Small Farmers and 21.42 days for others while it has varied between 14.26 days for Others and 26.66 for Non-Agricultural Labourers during Post-DWCRA period. Thus, the relative position of 'Others' has deteriorated and first position is occupied by Non-Agricultural labourers instead of Small Farmers during Post-DWCRA period. Moreover, the rise in average employment is not uniform among various categories and inter-category variation can be observed.

Relationship Between Educational Qualification of the Respondent and Employment Generation During Pre and Post-DWCRA Period

It can be noticed from Table-5.23 that the average employment during Pre-DWCRA period has ranged between 14.01 days per month for respondents who have upto primary level education and 30 days per month for Degree holders. It is to be noted that the average employment during Post-DWCRA period has increased for the respondents who are Illiterate, Primary and Secondary level education. Unfortunately, it has shown a fall for the respondents who could have education upto Intermediate and Degree. Interestingly, in these cases, though average employment shown a decline, total days of employment generated has increased. Thus, the decline in average days of employment is due to rise in the number of respondents. Total days of employment generated has shown a rise for all the respondents irrespective of their educational qualifications. Moreover, the rise is not uniform.

Table 5.23 : Educational Qualifications and Employment Generation During Pre and Post-DWCRA Period in Karimnagar District

Educational Qualifications	*Pre-DWCRA Employment*			*Post-DWCRA Employment*			*Difference of Avg. Emplo-ment*
	No. of Respon-dents	*Total Days*	*Avg.Emp Days (P. M.)*	*No. of Respon-dents*	*Total Days*	*Avg.Emp Days (P. M.)*	
Illiterates	88	1300	14.77	95	2063	21.71	6.94
Primary	59	827	14.01	66	1407	21.31	7.30
Secondary	31	504	16.25	48	882	18.37	2.12
Intermediate	5	102	20.40	9	148	16.44	-3.96
Degree	1	30	30.00	2	36	18.00	12.00
TOTAL	184	2763	15.01	220	4536	20.61	5.60

Source : Field Study.

Relationship Between Age and Employment Generation During Pre and Post-DWCRA Period

It can be observed from Table-5.24 that the total days of employment as well as average employment has shown a rise during Post-DWCRA period when compared to Pre-DWCRA period. The average employment during Pre-DWCRA period has varied between 14 days per month for the respondents whose age is above 50 years and 15.96 for who are in between 20-30 years. Interestingly, their relative positions are completely reversed during Post-DWCRA period where first position is occupied by the respondents who are of 50 years age with 23.60 days of average employment and last position is occupied by the respondents who are of 20-30 years with 19.88 days of average employment. However, this is due to rise in the number of respondents in this age group. Moreover, the difference between Pre and Post-DWCRA average employment has varied between 3.92 days for the age group of 20-30 years and 9.60 days for age group of above 50 years.

Table 5.24 : Relationship Between Age and Employment Generation During Pre and Post-DWCRA Period in Karimnagar District

Age	*Pre-DWCRA Employment*			*Post-DWCRA Employment*			*Difference of Avg. Emplo-ment*
	No. of Respon-dents	*Total Days*	*Avg.Emp Days (P. M.)*	*No. of Respon-dents*	*Total Days*	*Avg.Emp Days (P. M.)*	
20 - 30	60	958	15.96	79	1571	19.88	3.92
31 - 40	81	1150	14.19	90	1877	20.85	6.66
41 - 50	38	585	15.39	46	970	21.08	5.69
Above 50	5	70	14.00	5	115	23.60	9.60
TOTAL	184	2763	15.01	220	4536	20.61	5.60

Source : Field Study.

Additional Employment Generation

This indicates that in addition to employment generation for the respondent herself, in certain schemes, the respondents used to employ others too in running the scheme. The respondents either involve their family members or other than family members to run the trade. The relevant information is shown in Table-5.25.

It can be noticed from Table-5.25 that the sample respondents could employ as many as 88 persons. Out of them, 64 are family members and 24 are others. The additional employment generation is high in the trade Milch Animals and this is followed by Petty Coats. The additional employment generation is as low as 1 in three trades viz., Greeting Cards, Surf/ Blue/ Phenol and Embroidery Work. Moreover, in certain schemes, no any additional employment being generated. They are Leaf Plate Making, Thread Work, Cosmetic Sales, Lace Work, Tailoring, Others and No trade.

The involvement of family members is high in Milch animals and this is followed by Petty coats. In certain schemes, the respondents involved family members only. They are- Basket Making, Greeting Cards, Nawar Making, Veg/ Fruit Vending, Vegetable Cultivation and Embroidery Work.

Table 5.25 : Scheme-wise Analysis of Additional Employment Generation Under DWCRA in Karimnagar District

Trade	*Family Members*	*Other Members*	*Total*
Leather Works	2	1	3
Soft-Toys	1	1	2
Basket Making	8	–	8
Greeting Cards	1	–	1
Petty Coats	13	8	21
Leaf Plate Making	–	–	–
Thread Work	–	–	–
Cosmetic Sales	–	–	–
Nawar Making	2	–	2
Veg./ Fruit Vending	2	–	2
Surf/ Blue/ Phenoil	–	1	1
Lace Work	–	–	–
Readymade Dresses	2	6	8
Veg. Cultivation	8	–	8
Milch Animals	24	7	31
Tailoring	–	–	–
Embroidary Work	1	–	1
Others	–	–	–
No Trade	–	–	–
TOTAL	64	24	88

Source : Field Study.

Inspite of scheme-wise variation in regard to additional employment generation, one can notice that the DWCRA could create employment not only to the respondents but also to others also. Thus, 220 selected respondents in Karimnagar district could create employment to 88 persons additionally. In this way the programme is a success in terms of employment generation.

Employment Generation Exclusively by DWCRA

How many days of work per month exclusively generated by DWCRA is discussed in this part. The scheme-wise analysis in this regard is presented in Table-5.26. Out of selected 220 respondents, for 105 respondents, the additional days of work

Table 5.26 : Scheme-Wise Analysis of Employment Generation From DWCRA in Karimnagar District

Trade	*Days Per Month*					*Total*
	Below 5	*6 - 10*	*11 - 15*	*16 - 20*	*Above 20*	
Leather Works	1	6	4	–	1	12
Soft-Toys	6	6	–	–	–	12
Basket Making	9	6	3	–	–	18
Greeting Cards	3	1	–	–	–	4
Petty Coats	7	12	3	1	–	23
Leaf Plate Making	1	4	3	–	–	8
Thread Work	4	2	–	–	–	6
Cosmetic Sales	–	1	–	1	–	2
Nawar Making	–	4	–	–	–	4
Veg./ Fruit Vending	–	3	5	–	–	8
Surf/ Blue/ Phenoil	4	6	–	–	–	10
Lace Work	6	–	1	–	–	7
Readymade Dresses	1	5	1	–	–	7
Veg. Cultivation	4	2	3	1	–	10
Milch Animals	5	44	21	–	–	70
Tailoring	2	–	–	–	–	2
Embroidary Work	2	3	–	–	–	5
Others	2	–	–	–	–	2
No Trade	10	–	–	–	–	10
TOTAL	67 (30.5)	105 (47.7)	44 (20.0)	3 (1.4)	1 (0.5)	220 (10.0)

Source : Field Study.

generated exclusively by DWCRA is in the range of 6-10 days per month. This is followed by less than 5 days per month for 67 respondents and 11-15 days per month for 44 respondents. However, for one respondent, the additional work generated is more than 20 days per month. This respondent belongs to the scheme Leather Works. Three trades belonged to Petty coats, Cosmetic sales and Vegetable cultivation, the work generated by DWCRA is 16-20 days per month. Moreover, same trade has created different levels of work for different respondents. Thus, inter-scheme and intra-scheme variation is noticed in regard to employment generation exclusively by DWCRA.

Table-5.27 presents caste-wise data in regard to employment generation exclusively by DWCRA in terms of number of days of work per month. It can be observed from Table-5.27 that for the majority of Forward Caste and Scheduled Tribe respondents, the work generated exclusively by DWCRA is less than 5 days per month while for Backward Class and Scheduled Caste respondents, it is in between 6-10 days per month. Only one respondent is seen in above 20 days and she belongs to Forward Caste and out of 3 respondents who could get work in between 16-20 days per month, 2 belonged to Backward Class and One belonged to Scheduled Caste. However, Scheduled Tribe respondent can not be seen beyond 11-15 days of work per month.

Table 5.27 : Caste-wise Analysis of Employment Generation From DWCRA in Karimnagar District

Caste	*Days Per Month*					*Total*
	Below 5	*6 - 10*	*11 - 15*	*16 - 20*	*Above 20*	
F C	7	6	3	–	1	17
B C	40	65	21	2	–	128
S C	14	31	19	1	–	65
S T	6	3	1	–	–	10
TOTAL	67 (30.5)	105 (47.7)	44 (20.0)	3 (1.4)	1 (0.5)	220 (100.0)

Source : Field Study.

Impact of DWCRA on Income Generation

The main objective of DWCRA is to create employment so as to attain an improvement in their income levels. Therefore, the success of the programme is determined on the basis of its ability to increase earning capacity of the respondents.

The rise in earnings of the respondent is ascertained in two ways. One way is to examine income/earnings exclusively generated from DWCRA. Another way is to compare Post-DWCRA earnings with that of Pre-DWCRA earnings.

Income Generation Exclusively From DWCRA

The information in regard to earnings of the respondents exclusively from DWCRA (Scheme-wise) is presented in Table-5.28.

Table 5.28 : Relationship Between Scheme and Income Generation in Karimnagar District

(Income In Rs.)

Trade	*Nil*	*Below 250*	*251-500*	*501-750*	*751-1000*	*1001 1500*	*Total*
Leather Works	–	–	1	7	3	1	12
Soft-Toys	–	7	5	–	–	–	12
Basket Making	1	5	10	2	–	–	18
Greeting Cards	–	4	–	–	–	–	4
Petty Coats	10	3	5	2	2	1	23
Leaf Plate Making	–	–	7	1	–	–	8
Thread Work	4	2	–	–	–	–	6
Cosmetic Sales	1	–	1	–	–	–	2
Nawar Making	–	2	2	–	–	–	4
Veg./ Fruit Vending	–	–	3	3	2	–	8
Surf/ Blue/ Phenoil	–	5	4	1	–	–	10
Lace Work	–	5	2	–	–	–	7
Readymade Dresses	–	6	–	1	–	–	7
Veg. Cultivation	–	–	7	3	–	–	10
Milch Animals	6	9	27	6	9	13	70
Tailoring	–	2	–	–	–	–	2
Embroidary Work	–	2	3	–	–	–	5
Others	–	1	1	–	–	–	2
No Trade	4	6	–	–	–	–	10
TOTAL	26 (11.8)	59 (26.8)	78 (35.5)	26 (11.8)	16 (7.3)	15 (6.9)	220 (10.0)

Source : Field Study.

Table-5.28 denotes that out of 220 selected respondents, as many as 78 could get earnings in the range of Rs. 251-500 per month. This is followed by 59 respondents whose income is less than Rs. 250 per month. It is disheartening to note that the income generation from DWCRA is nil for 26 respondents.

Contrast to this, the income generation from DWCRA has exceeded Rs. 501 per month for 57 respondents. Out of them, 31 respondents could get an income in excess of Rs. 751 per month and among them, 15 could get the income in the range of Rs. 1001-1500 per month. Out of these 15 respondents, One each belonged to Leather works and Petty coats and 13 belonged to Milch Animals. Similarly, out of 26 respondents whose income from DWCRA is nil, one each belonged to Basket making, Cosmetic sales, 4 each belonged to Thread work, No trade, 6 belonged to Milch Animals and 10 belonged to Petty coats. Intra-scheme variation is relatively wider in terms of income generation per month in the scheme of Petty Coats and Milch Animals.

Table-5.29 indicates caste-wise information in regard to income generation under DWCRA in Karimnagar district. The respondents who belonged to Forward Caste, Backward Classes and Scheduled Castes can be found in all the ranges of income from nil to Rs. 1001-1500 per month. However, out of 15 respondents who could get income exclusively from DWCRA in the range of Rs. 1001-1500, One belonged to Forward Caste, 3 to Backward Classes and 11 belonged to Scheduled Castes. This indicates that the Success of the DWCRA in terms of income generation is relatively higher among Scheduled Castes and they are followed by Backward Classes. Moreover, the income generation per month did not exceed Rs. 501-750 for Scheduled Tribe respondents.

Table 5.29 : Relationship Between Caste and Income Generation in Karimnagar District

Caste	*Nil*	*Below 250*	*251-500*	*501-750*	*751-1000*	*1001 1500*	*Total*
F C	–	4	7	3	2	1	17
B C	11	40	51	12	11	3	128
S C	14	12	15	10	3	11	65
S T	1	3	5	1	–	–	10
TOTAL	26 (11.8)	59 (26.8)	78 (35.5)	26 (11.8)	16 (7.3)	15 (6.9)	220 (100.0)

Source : Field Study.

Comparative Analysis of Income Generation During Pre and Post-DWCRA Period

Table-5.30 presents scheme-wise information in regard to Pre and Post-DWCRA earnings of the selected respondents. Out of 220 selected respondents, only 167 were having

Table 5.30 : Scheme-wise Analysis of Income Generation During Pre and Post-DWCRA Period In Karimnagar District

(Income In Rs.)

Trade	Pre-DWCRA Income			Post-DWCRA Income			Difference
	No. of Respon-dents	Total Income	Avg. Income (P. M.)	No. of Respon-dents	Total Income	Avg. Income (P. M.)	of Avg. Income
Leather Works	11	4000	363.63	12	12900	1075.00	711.37
Soft-Toys	7	3800	542.85	12	6650	554.16	11.31
Basket Making	18	10250	569.44	18	15950	886.11	316.67
Greeting Cards	1	200	200.00	4	1050	262.50	62.50
Petty Coats	21	8400	400.00	23	15900	691.30	291.30
Leaf Plate Making	5	3000	600.00	8	6150	768.75	168.75
Thread Work	6	2450	408.33	6	3050	508.33	100.00
Cosmetic Sales	1	200	200.00	2	1100	550.00	350.00
Nawar Making	4	1650	412.50	4	2600	650.00	237.50
Veg./Fruit Vending	8	2900	362.50	8	7300	912.50	550.00
Surf/ Blue/ Phenoil	6	3500	583.33	10	6900	690.00	106.67
Lace Work	6	4500	75.00	7	6350	907.14	157.14
Readymade Dresses	5	2900	580.00	7	4550	650.00	70.00
Veg. Cultivation	10	4050	405.00	10	7600	760.00	355.00
Milch Animals	46	13900	302.17	70	59050	843.57	54.14
Tailoring	2	2800	1400.00	2	3150	1575.00	175.00
Embroidary Work	2	1200	600.00	5	2550	510.00	-90.00
Others	2	2400	1200.00	2	2900	1450.00	250.00
No Trade	6	4200	700.00	10	5150	515.00	-185.00
TOTAL	167	76300	456.88	220	170850	776.59	319.71

Source : Field Study.

independent earnings during Pre-DWCRA period. Total income as well as average income per month has shown a rise during Post-DWCRA period when compared to Pre-DWCRA period. The average income per month is Rs. 456.88 during Pre-DWCRA period and it has been increased to Rs. 776.59 during Post-DWCRA period.

The scheme-wise analysis reveals that the average income has shown a rise during Post-DWCRA period in 17 out of 19 schemes selected. The average income per month during Pre-DWCRA period has varied between Rs. 200 in Greeting Cards and Cosmetic sales and Rs. 1400 in Tailoring while it has ranged between Rs. 262.50 in Greeting cards and Rs. 1575 in Tailoring during Post-DWCRA period. However, negative growth is observed in Embroidery work and 'No trade'. It is to be noted that even in these two schemes, total income has shown a rise but average income per month has shown a fall because of increase in the number of respondents from 2 to 5 in Embroidery work and 6 to 10 in 'No trade'.

Further, the change in income is not uniform across trades and inter-scheme variation is noticed. Therefore, the difference in average income between Pre and Post-DWCRA period has varied between Rs. 11.31 in Soft-Toys and Rs. 711.37 in Leather Works keeping apart the schemes which show negative difference. Thus, the DWCRA is a success in terms of attaining improvement in earnings/ income.

Comparative Analysis of Pre and Post-DWCRA Earnings in Relation to Caste

Table-5.31 denotes that the number of respondents who earn independent income has increased from 167 during Pre-DWCRA period to 220 during Post-DWCRA period. Similarly, total income has increased from Rs, 76,300 per month to Rs. 1,70,850 per month and average income per month has increased from Rs. 456.88 during Pre-DWCRA period to Rs. 776.59 during Post-DWCRA period.

Further, the caste-wise analysis explains that the average income per month has shown a rise during Post-DWCRA

Table 5.31 : Caste-wise Analysis of Income Generation During Pre and Post-DWCRA Period in Karimnagar District

(Income In Rs.)

Caste	*Pre-DWCRA Income*			*Post-DWCRA Income*			*Difference*
	No. of Respon-dents	*Total Income*	*Avg. Income (P. M.)*	*No. of Respon-dents*	*Total Income*	*Avg. Income (P. M.)*	*of Avg. Income*
F C	11	6250	568.18	17	15000	882.35	314.17
B C	85	44450	522.94	128	93450	730.07	207.13
S C	61	20100	329.50	65	53650	825.38	495.88
S T	10	5500	550.00	10	8750	875.00	325.00
TOTAL	167	76300	456.88	220	170850	776.59	319.71

Source : Field Study.

period irrespective of the caste. However, the rise is not uniform among castes. Thus, inter-caste variation is noticed in this regard. The average income per month during Pre-DWCRA period has varied between Rs. 329.50 among Scheduled Caste and Rs. 568.18 among Forward Caste respondents. During Post-DWCRA period, it is in the range of Rs. 730.07 among Backward Class and Rs. 882.35 among Forward Caste respondents. Thus, highest position in terms of average earnings per month by Forward Caste respondents is retained even during Post-DWCRA period but last position is shifted from Scheduled Caste to Backward Class respondents. The difference between Pre and Post-DWCRA average income per month has varied between Rs. 207.13 among Backward Class and Rs. 495.88 among Scheduled Caste respondents.

On the whole, it can be stated that the average income during Pre-DWCRA period did not exceed Rs. 568.18 but it is above Rs. 730.07 during Post-DWCRA period. This clearly denotes the success of DWCRA in terms of achieving an improvement in earnings of the respondents.

Comparative Analysis of Pre and Post-DWCRA Earnings in Relation to Economic Category of the Respondents

Table-5.32 indicates that the average income per month has shown a rise for all the respondents irrespective of their economic category except 'Others'. Even for them, total income has shown a rise from Rs. 3900 during Pre-DWCRA period to Rs. 10,200 during Post-DWCRA period. But the fall in average income to this category is due to rise in the number of respondents during Post-DWCRA period.

Table 5.32 : Category-wise Analysis of Income Generation During Pre and Post-dwcra Period In Karimnagar District

(Income In Rs.)

Category	*Pre-DWCRA Income*			*Post-DWCRA Income*			*Difference*
	No. of Respon-dents	*Total Income*	*Avg. Income (P. M.)*	*No. of Respon-dents*	*Total Income*	*Avg. Income (P. M.)*	*of Avg. Income*
Small Farmers	17	8350	491.17	37	26200	708.10	216.93
Marginal Farmers	42	18650	444.04	51	50100	982.35	538.31
Agri. Labourers	55	17400	316.36	58	37650	649.13	332.77
Non-Agri. Labourers	9	5900	655.55	9	11050	1227.77	572.22
Rural Artisans	39	22100	566.66	46	35650	775.00	208.34
Others	5	3900	780.0	19	10200	536.84	-243.16
TOTAL	167	76300	456.88	220	170850	776.59	319.71

Source : Field Study.

The category-wise analysis also reveals that the average income per month during Pre-DWCRA period has varied between Rs. 316.36 among Agricultural Labourers and Rs. 780 among Others. It is in between Rs. 536.86 among Others and Rs. 1227.77 among Non-Agricultural Labourers. Thus, the category of 'others' who stood first during Pre-DWCRA period have gone down to last position during Post-DWCRA period. Moreover, first position is occupied by Non-Agricultural Labourers during Post-DWCRA period. Thus, the relative positions of various categories have undergone a change. Moreover, the rise in income is not uniform among various economic categories. Therefore, the difference between Pre and Post-DWCRA average income per month has varied between Rs. 208.34 among Rural Artisans and Rs. 572.22 among Non-Agricultural Labourers. Of course, it is 243.13 for Others.

Comparative Analysis of Pre and Post-DWCRA Earnings in Relation to Educational Qualifications

Table-5.33 explains that the total income has shown a rise during Post-DWCRA period when compared to Pre-DWCRA period. The average income per month during Pre-DWCRA period has varied between Rs. 414.10 to illiterates and Rs. 1000 to Degree holders. This is in the range of Rs. 688.54 for the respondents who could study upto secondary level and Rs. 852.23 for who could study upto primary level during Post-DWCRA period. Moreover, Post-DWCRA income has shown a decline for the respondents who could study upto intermediate and beyond. However, even among the people, total income has shown a rise but average income has declined which is due to rise in the number of respondents from 5 to 9 in Intermediate level education and 1 to 2 in Degree holders. The minimum income in the Post-DWCRA period is higher when compared to Pre-DWCRA period but this has not been maintained in regard to maximum income range.

Table - 5.33 : Relationship Between Educational Qualifications and Income Generation During Pre and Post-DWCRA Period in Karimnagar District

(Income In Rs.)

Educational Qualifications	*Pre-DWCRA Income*			*Post-DWCRA Income*			*Difference of Avg. Income*
	No. of Respon-dents	*Total Income*	*Avg. Income (P. M.)*	*No. of Respon-dents*	*Total Income*	*Avg. Income (P. M.)*	
Illiterate	78	32300	414.10	95	73600	774.73	360.63
Primary	53	23700	447.16	66	56250	852.27	405.11
Secondary	30	15500	516.66	48	33050	688.54	171.88
Intermediate	5	3800	760.00	9	6450	716.66	-43.34
Degree	1	1000	1000.00	2	1500	750.00	-250.00
TOTAL	167	76300	456.88	220	170850	776.59	319.71

Source : Field Study.

Comparative Analysis of Pre and Post-DWCRA Earnings in Relation to Age of the Respondent

It can be observed from Table-5.34 that the total income as well as average income per month has shown an increase for all the respondents irrespective of their age. However, the average income per month during Pre-DWCRA period has varied between Rs. 431.08 for the age group of 41-50 years and Rs. 560 for the age group of above 50 years. While it is in the range of Rs. 749.36 for the age group of 20-30 years and Rs. 1260 for the age group of above 50 years during Post-DWCRA period. Thus, the first position in terms of generating income per month is retained by the age group of above 50 years even during Post-DWCRA period. But the last position in this regard has been shifted from the age group of 41-50 years to the age group of 20-30 years. A close examination of the table reveals that the rise in the income is not uniform among all the age groups. Inter age group variation is noticed. Therefore, the difference between Pre and Post-DWCRA average income per month has varied between Rs. 316.68 for the age group of 31-40 years and Rs. 700 for the age group of above 50 years. Thus, the DWCRA is relatively more successful for the age group of above 50 years. Moreover, the success of the programme in terms of generating average income per month rises as the age of the respondent increases. Thus, there is a positive relationship between age of the respondent and income generation.

Table 5.34 : Age-wise Analysis of Income Generation During Pre and Post-DWCRA Period in Karimnagar District

(Income In Rs.)

Age	*Pre-DWCRA Income*			*Post-DWCRA Income*			*Difference*
	No. of Respon-dents	*Total Income*	*Avg. Income (P. M.)*	*No. of Respon-dents*	*Total Income*	*Avg. Income (P. M.)*	*of Avg. Income*
20 - 30	58	27550	475.00	79	59200	749.36	319.36
31 - 40	67	30000	447.76	90	68800	764.44	316.68
41 - 50	37	15950	431.08	46	36550	794.56	363.48
Above 50	5	2800	560.00	5	6300	1260.00	700.00
TOTAL	167	76300	456.88	220	170850	776.50	319.71

Source : Field Study.

Impact on Living Conditions

The ultimate aim of DWCRA is to attain an improvement in the quality of life of rural poor. Therefore, an analysis as to the impact of DWCRA on the living conditions of respondents assumes significance. The relevant information is presented in Table-5.35.

The various aspects that determine living conditions are immediate consumption needs like nutritious food/ better quality food, clothing and medical. In addition, the consumption issues which have long term implications are education, purchase of assets, savings, debt repayment, expansion of trade and others.

Table-5.35 explains how did the respondents utilise their earnings from DWCRA to improve their living conditions. As many as 137 out of 220 selected respondents gave preference to keep their earnings in savings and this is followed by 112 for education and third place goes to medical expenses. The expansion of trade occupied importance for 42 respondents. As low as 26 respondents utilised their earnings to consume better food while 24 for better clothing and 17 for debt repayment and 15 preferred to purchase assets. Thus, savings occupied first position.

Further, inter-scheme and intra-scheme variation is noticed in regard to utilisation of earnings.

Repayment

The regular repayment of loan is another indicator of the success of the programme. It is heartening to note that all the selected respondents in Karimnagar district are regular in repayment of loan irrespective of their scheme and caste.

SECTION - II

In line with the preceding chapters viz Chapter-III and IV, this section would examine the impact of DWCRA on the status of women within the family as well as in the society in Karimnagar district. In addition, their participation in political decision making is also discussed. The discussion about all these aspects are essential to determine the success of DWCRA in attaining women's empowerment.

Table 5.35 : Impact of DWCRA on Expenditure Pattern of the Selected Respondents in Karimnagar District

Trade	*Nutritional Food*	*Clothing*	*Medical*	*Education*	*Assets Purchased*	*Savings*	*Debt Rapayment*	*Exp. of Trade*	*Any Other*
Leather Works	2	–	2	5	1	8	1	5	3
Soft-Toys	4	2	4	6	–	5	–	2	5
Basket Making	–	–	3	9	2	6	–	3	1
Greeting Cards	–	–	1	3	–	4	–	–	2
Petty Coats	3	8	12	13	4	18	3	8	3
Leaf Plate Making	–	1	2	3	–	4	–	1	2
Thread Work	–	–	–	2	–	2	–	–	–
Cosmetic Sales	–	–	–	1	–	2	–	–	–
Nawar Making	–	–	1	2	–	2	–	–	–
Veg./ Fruit Vending	–	–	2	3	1	5	3	2	1
Surf/ Blue/ Phenoil	2	1	6	5	1	6	1	–	2
Lace Work	–	3	2	2	–	4	–	–	1
Readymade Dresses	2	3	5	5	1	6	1	3	3
Veg. Cultivation	–	–	3	5	–	4	1	2	–
Milch Animals	13	6	24	41	5	57	7	16	17
Tailoring	–	–	–	2	–	2	–	–	–
Embroidary Work	–	–	1	2	–	2	–	–	–
Others	–	–	1	1	–	–	–	–	–
No Trade	–	–	3	2	–	–	–	–	–
TOTAL	26	24	72	112	15	137	17	42	40

Source : Field Study.

Owing to the prevalence of patriarchy, though women earn and extend support for the sustenance of the family and play vital role for the maintenance of the family their role in decision making related to the household either marginal or negligible. In this context, an examination in regard to what extent women play active role in decision making related to the family affairs assumes important. The real success of the programme lies in its ability to improve the status of women and not in terms of mere rise in their income levels.

Owing to the prevalence of patriarchy, woman stands first in doing work related to the household but goes last in participation of household decision making as well as in consumption. The distributive rules of the household are against to women. In this context, an analysis as to the impact of DWCRA on the participation of women in household decision making assumes significance to ascertain any change in the distributive rules of household in favour of women.

The consumption decision of the household broadly can be divided into short run and long run where the former consists of purchase of daily needs while the latter includes education of the children, purchase of assets, arrangement of marriages to their children and expansion of trade.

Short-run Decision Making of the Household

The relevant information in regard to short-run decision-making of the household is presented in Tables-5.36 and 5.37. Out of 220 selected respondents, as many as 97 could take decision in regard to daily needs of the family on their own while in 66 cases husbands alone will take the decision and in 39 cases both wife and husband together take decision. Elders in the family take decision in the case of 18 respondents. The caste-wise analysis reveals that own decision is relatively lesser and conversely domination of husband in regard to short-run decision making of the family is relatively higher among Backward Class and Scheduled Caste respondents. Table-5.37 reveals that the educational qualifications of the respondent did not play any role in the determination of their participation in short-run decision making of the household.

Table 5.36 : Participation of Respondents in Short-run Decision Making Related to Daily Expenditure Caste-wise

Caste	*Own*	*Husband*	*Both*	*Others*	*Total*
F C	9	3	5	–	17
B C	58	40	19	11	128
S C	26	21	11	7	65
S T	4	2	4	–	10
TOTAL	97 (44.1)	66 (30.0)	39 (17.2)	18 (8.2)	220 (100.0)

Source : Field Study.

Table 5.37 : Education and Participation of Respondents in Decision Making Related to Daily Expenditure

Educational Qualifications	*Own*	*Husband*	*Both*	*Others*	*Total*
Illiterates	42	34	13	6	95
Primary	28	18	12	8	66
Secondary	23	13	9	3	48
Intermediate	2	1	5	1	9
Degree	2	–	–	–	2
TOTAL	97 (44.1)	66 (30.0)	39 (17.2)	18 (8.2)	220 (100.0)

Source : Field Study.

Long-run Decision Making Related to the Household

The decision in regard to purchase of consumer durables, expansion of trade, education of the children, arrangement of marriages and loans and repayment are categorised as long run decisions.

(i) Decision-making of the Purchase of Consumer Durables

Tables-5.38 and 5.39 present relevant matter. It can be observed from Table-5.38 that husbands alone take decision in the case of 101 respondents while both life partners together take decision in the case of 41 respondents. Own decision is relatively higher among Forward Caste and Scheduled Tribe respondents while husband's domination is relatively higher among Backward Class and Scheduled Caste respondents. Moreover, other elders in the family play vital role in this regard in the case of respondents belonged to Backward Class and Scheduled Caste.

Table 5.38 : Caste and Decision Making of the Purchase of Consumer Durables

Caste	*Own*	*Husband*	*Both*	*Others*	*Total*
F C	9	3	5	–	17
B C	31	66	23	8	128
S C	21	29	11	4	65
S T	5	3	2	–	10
TOTAL	66 (30.1)	101 (45.9)	41 (18.6)	12 (5.4)	220 (100.0)

Source : Field Study.

Table-5.39 states that as the level of education of the respondent increases, they will be consulted in taking decisions and therefore, taking decision by both is relatively higher among respondents who could study Intermediate and beyond. Similarly, husband's domination in this regard is relatively higher among illiterates and who could have upto Primary level education.

Table 5.39 : Education and Decision Making of the Purchase of Consumer Durables

Educational Qualifications	*Own*	*Husband*	*Both*	*Others*	*Total*
Illiterates	32	44	14	5	95
Primary	10	41	10	5	66
Secondary	21	14	11	2	48
Intermediate	2	2	5	–	9
Degree	1	–	1	–	2
TOTAL	66 (30.1)	101 (45.9)	41 (18.6)	12 (5.4)	220 (100.0)

Source : Field Study.

(ii) Decision-making in Regard to Expansion of Trade

Table-5.40 explains that in the case of 122 out of 220 respondents, the expansion of trade is determined by husbands. One can notice that though the trade belonged to wife, the decisions are taken by husbands. Only 35 respondents could take decision on their own while in 51 respondents both wife and husband together take decision. Interestingly, others make decision in 12 cases. No any caste-wise variation is noticed. However, the role of others can be seen in Backward Class and Scheduled Caste respondents only.

Table 5.40 : Caste and Decision Making in Regard to the Expansion of the Trade

Caste	*Own*	*Husband*	*Both*	*Others*	*Total*
F C	4	10	3	–	17
B C	17	72	31	8	128
S C	13	32	16	4	65
S T	1	8	1	–	10
TOTAL	35 (15.1)	122 (55.4)	51 (23.2)	12 (5.4)	220 (100.0)

Source : Field Study.

Table-5.41 explains that the domination of husband is relatively higher among respondents who could not study beyond secondary level education and further, domination of

Table 5.41 : Education and Decision Making in Regard to the Expansion of Trade

Educational Qualifications	*Own*	*Husband*	*Both*	*Others*	*Total*
Illiterates	15	58	13	9	95
Primary	13	36	15	2	66
Secondary	5	25	17	1	48
Intermediate	2	3	4	–	9
Degree	–	–	2	–	2
TOTAL	35 (15.1)	122 (55.4)	51 (23.2)	12 (5.4)	220 (100.0)

Source : Field Study.

other elders also can be traced among these respondents. As the level of education of the respondent is Intermediate and beyond then decision making by both wife and husband is relatively higher. Thus, education level of the respondent plays a role in the determination of participation in decision making related to the expansion of trade or purchase of assets related to trade.

(iii) Decision-making in Regard to Arrangement of Marriages

Table-5.42 explains that 99 out of 220 selected respondents jointly (wife and husband together) take decision as to the arrangement of marriages to the children, in 75 cases, husband alone takes decision. However, in 8 cases other elders in the family take decision. Thus, husband's domination is relatively higher among Scheduled Caste and Scheduled Tribe respondents while joint decision is relatively higher among Forward Caste and Backward Class respondents.

Table 5.42 : Caste and Decision Making in Regard to Marriages of the Children

Caste	*Own*	*Husband*	*Both*	*Others*	*Total*
F C	3	2	12	–	17
B C	22	30	72	4	128
S C	11	39	12	3	65
S T	2	4	3	1	10
TOTAL	38 (17.3)	75 (34.1)	99 (45.0)	8 (3.6)	220 (100.0)

Source : Field Study.

Table-5.43 states that the domination of husband is relatively more among illiterates while decision making by both wife and husband is relatively higher among literates.

(iv) Decision-making in Regard to Education of the Children

Table-5.44 denotes that 113 out of 220 selected respondents take decision in regard to education of their children jointly while in 62 cases, husband alone take decision. No any significant inter-caste variation is observed in this regard.

Table 5.43 : Education and Decision Making in Regard to Marriages of the Children

Educational Qualifications	*Own*	*Husband*	*Both*	*Others*	*Total*
Illiterate	9	46	35	5	95
Primary	13	16	36	1	66
Secondary	15	10	21	2	48
Intermediate	1	3	5	–	9
Degree	–	–	2	–	2
TOTAL	38 (17.3)	75 (34.1)	99 (45.0)	8 (3.6)	220 (100.0)

Source : Field Study.

Table 5.44 : Caste and Decision Making in Regard to Education of the Children

Caste	*Own*	*Husband*	*Both*	*Others*	*Total*
F C	2	5	10	–	17
B C	25	30	69	4	128
S C	11	21	31	2	65
S T	1	6	3	–	10
TOTAL	39 (17.7)	62 (28.2)	113 (51.4)	6 (2.7)	220 (100.0)

Source : Field Study.

Table-5.45 indicates that as the education level of the respondent increases, husband's domination in decision making

Table 5.45 : Education and Decision Making in Regard to Education of the Children

Educational Qualifications	*Own*	*Husband*	*Both*	*Others*	*Total*
Illiterate	12	39	40	4	95
Primary	8	12	45	1	66
Secondary	17	11	19	1	48
Intermediate	2	–	7	–	9
Degree	–	–	2	–	2
TOTAL	39 (17.7)	62 (28.2)	113 (51.4)	6 (2.7)	220 (100.0)

Source : Field Study.

as to the education of the children lesser. Thus, education level of the respondent makes them active in decision making.

(v) Decision-making in Regard to Debt and Re-payment

Table-5.46 indicates that out of 220 selected respondents, husband alone take decision in regard to debt and re-payment in the case of 146 respondents. Both wife and husband together take decision in 50 cases while own decision is observed only in 12 cases. The caste-wise analysis reveals that the domination of husband is relatively lesser among Forward Caste respondents.

Table 5.46 : Caste and Decision Making in Regard to Debt and Repayment

Caste	*Own*	*Husband*	*Both*	*Others*	*Total*
F C	3	4	10	–	17
B C	7	88	24	9	128
S C	1	48	14	2	65
S T	1	6	2	1	10
TOTAL	12 (5.4)	146 (66.4)	50 (22.7)	12 (5.4)	220 (100.0)

Source : Field Study.

Table-5.47 reveals that the education level of the respondent plays a positive role in making the respondent active in decision

Table 5.47 : Education and Decision Making in Regard to Debt and Repayment

Educational Qualifications	*Own*	*Husband*	*Both*	*Others*	*Total*
Illiterate	3	74	11	7	95
Primary	4	41	18	3	66
Secondary	4	29	14	1	48
Intermediate	1	2	5	1	9
Degree	–	–	2	–	2
TOTAL	12 (5.4)	146 (66.4)	50 (22.7)	12 (5.4)	220 (100.0)

Source : Field Study.

related to household. Therefore, husband's domination can not be seen among degree holders.

Ownership of Property

The ownership of property is one of the important factors which determine the control over resources. This is lacking among women though they earn income and contribute equally on par with husband to support the sustenance of the family. Unless they have ownership rights, women can not exercise any control over property. The seriousness of the problem is identified by Human Development Report'95 also. Therefore, an examination of this aspect with reference to the selected respondents assumes important. The relevant information is presented in Tables-5.48 and 5.49.

Table 5.48 : Caste-wise Analysis of Ownership of Property by the Selected Respondent

Caste	*Yes*	*No*	*Total*
F C	5	12	17
B C	17	111	128
S C	5	60	65
S T	–	10	10
TOTAL	27 (12.3)	193 (87.7)	220 (100.0)

Source : Field Study.

Table 5.49 : Education and Ownership Property by the Selected Respondents Caste-Wise

Educational Qualifications	*Yes*	*No*	*Total*
Illiterate	4	91	95
Primary	15	51	66
Secondary	3	45	48
Intermediate	5	4	9
Degree	–	2	2
TOTAL	27 (12.3)	193 (87.7)	220 (100.0)

Source : Field Study.

Table-5.48 explains that out of 220 selected respondents as many as 193 did not own any property. No any significant inter-caste variation is noticed. Table-5.49 reveals the relationship between education level of the respondent and property ownership. Out of 95 Illiterates as many as 91 do not own property and out of 66 who could study upto primary level education, 51 do not own property. Similarly, out of 48 respondents who could study upto secondary level, only 3 were owners of property. Moreover, the selected 2 degree holders do not own property.

The preceding analysis in regard to long-run decision making of the household has revealed one significant aspect i.e, as the education level of the respondent increases, their active participation in decision-making also rises. Thus, there is a positive relationship between education level of the respondent and their participation in decision-making. This indicates that while taking decisions husband used to consult wife whenever wife is educated. When it comes to ownership of property even the respondent purchases property of any form from her own earnings, the property is usually on the name of husband. In this aspect, education level of the respondent did not play any determinant role. This clearly explains stronghold of patriarchy in the determination of family relations even in regard to economic affairs. The structure of patriarchal family will not allow women to own property irrespective of their earnings and level of education. Consequently, they can not exercise any control over resources and as a result, their status will be weakened.

Domestic Work

Women are compelled to perform domestic work irrespective of their employment, income and level of education. Moreover, domestic work is significant particularly in poor rural families without which they can not survive. Inspite of its significance for the sustenance of the family, the domestic work is not recognised either by the family or by the society. However, women should devote time and energy to perform domestic work which consists of cleaning house, vessels, washing cloths, cooking, bringing water from distant places, maintaining kitchen garden, looking after children, bringing fire wood and over all maintenance of the house. The nature and extent of domestic work may not be uniform. Inter-caste variation due to economic factors may be noticed. The information as to the time spent on domestic chores is shown in Tables-5.50 and 5.51. It is mere quantitative information. There are no any prescribed working hours and women have to perform it depending upon the requirement of the household irrespective of day and night or holidays or tiredness, stress and strain. Thus, qualitatively it is entirelya different aspect and will be difficult to fix in numbers.

Table 5.50 : Caste-wise Analysis of Number of Hours Spent on Domestic Work

Caste	*1 - 2*	*3 - 4*	*5 - 6*	*Above 6*	*Total*
F C	3	3	9	2	17
B C	12	47	72	25	128
S C	3	32	37	5	65
S T	1	2	5	2	10
TOTAL	19 (8.6)	44 (20.0)	123 (55.9)	34 (15.5)	220 (100.0)

Source : Field Study.

Table 5.51 : Education and Number of Hours Spent on Domestic Work

Educational Qualifications	*1 - 2*	*3 - 4*	*5 - 6*	*Above 6*	*Total*
Illiterate	5	17	55	18	95
Primary	5	12	40	9	66
Secondary	7	11	23	7	48
Intermediate	1	4	4	–	9
Degree	–	–	1	–	2
TOTAL	19 (8.6)	44 (20.0)	123 (55.9)	34 (15.5)	220 (100.0)

Source : Field Study.

Table-5.50 indicates that out of 220 selected respondents, 123 would spend 5-6 hours per day on domestic work and 44 spend 3-4 hours and 34 have to spend more than 6 hours per day but 19 respondents spend only 1-2 hours per day. No significant caste-wise variation is noticed. However, number of hours spent on domestic work is relatively higher among Backward Class and Scheduled Tribe respondents.

Table-5.51 explains that among the respondents who spend more than 6 hours on domestic work, the respondents who could study upto Intermediate and beyond can not be seen.

Table-5.52 denotes that out of 220 selected respondents, as many as 80 respondents would not get any assistance from family members in performing domestic work while 73 get assistance either from children or from other family members and only 67 used to get assistance from the husband. The caste-wise analysis explains that the husband extends support in 7 out of 17 among Forward Caste, 41 out of 128 among Backward Class, 16 out of 65 among Scheduled Caste and 3 out of 10 among Scheduled Tribe respondents. Thus, husband's help in performing domestic work is relatively lesser among Scheduled Caste respondents.

Table 5.52 : Caste and Assistance Received in Performing Domestic Work

Caste	*Husband*	*Children*	*Others*	*Own*	*Total*
F C	7	–	4	6	17
B C	41	22	25	40	128
S C	16	14	6	29	65
S T	3	1	1	5	10
TOTAL	67 (30.5)	37 (16.8)	36 (16.4)	80 (36.4)	220 (100.0)

Source : Field Study.

Table-5.53 reveals that as the education level of the respondent increases, husband's assistance in doing domestic work also rises.

Table 5.53 : Education and Assistance Received in Performing Domestic Work

Educational Qualifications	*Husband*	*Children*	*Others*	*Own*	*Total*
Illiterate	20	21	7	47	95
Primary	20	9	13	24	66
Secondary	20	7	13	8	48
Intermediate	6	–	2	1	9
Degree	1	–	1	–	2
TOTAL	67 (30.5)	37 (16.8)	36 (16.4)	80 (36.4)	220 (100.0)

Source : Field Study.

Family Purchasing Priorities

The theories of consumption function have discussed several variables which determine consumption but have ignored gender aspect of the phenomenon. Though the rise in the income leads to rise in the consumption of the family, the women, who are responsible for the rise in the income, their preferences and priorities are ignored.

The preceding section in this chapter has revealed that the DWCRA has resulted in the rise in the income of the respondents. The information in regard to family purchasing priorities has been shown in Tables-5.54 and 5.55.

Table 5.54 : Caste-wise Analysis of Family Purchasing Priorities

Caste	*Goods Used by Male Members of the Family*	*Consumer Durables*	*Savings*	*Exp. of the trade*	*Total*
F C	3	6	6	2	17
B C	19	51	50	8	128
S C	10	19	30	6	65
S T	2	5	2	1	10
TOTAL	34 (15.5)	81 (36.8)	88 (40.0)	17 (7.7)	220 (100.0)

Source : Field Study.

Table-5.54 states that out of 220 respondents selected, 88 gave priority to save, 81 to purchase consumer durables, 34 to purchase goods which are exclusively used by the male members of the family and only 17 preferred to utilise increased income for the purpose of expansion of trade. Though they could get improved incomes due to trade, they gave least preference for the expansion of trade. The caste-wise analysis reveals that 2 out of 17 Forward Castes, 8 out of 128 Backward Classes, 6 out of 65 Scheduled Castes and 1 out of 10 Scheduled Tribe respondents gave preference for the expansion of trade. Moreover, majority of Forward Caste, Backward Classes and Scheduled Tribe respondents gave priority to purchase consumer durables. This clearly indicates strong impact of growing consumerism even on poor rural families. This impact is relatively lesser among Scheduled Caste respondents.

Table-5.55 indicates that the purchasing priorities of the selected households did not affect by the education level of the respondents.

Table 5.55 : Education and Family Purchasing Priorities

Educational Qualifications	*Goods Used by Male Members of the Family*	*Consumer Durables*	*Savings*	*Exp. of the trade*	*Total*
Illiterate	18	32	37	8	95
Primary	10	26	25	5	66
Secondary	5	19	21	3	48
Intermediate	1	4	3	1	9
Degree	–	–	2	–	2
TOTAL	34 (15.5)	81 (36.8)	88 (40.0)	17 (7.7)	220 (100.0)

Source : Field Study.

Further, the field study has revealed the fact that in the case of majority of respondents, the purchasing priorities of the family are decided by the husband only.

Harassment

Even today, women irrespective of their caste, earning capacity and educational qualifications suffer from the harassment by the family members owing to the prevalence of patriarchy. The relevant information is presented in Tables-5.56 and 5.57.

Table-5.56 presents that 163 out of 220 selected respondents did not face any harassment by the family members. However, 57 out of 220 are subjected to harassment. Still the seriousness of the problem can not be ignored. Thus, 4 out of 17 Forward Caste, 27 out of 128 Backward Classes, 24 out of 65 Scheduled Caste and 2 out of 10 Scheduled Tribe respondents are subjected to harassment. The problem is relatively higher among Scheduled Caste respondents.

Table 5.56 : Caste and Harrassment in the Family

Caste	*Yes*	*No*	*Total*
F C	4	13	17
B C	27	101	128
S C	24	41	65
S T	2	8	10
TOTAL	57 (25.9)	163 (74.1)	220 (100.0)

Source : Field Study.

Table-5.57 explains that the harassment is relatively higher among illiterates and respondents who have upto primary

Table 5.57 : Education Level and Harassment in the Family

Educational Qualifications	*Yes*	*No*	*Total*
Illiterate	35	60	95
Primary	18	48	66
Secondary	3	45	48
Intermediate	1	8	9
Degree	–	2	2
TOTAL	57 (25.9)	163 (74.1)	220 (100.0)

Source : Field Study.

education. No harassment is seen among degree holders. Thus, the level of education of the respondent plays a positive role in mitigating the problem of harassment meted out to women.

The women are subjected to harassment within the family either by husband or by mother-in-law or by sister-in-law. The relevant information is presented in Tables-5.58 and 5.59.

Table 5.58 : Caste-wise Analysis of Harassment From Whom

Caste	*Mother-in-law*	*Sister-in-law*	*Husband*	*Total*
F C	1	–	3	4
B C	8	3	16	27
S C	3	2	19	24
S T	–	–	2	2
TOTAL	12 (21.0)	5 (8.8)	40 (70.2)	57 (100.0)

Source : Field Study.

Table-5.58 denotes that out of 57 respondents who are subjected to harassment, as many as 40 are harassed by husband, 12 are by mother-in-law and only 5 are by sisters-in-law. Thus, the husband is the main enemy within the family who harass the wife.

The caste-wise analysis reveals that the harassment by mother-in-law can not be seen among Scheduled Tribe respondents. Moreover, it is relatively higher among Backward Class respondents. Further, harassment by sister-in-law can not be observed among Forward Caste and Scheduled Tribe respondents. However, harassment by husband can be found in all the respondents irrespective of the caste.

Table-5.59 explains that the harassment by mother-in-law can not be seen when the respondent is educated at the level of Intermediate and beyond. Further, the harassment by sister-in-law is observed among Illiterates and among the respondents who could study upto primary level. Moreover, harassment by husband can not be seen among Degree holders. Thus, the level of education of education of the respondent plays a vital role in lessening the problem of harassment. In other words, the assertiveness of women increases as their level of education increases.

Table 5.59 : Education Level and Harassment From Whom

Educational Qualifications	*Mother-in-law*	*Sister-in-law*	*Husband*	*Total*
Illiterate	8	2	25	35
Primary	3	3	12	18
Secondary	1	–	2	3
Intermediate	–	–	1	1
Degree	–	–	–	–
TOTAL	12 (21.0)	5 (8.8)	40 (70.2)	57 (100.0)

Source : Field Study.

The information as to the nature of harassment is presented in Tables-5.60 and 5.61.

Table-5.60 explains that out of 57 respondents who ar subjected to harassment, as many as 32 (56.1 percent) are from wife-beating. It can be found in all the castes. Further, dowry is a problem for 15 (26.3 percent) women and Scheduled Tribe respondents can not be found in this and 6 women face harassment in performing domestic work and Forward Caste respondents can not be seen in this aspect.

Table 5.60 : Caste-wise Analysis of Nature of Harassment

Caste	*Dowry*	*Work*	*Wife Beating*	*Other*	*Total*
F C	1	–	3	–	4
B C	7	3	14	3	27
S C	7	2	14	1	24
S T	–	1	1	–	2
TOTAL	15 (26.3)	6 (10.5)	32 (56.1)	4 (7.1)	57 (100.0)

Source : Field Study.

Table-5.61 reveals that wife-beating and harassment in doing work can not be found if the respondent is educated at the level of Intermediate and beyond. Further dowry problem can not be observed among degree holders.

Table 5.61 : Education Level and Nature of Harassment

Educational Qualifications	*Dowry*	*Work*	*Wife Beating*	*Other*	*Total*
Illiterate	9	5	19	2	35
Primary	4	–	12	2	18
Secondary	1	1	1	–	3
Intermediate	1	–	–	–	1
Degree	–	–	–	–	–
TOTAL	15 (26.3)	6 (10.5)	32 (56.1)	4 (7.1)	57 (100.0)

Source : Field Study.

Protest Against Harassment

The selected respondents belonged to DWCRA group. This will provide confidence among members in two ways. One way is by providing employment and making them to earn income and other way is by inculcating the habit of living in groups. DWCRA works as a group and therefore, arranges meeting of the members regularly to discuss about the financial aspects. The meetings invariably make them to discuss their personal problems including harassment. Since all of them 'travel on the same boat', they try to fight against the problem as a group too.

The field work has revealed that out of 57 respondents who are subjected to harassment, only 18 could protest. Among them, 3 out of 4 Forward Caste, 10 out of 27 Backward Class, 5 out of 24 Scheduled Caste respondents can be seen. Moreover, no any relationship is observed between protest and educational qualifications of the respondent.

Only 16 respondents could inform about the problem to the group members. No Scheduled Tribe respondent can be found in this aspect. Out of these 16, in 10 cases, the DWCRA groups tried to initiate action in the form of counselling to family members, giving advice or warning to family members who harass the respondent. However, the problem is solved in 3 cases. Though the achievement is little in quantitative terms, qualitatively, it is bigger. Because, the respondents no longer feel that it is their personal problem. Gradually, they understood social basis of the problem. They try to fight against it as an individual and as a group too. This will raise their confidence. Consequently, they can assert their position in the family which positively improves their status within the family as well as in the society. This will clear the way for the attainment of women empowerment.

Social Awareness

The group of women under DWCRA meets regularly to discuss about the economic aspects of the programme like savings, loan repayment, marketing of the product and expansion of trade. This invariably makes them aware of bank procedures, market conditions etc. The discussion in regard to family as well as social problems becomes indispensable in their meetings. Out of 220 selected respondents, 26 are discussing about the social problems also and most of them used to discuss the local problems which will naturally be their immediate concern. Thus, DWCRA groups also improves social awareness of the respondents.

Social Activities

Social awareness and involvement in social activities can not be separated. They are mutually dependent. One can not be isolated from the other. The discussion about social problem in the group meetings improves their social awareness. This naturally compels them to involve in social activities. The field study has revealed that out of 220 selected respondents as many as 75 are involved in protesting attrocities on women, 69 used to fight against social evils and 58 against liquor consumption and 18 on other related problems. The majority of respondents in their respective castes viz 6 out of 17 Forward Caste, 23 out of 65 Scheduled Caste involved in fighting against social evils, 45 out of 128 Backward Classes 6 out of 10 Scheduled Tribe respondents are involved in protesting against atrocities on women, of course, majority of Backward Classes respondents are also involved in fighting against liquor consumption. The involvement of respondents in various social activities is not determined by their educational qualifications.

'Janmabhoomi' is a social programme initiated by the Govt. of Andhra Pradesh to construct rural infrastructure as well as to improve awareness of the rural people on various socio-economic issues. The field work has revealed that out of 220 selected respondents, 79 have participated in 'Janmabhoomi' programme. Out of them, 6 out of 17 Forward Caste 59 out of 128 Backward Classes, 9 out of 65 Scheduled Caste and 5 out of 5 Scheduled Tribe respondents can be seen. However, education level of the respondent did not play only role in making them to participate in 'Janmabhoomi'.

Political Awareness

The active participation of women in social and political decision-making is a pre-condition for the attainment of women's empowerment. Human Development Report '95 also recognises its significance. Political awareness starts with the franchise of vote. The edifice of democracy based on proper exercise of right to vote. The field work has explained that out of 220 selected respondents as many as 214 could exercise their right to vote. Out of 6 respondents who did not exercise their right to vote, 2 belonged to Forward Caste and 4 belonged to Backward Class respondents. Further, they belonged neither to illiterates nor to degree holders. Thus, 3 of them belonged to the respondents who could study upto primary education, 2 upto secondary education and one upto Intermediate level.

Though vote casting is a necessary condition for political awareness, it will not determine it totally. The information is also elicited as to the basis to elect the representative. Out of 214 who exercise vote casting, 135 gives importance to party and 79 gives preference to personal qualities of the contestant. The field study has revealed that the majority of Forward Caste respondents gave importance to person while the majority of Backward Classes, Scheduled Caste and Scheduled Tribe respondents gave preference to the party to which the contestant belonged to. Further, the respondents who could study beyond secondary education used to exercise their right to vote casting on the basis of the person.

Further, independent assessment of the contestant, independent decision as to vote casting assumes significance in the determination of political awareness of the respondent. The relevant information is presented in Tables-5.62 and 5.63.

Table-5.62 explains that out of 214 selected respondents 90 could exercise vote on their own while 102 are influenced by their respective husband and 22 are by others. Among the respondents who take independent decision in this regard, 12 out of 15 Forward Caste, 52 out of 124 Backward Classes, 23 out of 65 Scheduled Caste and 3 out of 10 Scheduled Tribe respondents. Influence of husband on wife in casting her vote is relatively higher among Backward Classes and Scheduled Tribe respondents.

Table 5.62 : Caste-wise Analysis of Decision Making in Regard to Vote Casting

Caste	*Own*	*Husband*	*Others*	*Total*
F C	12	3	–	15
B C	52	63	9	124
S C	23	30	12	65
S T	3	6	1	10
TOTAL	90 (42.0)	102 (47.7)	22 (10.3)	214 (100.0)

Source : Field Study.

It is interesting to note from Table-5.63 that degree holders could take decision independently in casting their vote and have not been influenced either by husband or by others. The majority of illiterates as well as who have upto primary education are influenced either by husband or by others to cast their vote.

Participation in Political Decisions

The active participation of respondents in political decision making assumes significance for the attainment of their empowerment. The importance of this aspect is also identified by the Human Development Report '95.

Table 5.63 : Education Level and Decision Making in Regard to Vote Casting

Educational Qualifications	*Own*	*Husband*	*Others*	*Total*
Illiterate	32	52	11	95
Primary	23	33	7	63
Secondary	27	16	3	46
Intermediate	6	1	1	8
Degree	2	—	—	2
TOTAL	90 (42.0)	102 (47.7)	22 (10.3)	214 (100.0)

Source : Field Study.

Though 214 out of 220 selected respondents exercises their right to vote, 30 are actively involved in local politics. The field study has revealed that the active involvement of women in local policies is relatively lower among Backward Classes. Moreover, higher the education, lower will be the participation in local politics and vice versa.

Out of 30 respondents who actively involve in local politics, only 17 themselves participated in local politics while 10 are involved in canvassing and 3 tried to encourage the contestant. Among the respondents who directly participated in local politics, 1 out of 2 Forward Caste, 8 out of 12 Backward Classes, 7 out of 14 Scheduled Caste and 1 out of 2 Scheduled Tribe respondents can be found. Interestingly, all of them are educated below the secondary level.

Achievements of DWCRA

The field study has also elicited information as to the assessment in regard to the achievement of DWCRA on their lives in the opinion of respondents themselves. Out of 220 selected respondents, 84 feel an improvement in their economic status while 40 opined that the improvement is in their social status only. Further, 79 respondents have felt an improvement both in economic and social status also. Moreover, 17 are of the opinion that the DWCRA has resulted in the progress of their status within the family. Thus, the progress in the economic status has resulted in the improvement in their social status too in the case of 79 respondents. Out of them, 4 out of 17 Forward Caste, 44 out of 128 Backward Classes, 30 out of 65 Scheduled Caste and 1 out of 10 Scheduled Tribe respondents are found. The achievement of DWCRA in terms of an improvement in their status is not uniform among all the castes and inter-caste variation is noticed in this regard.

The data in regard to education qualifications of the respondents and the achievement of DWCRA reveals that 49 out of 95 Illiterates feel an improvement in their economic status while 35 out of 66 respondents who could study upto primary level feel an improvement in their economic as well as social status. Similarly, as many as 18 out of 48 respondents who could study upto secondary level also feel an improvement in their social and economic status and 3 out of 9 respondents who could study upto Intermediate opine an improvement in their social status only. Out of 2 degree holders 1 felt an improvement in their social status and other one on her status with in the family.

6

A Comparative Analysis

In preceding chapters viz., III, IV and V the impact of DWCRA on rural women in Khammam, Warangal and Karimnagar was discussed respectively. The present chapter is devoted to analyse the comparative performance of DWCRA in selected three districts. Moreover, the present chapter confines to economic impact only. In other words, the performance of DWCRA in terms of employment and income generation so as to achieve an improvement in the quality of life of rural people. For the purpose of convenience, this chapter is divided into two sections. Section-I will present a comparative analysis of characteristics of the sample, socio-economic background of the sample respondents, selection of trade and problems in running the trade while Section-II will be devoted to examine the relative performance of DWCRA in terms of employment and income generation and its effect on the consumption pattern of the selected respondents.

SECTION - I

Characteristics of Sample Respondents:

1. In Khammam district 300 respondents are selected from 23 villages representing 19 trades and they belonged to Agricultural and Allied activities, Food processing activities, Manufacturing activities, Tailoring and Business activity. Among them, Milch Animals occupies first position in terms of number of beneficiaries and this is followed by

Tailoring activity and third place occupied by Pickles/ Edible items making.

In Warangal district, 300 respondents are selected from 20 villages representing 24 trades. In addition to activities appeared in Khammam district. Artistic activities like Embroidery Work, Lace Work and Thread Work are found in this district. Further, the activity 'No Trade' indicates that the DWCRA members do not involve in any productive activity rather the funds will be utilised to run 'Chit' among themselves. Even in Warangal, Milch Animals occupied first position in terms of number of respondents followed by Chappals making.

In Karimnagar district, 220 respondents are selected from 18 villages representing 19 trades. All the trades that appear in Warangal district can be found in Karimnagar. Even in this district Milch Animals occupies first position in terms of number of respondents and which is followed by Petty Coats making.

Thus, in all the selected three districts, the trade Milch Animals occupy first position in terms of number of respondents which indicates the significance of Agricultural and Allied activities in rural India.

2. The caste-wise distribution of sample respondents in Khammam district indicates that Backward Classes stand first, Forward Caste, Schedule Tribe and Schedule Caste respondents occupy 2nd, 3rd and 4th position respectively.

In Warangal district, Backward Classes stand first, Scheduled Caste, Forward Caste and Scheduled Tribe respondents occupy 2nd, 3rd and 4th position respectively in this regard. Similar distribution of sample respondents among different castes will be found even in Karimnagar district.

In all the three selected districts, Backward Class respondents occupy dominant position in terms of their number. However, Scheduled Caste respondents occupy 2nd position in Warangal and Karimnagar districts while they occupy last position in Khammam district.

Moreover, Backward Class respondents can be found in relatively more number of trades in all the selected three districts. This indicates that the scope of selecting trades is relatively more wider for Backward Class respondents.

3. The category-wise distribution of sample in Khammam district indicates that Marginal Farmers are highest in number and Rural Artisans occupy 2nd position. While in Warangal district also Marginal Farmers retained their position but second position is occupied by 'Others', whereas in Karimnagar district Agricultural Labour occupy first position and Marginal Farmers stand 2nd place.

In Khammam district, the majority of Forward Caste and Scheduled Tribe respondents are either Small or Marginal Farmers and the majority of Backward Class respondents are Rural Artisans and Scheduled Caste respondents are Agricultural labourers.

In Warangal district, the economic category of Forward Caste respondents is retained. Further, the majority of Backward Class respondents are also either Small or Marginal Farmers while the majority of Schedule Caste respondents are Rural Artisans.

In Karimnagar, Forward Caste and Backward Class respondents retained their position of economic category and majority of Scheduled Caste respondents are Agricultural Labourers as there in Khammam district while the majority of Scheduled Tribe respondents are Rural Artisans. In all the selected three districts, the majority of Forward Caste respondents are having some land base but Backward Class respondents are either Small or Marginal Farmers or Rural Artisans while the majority of Schedule Caste and Schedule Tribe respondents are either Agricultural Labourers or Rural Artisans.

4. The scope of selecting trades is relatively more wider for the category of Marginal Farmers in all the three selected districts.

Socio-economic Background of the Selected Respondents:

In all the three selected districts more than the 76 percent of the sample respondents are in the age group of 20-40 years. Similarly, in all the three districts more than 73 percent of the sample respondents are either illiterates or who could have only upto primary level education. In the same way, the marital status of more than 85 percent of selected respondents in all the three districts is 'married. Further, the primary occupation of the households of the majority of the selected respondents in all the three districts is 'Agriculture' and this is followed by `Agricultural Labour in Khammam and Karimnagar districts while it is `Rural Artisans' in Warangal district. All this analysis clearly indicates uniformity in the socio-economic background of selected respondents in all the three selected districts.

The relationship between caste and educational qualification of the selected respondents in Khammam district reveals that the Forward Caste respondents have relatively more scope for higher education though majority of them could have upto primary education. Contrastingly, Scheduled Tribe respondents have relatively lesser scope for higher education. In Warangal district, the position of Scheduled Tribe respondents in terms of getting an opportunity for higher education is retained but the scope in this regard is relatively more for Backward Class respondents instead of Forward Caste. Similar trend is noticed in Karimnagar district also but in addition to Scheduled Tribe, Scheduled Caste respondents too having relatively lesser opportunities for higher education.

Thus, the comparative analysis clearly indicates that either Forward Caste or Backward Class respondents get relatively more opportunities for higher education when compared to Scheduled Caste and Scheduled Tribe respondents.

Caste and Family

The size of family has been identified as one of the indicators of socio-economic status of that family and the size of the family and socio-economic status are inversely related.

In Khammam district, the size of the family for majority of the respondents is in between 3-4 irrespective of the caste. However, the percentage of respondents who are in this range has declined as one moves from Forward Caste to Scheduled Tribe. Further, among the respondents whose size of the family is 7 and above, Scheduled Tribes are relatively more.

But a different picture can be seen in Warangal district in this regard. Though the size of the family is in between 3-4 in 42.3 percent of the sample. The caste-wise analysis reveals the family size is relatively higher among Scheduled Tribe respondents and this is followed by Scheduled Caste respondents.

In Karimnagar district, the relationship between caste and size of the family is similar to that of Khammam district.

Thus, in all the three districts the family size is relatively higher among Scheduled Tribe respondents. This indicates the significance of social status in the determination of family size.

Caste and House Possession

In Khammam district, 135 out of 300 respondents selected reside in Pucca houses. Among them, majority belonged to Forward Castes, Backward Classes and Scheduled Castes while 51 percent of Scheduled Tribe respondents reside in RCC houses. Of course, not less than 26.7 percent of Forward Caste, Backward Class and Scheduled Caste respondents reside in Kutcha houses.

In Warangal district, 44.1 percent of Forward Caste, 64.7 percent of Backward Class and 42.5 percent of Scheduled Caste respondents reside in Pucca houses while as high as 66.7 percent of Scheduled Tribe respondents reside in Kutcha houses. The percentage of respondents who reside in RCC houses is relatively higher among Forward Caste and it is followed by Scheduled Caste respondents. Further, 27.7 percent of Scheduled Caste respondents reside in rented houses.

In Karimnagar district, majority of selected respondents reside in Pucca houses irrespective of the caste. The percentage of respondents who reside in Kutcha houses will become higher as one moves from Forward Caste to Scheduled Tribe and no Scheduled Tribe respondent is residing in RCC houses.

Thus, one common feature that can be observed in all the three districts is that the majority of selected respondents reside in Pucca houses. But, in Khammam district, the percentage of respondents who reside in RCC houses is relatively higher among Scheduled Tribe respondents while it is nil in Warangal and Karimnagar districts.

Caste and Asset Position

In Khammam district, 109 out of 300 selected respondents have possessed assets in the range of Rs. 1001-3000/-. The percentage of respondents who are in the range of assets in between Rs. 3001-5000/- is relatively higher among Scheduled Caste and Scheduled Tribe respondents. However, the percentage of respondents who are having rupees more than 15000/- is relatively higher among Forward Caste respondents.

In Warangal district, 67 out of 300 selected respondents are having assets in the range of Rs. 3001-5000/-. The assets of Scheduled Tribe respondents did not exceed Rs. 10000/-. Other wise, no significant inter caste variation is noticed. Similar picture can be seen even in Karimnagar district.

Thus, in all the selected three districts, the position of Scheduled Tribe respondents is relatively weaker in terms of assets.

Caste and Savings Position

In Khammam district 177 out of 300 selected respondents are not in a position to save. It can be noticed that 61.3 percent of Forward Caste respondents are able to save while 66.9 percent Backward Classes, 62 percent of Scheduled Caste and 63.8 percent of Scheduled Tribe respondents are unable to save. Further, among the respondents who could save, majority of Forward Caste and Backward Class respondents preferred to keep their savings in Banks while majority of Scheduled Caste and Scheduled Tribe respondents preferred to keep their savings in Chits.

In Warangal district, 181 out of 300 selected respondents could save. The percentage of respondents who could not save is relatively higher among Scheduled Tribe respondents. Otherwise, no significant caste-wise variation is noticed. Moreover, the majority of respondents preferred to keep their savings in Chits irrespective of the caste.

In Karimnagar district, 136 out of 220 selected respondents could not save. The percentage of respondents who could save is gradually on the decline as one moves from Forward Caste to Scheduled Tribe and further no Scheduled Tribe is in a position to save. Moreover, the majority of Backward Class and Scheduled Caste respondents preferred to keep their savings in Chits.

In all the three districts, the position of Scheduled Tribe respondents in terms of savings is relatively weaker. Moreover, the majority of respondents are preferring to keep their savings in Chits. Of course, the percentage of respondents who prefer Banks is relatively higher among Forward Caste respondents in all the three districts.

Selection of Trade

As the sample respondents are mainly characterised by Illiteracy or low level of education, they could not select the trade on their own. Interestingly, in all the three districts selected, DRDA officials have played a vital role in extending support to the respondents in the selection of trade.

Problems in Running the Trade

The main problems confronted by the respondents in running the trade are related to the procurement of raw-materials and marketing of the product.

In Khammam district, 215 out of 300 respondents selected did not have any problem in regard to the procurement of raw-material. The 85 respondents who face problem in this regard belonged to 11 out of 19 trades selected while problem in marketing the product is faced by 109 respondents. Inadequate demand and transportation are the major problems for 77.1

percent of respondents and remaining are confronting problems from quality of the product and competition.

In Warangal district too, 224 out of 300 selected respondents did not face any problem in the procurement of raw-material. The 76 respondents who face problems in this regard belonged to 14 out of 24 trades selected. Moreover, 216 respondents do not face problem in regard to sale of the product. In line with Khammam district, inadequate demand and transportation are the major problems.

In Karimnagar district, 161 out 220 respondents selected do not have problems in regard to the procurement of raw-material and 59 respondents who face the problem belonged to 9 out of 19 trades selected. Similarly, 141 respondents do not have any marketing problem. However, inadequate demand and competition are the major problems confronted by the respondents in this district.

Thus, in all the three selected districts, the majority of respondents face problems neither in the procurement of raw-material nor in marketing the product. Further, inadequate demand is found to be a common problem in all the three districts while second major problem is transportation in Khammam and Warangal while it is competition in Karimnagar district.

However, DRDA used to organise DWCRA bazars to mitigate the marketing problem. In Khammam district, 66 out of 300 respondents exclusively depend upon DWCRA Bazars for sale while 107 could utilise both own source as well as DWCRA Bazars and only 127 exclusively depend upon own source for selling the product.

In Warangal district, 50 respondents exclusively depend upon DWCRA Bazar for sale while 58 on both sources own as well as DWCRA Bazars and as many as 192 respondents exclusively depend upon own sources for marketing the product.

In Karimnagar district, 49 out of 220 respondents selected exclusively depend upon DWCRA Bazars for sale and 34 depend upon both sources while as many as 137 exclusively depend upon own source for sale of the product.

Thus, DWCRA Bazars play a vital role in extending support to the respondents in selling the product. However, the percentage of respondents who utilise this facility is relatively higher in Khammam district when compared to Warangal and Karimnagar districts. The strengthening of DWCRA Bazars is required to lessen the marketing problem of the respondents.

SECTION - II

The comparative performance of DWCRA in terms of generating employment and income and its impact on consumption levels of rural poor in the selected three districts viz., Khammam, Warangal and Karimnagar is analysed in this section.

Comparative Analysis of Pre and Post-DWCRA Employment Generation

This is examined in relation to scheme, caste, category, educational qualifications and age of the respondents.

(i) Scheme-wise Analysis : In Khammam district, out of 300 selected respondents, 273 were employed during Pre-DWCRA period. Total days of employment has increased from 4144 days during Pre-DWCRA period to 6986 days during Post-DWCRA period. Consequently, the average employment in terms of number of days per month has increased from 15.17 during Pre-DWCRA period to 23.28 days during Post-DWCRA period. Moreover, Post-DWCRA employment has increased for all the respondents irrespective of the scheme. However, inter-scheme variation is noticed in regard to employment generation. The average employment has varied between 16.30 days in Woolen work and 30 days in Fish vending. Moreover, the average employment per month has exceeded 20 days during Post-DWCRA period in 17 out of 19 schemes selected. Further, the difference between Pre and Post-DWCRA average employment has varied between 4.50 in Sheep rearing and 12.39 in Baniyans making.

In Warangal district, the number of respondents who are employed has been increased from 287 during Pre-DWCRA period to 300 during Post-DWCRA period. Total days of employment as well as average employment in terms of days per month has increased for all the respondents irrespective of the scheme. The average employment has increased from 16.34 days during Pre-DWCRA period to 24.23 days during Post-DWCRA period. The average employment has varied between 15.50 days in Piggery and 29.44 days in Veg./ Fruit vending during Post-DWCRA period. In all the schemes except in four, the average employment has exceeded 20 days per month. Inter-scheme variation can be observed in regard to employment generation during Post-DWCRA period. Therefore, the difference between Pre and Post-DWCRA average employment has varied between 0.07 in 'No Trade' and 15.83 in Tailoring.

In Karimnagar district, the number of respondents who are employed increased from 184 during Pre-DWCRA period to 220 during Post-DWCRA period. The total days of employment as well as average employment in terms of days per month has increased during Post-DWCRA period. The average employment has increased from 15.01 days during Pre-DWCRA period to 20.61 days during Post-DWCRA period. However, the rise is not uniform among all the schemes and inter-scheme variation is noticed. The average employment during Post-DWCRA period has varied between 8 days in Greeting Cards and 25.80 days in Vegetable Cultivation. Further, the difference between Pre and Post-DWCRA employment is negative in three schemes viz., Soft-toys, Greeting Cards and 'No Trade'. Interestingly, in all these three schemes, total days of employment generated has shown a rise but due to rise in the number of respondents who are employed in these schemes, the average employment has declined during Post-DWCRA period.

Thus, in all the selected three districts - Khammam, Warangal and Karimnagar, the DWCRA is a success in terms of employment generation. The Post-DWCRA employment is on the rise when compared to Pre-DWCRA employment in all the three districts.

The average employment in terms of days per month during Post-DWCRA period is relatively higher in Warangal with 24.23 days and this is followed by Khammam with 23.28 days and Karimnagar occupied last position in this regard with 20.61 days.

The inter-scheme variation is relatively lesser in Khammam and higher in Karimnagar.

The best schemes in Khammam where the average employment is more than 25 days per month during Post-DWCRA period are Fish Vending, Baniyans Making, Vegetable Cultivation, Milch Animals, Surf/ Blue/ Phenol and Kiranam and sale of Agricultural produce (6 out of 19 schemes).

The same in Warangal are Soft-toys, Chappals making, Veg./ Fruit vending, Milch Animals, Fish vending, Tailoring, Kiranam, Weaving and Thread work (9 out of 24 schemes).

In Karimnagar, they are Leaf Plate making, Vegetable cultivation, Tailoring and others (4 out of 19 schemes). Thus, inter-district variation is observed in terms of employment generation as well as in terms of number of schemes successful in this regard.

(ii) Caste-wise Analysis : In Khammam district, total days of employment generated as well as average employment in terms of number of days per month has increased for all the respondents irrespective of the caste. However, inter-caste variation is noticed in this regard. The average employment during Post-DWCRA period has varied between 21.78 days among Forward Caste and 25.08 days among Scheduled Tribe respondents. Moreover, the difference between Pre and Post-DWCRA average employment has varied between 7.57 days for Scheduled Tribes and 8.45 for Backward Class respondents.

Similarly, in Warangal district also total as well as average employment during Post-DWCRA period has increased for all the respondents irrespective of the caste. However, inter-caste variation is observed and the average employment in terms of number of days per month during Post-DWCRA period has varied between 15.50 days among Scheduled Tribe and 26.63

days among Scheduled Caste respondents. Further, the difference between Pre and Post-DWCRA employment is higher among Scheduled Caste and least among Scheduled Tribe respondents.

In Karimnagar district too, the total as well as average employment in terms of number of days per month during Post-DWCRA period has increased for all the respondents irrespective of the caste. However, the average employment during Post-DWCRA period has varied between 17.05 days among Forward Caste and 21.90 days among Scheduled Caste respondents. Thus, inter-caste variation is noticed.

Thus, the employment generation in terms of average employment during Post-DWCRA period has increased for all the respondents irrespective of the caste in all the three selected districts.

The inter-caste variation in this regard is relatively higher in Warangal district when compared to Khammam and Karimnagar district.

The performance of Forward Caste respondents in terms of average employment during Post-DWCRA period is least in Khammam and Karimnagar districts while the last position is occupied by Scheduled Tribe respondents in Warangal.

Interestingly, the highest position in terms of employment generation during Post-DWCRA period is occupied by Scheduled Caste respondents in Warangal and Karimnagar while Scheduled Tribe respondents occupy this position in Khammam district. Thus, inter-district variation can be observed.

In this way, the DWCRA is relatively more successful in terms of employment generation among Scheduled Caste respondents in Warangal and Karimnagar while among Scheduled Tribe respondents in Khammam district.

Further, Scheduled Tribe respondents who are successful in Khammam stood last in Warangal.

(iii) Category-wise Analysis : In Khammam, the total days of employment generated as well as average employment in terms

of days of work per month per respondent has increased during Post-DWCRA period irrespective of their economic category. The average employment has varied between 21.41 days for 'others' and 25.05 days for Non-Agricultural labourers. Moreover, the difference between average employment during Pre and Post-DWCRA periods has varied between 1.68 days for Others and 10.28 days for Non-Agricultural labourers. Thus, inter-category variation is noticed. Further, the category of 'others' who stood first in terms of average employment moved down to 'last' position during Post-DWCRA period.

In Warangal too, Post-DWCRA employment has increased irrespective of the category. The average employment has varied between 21.72 days among Non-Agricultural labourers and 26 days among Rural Artisans. Further, the rise in employment is not uniform among all the economic categories. The difference between Pre and Post-DWCRA average employment has varied between 3.82 days among Agricultural labourers and 10 days among Small Farmers. The first position in terms of average employment has been shifted from Agricultural labourers during Pre-DWCRA period to Rural Artisans during Post-DWCRA period.

Similarly, even in Karimnagar district, total days of employment as well as average employment in terms of days per month has increased during Post-DWCRA period irrespective of their economic category except for 'Others'. Further, the average employment has varied between 14.26 days among 'others' and 26.66 days among Non-Agricultural Labourers. The first position in terms of average employment is occupied by Non-Agricultural Labourers during Pre-DWCRA period has been retained during Post-DWCRA period.

Thus, the DWCRA is a success in terms of employment generation among all the economic categories in all the selected three districts.

The inter-category variation in this regard is relatively lesser in Khammam district and higher in Karimnagar.

Moreover, the success of DWCRA in terms of employment generation as indicated by difference between Pre and Post-

DWCRA employment is relatively higher among Non-Agricultural Labourers in Khammam district and they secure first position in terms of average employment during Post-DWCRA period. In Warangal, DWCRA has added relatively more employment to Small Farmers but first position in this regard is occupied by Rural Artisans. In Karimnagar, Non-Agricultural Labourers stand first.

Thus, in Khammam and Karimnagar, Non-Agricultural Labourers occupied first position in terms of average days of employment per month while Rural Artisans occupy first position and Non-Agricultural Labourers occupy last position in Warangal.

(iv) Educational Qualifications and Employment Generation : In Khammam, the total days of employment and average employment has increased for all the respondents irrespective of their educational qualifications. The average employment has varied between 20.54 days among respondents who could study upto Intermediate and 25 days among Illiterates. The DWCRA has generated relatively more employment among Degree holders as indicated by the difference between Pre and Post-DWCRA employment.

In Warangal also, the employment generation has shown a rise among all the respondents irrespective of their educational qualifications. The average employment has varied between 19.42 days among Intermediate holders and 27.85 days among Degree holders. Moreover, the DWCRA has added more employment to Degree holders as indicated by the difference between Pre and Post-DWCRA employment.

In Karimnagar, the average employment during Post-DWCRA period has increased for all the respondents but it has shown a decline among respondents who could study upto Intermediate. The first position is occupied by Illiterates but DWCRA has added more average employment to Degree holders.

Thus, in all the three selected districts, DWCRA is a success in terms of employment generation for all the respondents irrespective of their educational qualifications except for the respondents who could study upto Intermediate in Karimnagar. Interestingly, the DWCRA is relatively more successful in making addition to the average employment among Degree holders in Khammam and Warangal. While it made a negative impact on them in Karimnagar.

However, Illiterates occupy first position in terms of average employment in Khammam and Karimnagar while it is by Degree holders in Warangal. Thus, the success of the DWCRA in terms of employment and its relation to the educational qualifications of the respondent has shown a contrast picture among three districts. The Illiterates are successful in Khammam and Karimnagar while Degree holders are successful in Warangal. Thus, Inter-district variation is observed in this regard.

(v) Age-wise Analysis : In Khammam, the average employment has shown a rise during Post-DWCRA period for all the respondents irrespective of their age group. The average employment has varied in a small range of 23.12 days among the age group of 20-30 years and 23.90 among 41-50 years age group. While it is 19.14 among the respondents whose age is above 50 years. The additional employment created by DWCRA did not show any significant variation.

Similar situation can be seen even in Warangal. The average employment during Post-DWCRA period did not vary significantly among the respondents who belonged to different age groups. But, the DWCRA has generated relatively more employment to the respondents whose age is above 50 years.

In Karimnagar too, the average employment has increased for all the respondents irrespective of their age group. Moreover, the average employment during Post-DWCRA period is continuously on the rise when one moves from the age group of 20-30 years to above 50 years. Moreover, the DWCRA has added more employment to the age group of above 50 years.

Thus, DWCRA is a success in terms of employment generation in all the three districts irrespective of the age of the respondent. The performance of the age group of 41-50 years is relatively better in Khammam while it is occupied by the age group of above 50 years in Warangal and Karimnagar. Thus, the DWCRA is relatively more successful among higher age groups. Further, the difference between Pre and Post-DWCRA employment is relatively higher for the age group of above 50 years in all the three districts. The inter-district variation is less in regard to the relationship between employment generation and age group of the respondent.

Comparative Analysis of Employment Generation Exclusively by DWCRA

In Khammam, the employment generation in terms of days of work per month exclusively created by DWCRA is 6-10 days for 101 respondents, 11-15 days for 97, 16-20 days for 23 and more than 20 days for 3 respondents while it is less than 5 days for 76 respondents. Inter-scheme as well as Intra-scheme variation is also observed. Therefore, only 11 schemes could provide employment beyond 16 days per month for 26 respondents. Similarly, except 2 schemes - Samber/ Rasam powder and Leaf Plate making - all the remaining schemes can be found in the employment generation as low as less than 5 days per 76 respondents.

In Warangal, the employment generation exclusively by DWCRA is less than 5 days per month for 104 out of 300 respondents and they belonged to 20 schemes out of 24 selected. The employment generation is in excess of 16 days per month for 42 respondents who belonged to 13 schemes. Thus, Inter-scheme and Intra-Scheme variation is noticed in regard to employment generation.

In Karimnagar, the employment generation is 6-10 days per month for 105 out of 220 respondents and 67 respondents could get employment even less than 5 days per month and they belonged to 16 out of 19 schemes selected. It is to be noted that only one scheme Leather Works has generated employment in excess of 20 days per month for only one respondent and 3 belonged to 3 schemes in the range of 16-20 days per month. Thus, Inter-scheme and Intra-Scheme variation is observed in this regard.

Thus, the employment exclusively generated by DWCRA in terms of days of work per month in all the three districts is positive and inter-scheme as well as intra-scheme variation is noticed in this regard.

The percentage of respondents who could get employment more than 11 days per month due to DWCRA is relatively higher in Khammam while Warangal occupies second place and Karimnagar stands last on this account.

The number of schemes which could provide employment more than 20 days per month is relatively higher in Warangal (9 schemes), this is followed by Khammam (3 Schemes) while Karimnagar occupies last place (One scheme with one respondent).

The intra-scheme variation is relatively more wider in Warangal whereas Karimnagar stands last in this regard. However, the performance of Karimnagar is relatively weaker in terms of employment generation. Thus, inter-district variation is observed.

Caste-wise Analysis : In Khammam, the intra-caste variation is relatively wider among Forward Caste respondents and it is smaller among Schedule Caste respondents. Thus, Forward Caste respondents can be found in all the ranges of employment from less than 5 days to more than 20 days while Schedule Caste respondents can not be seen beyond the range of 11-15 days of work per month. The percentage of respondents who are in the lower range of less than 5 days of employment per month is relatively higher among Scheduled Tribe respondents and they are followed by Backward Class respondents.

In Warangal, except Scheduled Tribe respondents, all the respondents can be found even in the range of employment which is above 20 days. Moreover, majority of the Forward Caste respondents can be seen in the range of employment below 5 days per month.

In Karimnagar, the only one respondent who could get employment more than 20 days per month belonged to Forward Caste. Moreover, Scheduled Tribe respondents can not be seen beyond the range of 11-15 days of employment per month. The employment generation is relatively lesser among Scheduled Tribe respondents and they are followed by Forward Caste respondents.

Thus, in all the three districts inter-caste as well as intra-caste variation can be observed in regard to employment generation exclusively by DWCRA. Intra-caste variation is relatively more wider among Forward Caste respondents in all the three districts. However, in Warangal, intra-caste variation is wide among Forward Caste, Backward Class and Scheduled Caste respondents. The employment generation is relatively less and it did not exceed 11-15 days per month for Scheduled Caste respondents in Khammam while this position can be seen among Scheduled Tribe respondents in Warangal and Karimnagar districts.

Consequential Employment Generation

It is heartening to notice that the DWCRA has created employment not only to the respondents but also to others because the respondents also utilise either services of their family members or employ others to run the scheme, this is called as consequential employment.

In Khammam, the selected respondents employed 138 persons and among them 88 are family members and 50 are others. All the schemes have created consequential employment except four schemes viz., Fish vending, Candle making, Carpets and Veg/ Fruit vending.

In Warangal, 154 members are employed and out of them, 121 are family members while 33 are others. However, seven out of 24 schemes selected did not create consequential employment. They are Lace work, Candle making, Mushrooms, Samber/ Rasam Powders, Woolen work, Fish vending and No Trade. Further, in 9 schemes, others are employed. Thus, the majority schemes have utilised the services of their family members.

In Karimnagar, 88 members are employed and out of them 64 are family members and 24 are others. Further, 7 out of 19 schemes selected did not create consequential employment. Moreover, only 6 schemes could employ others but 11 schemes used to utilise the services of the family members.

Thus, positive consequential employment generation can be observed in all the three selected districts. Further, the utilisation of services of the family members is relatively higher in all the three districts. However, inter-scheme variation is noticed in this regard and 4 schemes in Khammam, 7 schemes each in Warangal and Karimnagar districts did not create consequential employment.

Comparative Analysis of Pre and Post-DWCRA Income Generation

The relative performance of three selected districts - Khammam, Warangal and Karimnagar - in terms of generating income to the respondents is discussed. The difference between Pre and Post-DWCRA income is analysed in relation to scheme, caste, category, educational qualifications and age of the selected respondents.

Scheme-wise Analysis:

In Khammam district, the average income per month has increased from Rs. 364.06 during Pre-DWCRA period to Rs. 972.70 during Post-DWCRA period. The average income during Pre-DWCRA period has varied between Rs. 225 in Woolen works and Rs. 522.22 in Sambar/ Rasam powders while it has varied between RS. -75 in Woolen works and Rs. 1964.70 in Milch Animals during Post-DWCRA period. Moreover, the rise in average income is not uniform among schemes. Keeping apart Woolen works which show negative income during Post-DWCRA period, in the remaining schemes, the difference between Pre and Post-DWCRA income has varied between Rs. 45 in Candle Making and Rs. 1616.98 in Milch Animals.

In Warangal district, the average income per month has increased from Rs. 542.97 during Pre-DWCRA period to Rs. 996.06 during Post-DWCRA period. Except in Mushrooms, the average income has increased for all the respondents irrespective of the scheme. The difference between Pre and Post-

DWCRA average income has varied between Rs. 17.30 in 'No Trade' and Rs. 944.87 in Cut-Pieces Selling. Of course, it is negative in Mushrooms. Moreover, the average income per month during Post-DWCRA period has varied between Rs. 500 in Beedi Making and Rs.1544 in Chappals Making.

In Karimnagar, the average income has increased for all the schemes except Embroidery work and No Trade. It is in the Post-DWCRA period it has varied between Rs. 262.50 in Greeting cards and Rs. 1575 in Tailoring. Further, the difference between Pre and Post-DWCRA average income per month has varied between Rs. 11.31 in Soft-Toys and Rs. 711.37 in Leather Works keeping part negative difference in Embroidery Work and No Trade.

Thus, the average income per month during Post-DWCRA period has increased in all the three districts. It has reached to Rs. 972.70 in Khammam, Rs. 996.06 in Warangal and Rs. 776.59 in Karimnagar. The Warangal stands first in terms of generation of average income per month and it is followed by Khammam and Karimnagar respectively. The average difference between Pre and Post-DWCRA average income per month which indicates addition made by DWCRA is highest at Rs. 608.66 in Khammam and Karimnagar stands last in this regard with Rs. 319.71. Thus, inter-district variation can be observed where the performance of Karimnagar is last.

In addition, inter-scheme variation is noticed in all the three districts. The change in the average income per month is negative in Woolen works in Khammam, Mushrooms in Warangal while Embroidery work and No Trade in Karimnagar. In terms of attaining highest average income per month, Khammam stands first with Rs. 1964.70 in Milch Animals. The variation between Warangal and Karimnagar is little in this regard with Rs. 1585.71 in Weaving in Warangal and Rs. 1575 in Tailoring in Karimnagar district.

Caste-wise Analysis of Pre and Post-DWCRA Income Generation

In Khammam, the average income per month during Post-DWCRA has increased for all the respondents irrespective of the caste and the performance of respondents has declined as one moves from Forward Caste to Scheduled Tribe.

In Warangal, the average income per month during Post-DWCRA period has shown a significant progress for all the respondents except Forward Caste respondents. The rise in income has varied between Rs. 333.34 for Scheduled Tribe and Rs. 682.67 for Scheduled Caste respondents. Moreover, Scheduled Caste respondents stand first in this regard and they are followed by Backward Class respondents.

In Karimnagar too, the average income per month during Post-DWCRA period has increased for all the respondents irrespective of the caste. However, Forward Caste respondents stand first and they are followed by Scheduled Tribe and last place occupied by Backward Class respondents.

Thus, the average income per month during Post-DWCRA period has increased for all the respondents irrespective of the caste in all the three districts except Forward Caste respondents in Warangal. Interestingly, the Forward Caste respondents who failed to attain progress in terms of income generation in Warangal district, have stood first in this regard in Khammam and Karimnagar districts. Further, Scheduled Caste respondents stand first in Warangal and have occupied third position in Khammam and Karimnagar. In this way, inter-district as well as inter-caste variation is observed in regard to income generation.

Category-wise Analysis

In Khammam, the average income per month during Post-DWCRA period has increased for all the respondents irrespective of their economic category. Further, respondents who belonged to Small Farmers occupied first position with Rs. 1107.73 and they are followed by Marginal Farmers with average income of Rs. 1104.59 per month.

In Warangal, the average income per month during Post-DWCRA period has increased for all the respondents irrespective of their economic category except for Non-Agricultural Labourers. The Rural Artisans occupied first position in terms of average income per month during Post-DWCRA period and they are followed by 'Others'.

Similarly, in Karimnagar, the average income per month during Post-DWCRA period has increased for all the respondents irrespective of their economic category except 'Others'. Moreover, Non-Agricultural Labourers occupy first position with average income of Rs. 1227.77 per month and they are followed by Marginal Farmers with the average income of Rs. 982.35 per month.

Thus, Khammam is successful in terms of attaining rise in the average income per month during Post-DWCRA period for all the respondents irrespective of their economic category. But, Warangal is able to attain this for all the economic categories except Non-Agricultural Labourers while Karimnagar failed to raise average income of 'Others'. Inter-category variation is observed in all the three districts. Moreover, the relative performance of various economic categories has varied from district to district. In Khammam, the respondents who belonged to the economic category of Small Farmers stand first in this regard and 'Others' occupied last position while in Warangal Rural Artisans occupied first position and Small Farmers occupied last position whereas in Karimnagar, Non-Agricultural Labourers occupied first position and 'Others' occupied last position. Thus, Small Farmers who occupied first position in Khammam have occupied last position in Warangal while 'Others' occupied last position in Khammam as well as in Karimnagar districts.

Comparative Analysis of Pre and Post-DWCRA Income in Relation to Educational Qualifications of the Respondents

In Khammam, the average income per month during Post-DWCRA period has increased for all the respondents irrespective of their educational qualifications. However, the rise in income is not uniform. Therefore, the difference between Pre and Post-DWCRA average income per month has varied between Rs. 357.79 for Intermediate and Rs. 1375 among Degree holders. Interestingly the Degree holders have occupied first position and second place is occupied by Illiterates while last position is occupied by the respondents who could study upto Intermediate level.

In Warangal, the rise in average income per month during Post-DWCRA period is negative for the respondents who could study upto Intermediate level while Degree holders occupied first position with Rs. 2014.28.

In Karimnagar, the rise in average income per month during Post-DWCRA period is positive for the respondents who could study upto Secondary level and less. Further, the respondents who could study upto Primary level occupied first position and Intermediate holders stood last position.

Thus, in all the three selected districts, the respondents who could study upto Intermediate level stood last in terms of attaining rise in the average income per month. Further, the degree holders who occupied first position in Khammam and Warangal have shown negative average income in Karimnagar. Thus, Inter-district variation is wide in regard to Degree holders while it is uniform for Intermediate holders.

Age-wise Analysis

In Khammam, the average income per month during Post-DWCRA period has increased for all the respondents irrespective of their age-group. However, the rise in the income is not uniform among various age-groups and the respondents in the age group of 41-50 years occupied first position with Rs. 1161.90 per month while the respondents who are in the age group of 20-30 years stood last with Rs. 867.30 per month.

In Warangal too, the rise in average income can be observed for all the respondents irrespective of their age group. Interestingly, the respondents who are in the age group of 20-30 years stand first and the age group of above 50 years occupied second position in this regard.

In Karimnagar also, the average income per month has increased for all the respondents irrespective of their age group. The age group of above 50 years have occupied first position in this regard and second position is occupied by the age group of 41-50 years.

In all the three districts, the age group of 41-50 years and above 50 years have occupied either first or second position in terms of earning average income per month while the age-group of 20-30 years who were last in Khammam have occupied first position in Warangal. Thus, uniformity can be observed in regard to the performance of the age group of 41-50 years and above 50 years. But, inter-district variation is relatively wider for the age-group of 20-30 years in regard to their performance in terms of average earnings per month.

Comparative Analysis of Income Generation Exclusively by DWCRA

In Khammam district, 163 out of 300 respondents could get an income in excess of Rs. 501 per month exclusively by DWCRA. Out of them, 25 could get monthly earnings in the range of Rs. 751-1000 and for 37 respondents, it is Rs. 1001-1500. It is to be noted that 8 respondents did not get any additional income. Moreover, inter-scheme and intra-Scheme variation can be noticed in regard to additional earnings from DWCRA.

In Warangal district, 134 out of 300 respondents could get an income in excess of Rs. 501 per month exclusively from DWCRA. Out of them, 49 could get an income in the range of Rs. 751-1000 per month while 37 could get additional earnings in the range of Rs. 1001-1500 per month. Moreover, 10 respondents did not get any additional income. Further, inter-scheme and intra-Scheme variation can be observed on this account.

In Karimnagar district, 57 out of 220 respondents could get additional monthly earnings in excess of Rs. 501 and out of them, 15 could get it in the range of Rs. 1001-1500 while 16 respondents are in the range of Rs. 751-1000. It is to be noticed that 26 respondents were unable to get any additional earnings at all from DWCRA.

Thus, the performance of Khammam district in terms of additional earnings exclusively generated by DWCRA is relatively better when compared to Warangal and Karimnagar districts while Karimnagar stands last in this regard. Thus, inter-district variation is observed.

Caste-wise Analysis in Regard to Additional Earnings Generated by DWCRA

In Khammam district, the 8 respondents who did not get any additional income from DWCRA belonged to Forward Castes and Backward Classes. In contrast to it, out of 37 respondents who could get additional earnings in the range of Rs. 1001-1500 per month, 19 belonged to Forward Castes, 17 belonged to Backward Classes while only One respondents belonged to Scheduled Castes but no Scheduled Tribe respondent can be observed in this range of income. Thus, intra-caste variation is more wider among Forward Caste and Backward Class respondents.

Similarly, in Warangal district, out of 10 respondents whose additional income is nil, One belonged to Forward Caste while 9 belonged to Backward Classes. However, in the income range of Rs. 1001-1500, no Scheduled Tribe respondents is found. Thus, intra-caste variation is relatively higher among Forward Caste and Backward Class respondents. Further, the additional income from DWCRA is always in excess of Rs. 251 per month for Scheduled Caste respondents.

In Karimnagar, Forward Caste respondents can not be found in 'Nil' additional income while Scheduled Tribe respondents can not be observed beyond the income range of Rs. 501-750 per month.

Thus, the Forward Caste respondents can be found in the higher ranges of earnings in all the selected three districts. However, the intra-caste variation is relatively wider among Forward Caste and Backward Class respondents in Khammam and Warangal districts.

The Scheduled Tribe respondents are not found in higher ranges of income in all the three districts. Further, the performance of Scheduled Caste respondents in terms of additional earnings per month is relatively better in Karimnagar district when compared to Khammam and Warangal districts.

Thus, general inference can be drawn in regard to intra-caste variation in all the selected three districts.

Impact on Consumption Pattern of the Respondents

In Khammam, as many as 197 preferred to keep their earnings in savings, 183 preferred education and 114 spent on health while least preference can be found on the purchase of consumer durables. Moreover, only 32 respondents have spent on expansion of trade.

In Warangal, 218 out of 300 respondents kept their earnings in savings. This is followed by 181 in education for their children while third preference goes to health and 58 respondents spent on the expansion of trade whereas least preference is given for clothing.

In Karimnagar, 137 out of 220 respondents gave preference for savings and this is followed by 112 on education while 42 spent on expansion of trade and last preference can be found for the purchase of consumer durables.

In all the three districts, impact on consumption is uniform where first preference is on savings and this is followed by education. Moreover, negligible preference is being given on expansion of trade. Thus, no significant inter-district variation is observed in regard to impact of DWCRA on consumption pattern of the respondents. In all the selected three districts, repayment of loan is regular irrespective of the scheme, caste, category, age and educational qualifications of the respondents. No inter-district variation is observed in this regard.

7

Status of Women – A Comparative Analysis

The relative performance of DWCRA in selected three districts of Khammam, Warangal and Karimnagar in terms of generating employment, income, rise in consumption levels and repayment has been analysed in Chapter-VI. Though economic success of the programme is necessary but not sufficient condition to achieve an improvement in the status of women. Their position within the family as well as in the society is also equally influenced by socio-cultural conditions determined by patriarchy. Since DWCRA consists of women respondents, a specific examination of their status assumes significance to estimate overall impact of the programme on rural women. The relative performance of this aspect is analysed in this present chapter. The section-II of Chapter-III, IV and V is the basis for this chapter.

Status of Women Within the Family

Patriarchy determines and dictates distributive rules in the family which will not allow women to participate in the decision-making of the household irrespective of their visible and invisible contribution for the sustenance of the family. Moreover, it assigns the responsibilities of domestic work to women. In addition, women are harassed by husband as well as other members in the family. A positive change in all these aspects determines an improvement in the status of women within the family. Moreover, women's active participation in decision-making related to the household, society and political decision determines their empowerment.

Short-run Decision-making of the Household

The short-run decision of the household are connected to daily expenses of the household.

In Khammam district, out of 300 selected respondents, 185 (61.7 percent) take decision in this regard on their own, in 57 (19 percent) cases both husband and wife together take decision, in 37 (12.3 percent) cases, husbands alone decide while in 21 (7 percent) cases, other members of the family dominate. No significant caste-wise variation is noticed. The joint decision is higher among respondents who could study intermediate and beyond.

In Warangal district, out of 300 selected respondents, 206 (68.7 percent) have take decision on their own in regard to the purchase of daily needs, in 42 (14 percent) cases, both husband and wife together take decision while in 34 (11.3 percent) cases, husband alone decides where as in 18 (6 percent) cases, other members of the family determine it. The phenomenon of the role of other members of the family can not be found among Forward Caste respondents. Except this, no any significant caste-wise variation is observed. However, if the educational qualification of the respondent is Intermediate and more, then either they take decision on their own and jointly take decision in this regard.

In Karimnagar district, out of 220 respondents selected, 97 (44.6 percent) could take decision on the own, while in 66 (30 percent) cases, husband dominates where as in 39 (17.2 percent) cases, both husband and wife jointly take decision and in 18 (8.2 percent) cases, other members of the family decide this aspect. The domination of other members of the family can not be found in Forward Caste and Scheduled Tribe respondents. Otherwise, no significant caste-wise variation is observed. Further, domination of husband is negligible when the respondents is educated upto Intermediate or more.

The relative performance of the selected three districts in regard to participation of women in day to day expenditure of the family explains that the domination of husband is relatively higher in Karimnagar district. Further, the role of 'other members' of the family can not be seen among Forward Caste respondents in Warangal while among Forward Caste and Scheduled Tribe respondents in Karimnagar district. Apart from this, no any significant caste-wise variation can be observed in this regard. The educational qualifications of the respondents played a role in the determination of their participation in short-run decisions of the family. Therefore, husband's domination is negligible when women is educated at the level of Intermediate and more. Thus, no any significant inter-district variation is observed.

Long-run Decision Making of the Household

These decisions are called long-run decisions as they have long-run implications on the household.

(i) Purchase of Consumer Durables/Assets : In Khammam district, out of 300 selected respondents, 140 (46.7 percent) could take decision on their own while in 74 (24 percent) cases, both wife and husband together takes decision and in 68 (22.7 percent) cases, husband alone determines and lastly, in 18 (6 percent) cases, other members of the family decides. No significant caste-wise variation is observed except 'no role of others' among Scheduled Caste respondents. However, joint decision is higher among the respondents who are highly qualified.

In Warangal district, out of 300 selected respondents 161 (53.7 percent) could take decision on their own in regard to purchase of consumer durables/ assets. In the case of 66 (22 percent) joint decision can be found while in 50 (16.7 percent) cases, husband alone decides and in 23 (7.6 percent) cases, other members of the family take decision in this aspect. No significant caste-wise variation is observed. However, the domination of husband and others is nil when wife is educated at the level of Intermediate and beyond.

In Karimnagar district, in the case of 101 out of 220 respondents (45.9 percent), husband alone decides while 66 (30.1 percent) respondents take decision on their own and joint decision is found in 41 (18.6 percent) cases and role of others can be seen in 12 (5.4 percent) cases. Domination of husband is relatively higher among Backward Class respondents while the role of others can not be found among Forward Caste and Scheduled Tribe respondents. The domination of husband as well as other members of the family can not be seen in cases where wife is a degree holder.

Thus, the domination of husband is relatively higher in Karimnagar district when compared to Khammam and Warangal in regard to purchase of consumer durables/ assets. Further, no any significant caste-wise variation is noticed in Khammam and Warangal districts while in Karimnagar, the domination of other members of the family can not be seen among Forward Caste and Scheduled Tribe respondents. In all the three selected districts, the domination of husband as well as others is either nil or marginal when the wife is educated at the level of Intermediate and beyond.

(ii) Decision-making in Regard to Expansion of Trade : In Khammam, in the case of 176 (58.7 percent) out of 300 selected respondents, husband alone decides as to the decision in regard to expansion of trade. Both wife and husband together take decision in the case of 83 (27.7 percent) respondents while others decide in 23 (7.7 percent) cases and only 18 (6 percent) respondents could take decision independently. No significant caste-wise variation is observed except no role of others among Scheduled Caste respondents. Further, only joint decision is observed among degree holders.

In Warangal, in 121 (40.3 percent) cases, out of 300 selected respondents husband alone decides and this is followed by joint decision in the case of 99 (33 percent) respondents while third place goes to the role of others in the case of 50 (16.7 percent) respondents and only 30 (10 percent) respondents take decision independently in this regard. Interestingly, the role of others can be found even when the respondent is a degree holder.

In Karimnagar district, in the case of 122 (55.4 percent) out of 220 respondents, husband domination can be found. This is followed by joint decision in the case of 51 (23.2 percent) respondents while others dominate in the case of 12 (5.4 percent) respondents and 35 (15.1 percent) could take decision on their own. The role of others can not be seen among Forward Caste and Scheduled Tribe respondents but the domination of husband is relatively higher among Scheduled Tribe respondents. Further, joint decision alone can be found among degree holders.

The domination of husband in regard to decision-making as to the expansion of trade is relatively higher in Khammam district and it is relatively lower in Warangal district. The independent decision by the respondent is relatively higher in Karimnagar district and it is relatively lower in Khammam. Further, joint decision alone can be found among degree holders in Khammam and Karimnagar districts. Inspite of this inter-district variation, on the whole, it can be stated that the phenomenon of domination of husband is higher in all the three selected districts and in contrast to it, independent decision by the respondent is low in all the three districts.

The expansion of trade is a significant activity which enables the respondent to earn more in the long-run and moreover, it is exclusively related to the respondent. But in this important activity, her independent role is marginal and even among degree holders, the joint decision but not independent decision can be observed. This clearly indicates the extent of patriarchal culture rooted in the minds of people.

(iii) Decision-making in Regard to Arrangement of Marriages to the Children : In Khammam, joint decision can be observed in this regard among 156 (52 percent) respondents and it is followed by the domination of husband in the case of 96 (32 percent) respondents and 39 (13 percent) respondents take decision on their own and others decide in the case of 9 (3 percent) respondents. The domination of husband is relatively higher among Scheduled Tribe respondents while joint decision is relatively higher among Scheduled Caste respondents.

Further, joint decision is gradually increased as the level of education of the respondent increases and joint decision alone can be seen among degree holders.

In Warangal, joint decision in this regard can be seen in the case of 222 (71 percent) respondents while husband alone takes decision in 35 (11.7 percent) cases and respondent alone decides in the case of 13 (4.3 percent) respondents but the role of others is dominant in the case of 30 (10 percent) respondents. No any remarkable caste-wise variation is noticed. Further, joint decision alone can be observed among degree holders.

In Karimnagar, both wife and husband used to take decision in the case of 99 (45 percent) respondents and this is followed by 75 (34.1 percent) where husband alone decides but 38 respondents take decision independently and others intervene in the case of 8 (3.5 percent) respondents. The domination of husband is relatively higher among Scheduled Caste respondents and it is relatively lower among Forward Caste respondents. Further, the joint decision alone can be seen among degree holders.

Thus, the inter-district comparison reveals that the joint decision is relatively higher in regard to decision making as to the arrangement of marriages to their children in Warangal district and it is followed by Khammam district. The domination of husband is relatively higher among Scheduled Tribe respondents in Khammam while it is higher among Scheduled Caste respondents in Karimnagar district. Further, in all the three selected districts, the wife and husband together take decision among degree holders. However, in majority cases, wife is consulted in arranging marriages to their children in all the three districts. It is more so among degree holders in all the three districts.

(iv) Decision-making in Regard to Education of the Children : In Khammam district, 147 (49 percent) out of 300 selected could take the decision jointly in regard to education of their children while in 82 (27.3 percent) cases, the husband alone decides and 63 (21 percent) respondents take decision on their own whereas in 8 (2.7 percent) cases, others dominate. Role of others is nil

among Forward Caste and Schedule Caste respondents. Among degree holders, joint decision alone can be found.

In Warangal district, 141 (47 percent) out of 300 selected could take the decision jointly in this regard and it is followed by 109 (36.3 percent) respondents where husband alone decides while 30 (10 percent) respondents could take the decision on their own and further, others decide in the case of 20 (6.7 percent) respondents. The domination of husband and others is nil when the respondent is educated upto Intermediate and beyond.

In Karimnagar district, 113 (51.4 percent) could take the decision jointly while husband dominates in 62 (28.2 percent) cases. However, the role of others can not be seen among Forward Caste and Scheduled Tribe respondents. Moreover, if the wife is educated upto Intermediate, then either they decide on their own or they decide jointly. Further, joint decision alone can be found among degree holders.

In all the selected three districts, the joint decision is relatively higher in this regard. However, educational qualifications of the respondent play a positive role in making her active in the participation of decision making related to the education of their children. Thus, there is no any inter-district variation is observed in this regard.

(v) Decision-making in Regard to Debt and Re-payment : In Khammam district, in 146 (48.7 percent) cases, husband alone decides while joint decision can be found in 113 (37.7 percent) respondents. The role of others in this regard is nil among Scheduled Caste respondents. Further, joint decision alone can be seen among Degree holders.

In Warangal district, 141 (47 percent) out of 300 respondents could take the decision in regard to debt and re-payment of the household jointly while husband's domination can be found in 109 cases and role of others is observed in the case of 20 respondents belonged to all the castes except Scheduled Tribe respondents. Further, either own decision or joint decision can be noticed when the respondent could study upto Intermediate and beyond.

In Karimnagar district, 146 (66.4 percent) out of 220 respondents are dominated by husband in this regard while joint decision can be seen in the case of 50 (12.3 percent) respondents and others role can be seen in 12 (5.4 percent) cases. However, others have no role to play among Forward Caste respondents. Further, joint decision alone can be seen among degree holders.

Thus, joint decision in this regard is relatively higher in Khammam and Warangal districts while the domination of husband is relatively higher in Karimnagar district. Inter-district variation is noticed in regard to role of others. However, in all the three selected districts, joint decision alone can be found among Degree holders which indicates that if the respondent is highly educated, then husband used to discuss with her as to the debt and re-payments of the household.

Ownership of Property

The Ownership of property determines control over resources which is identified as one of the important factors to attain women's empowerment.

In Khammam district, out of 300 respondents as many as 277 (92.3 percent) do not own any property. No significant caste-wise variation is noticed. Interestingly, among the 23 respondents who own property, the degree holders are not seen in them.

In Warangal district, 266 (88.7 percent) respondents do not own property on their names. Further, ownership of property is relatively higher among Forward Caste respondents. But, educational qualifications of the respondent did not influence the ownership of property.

In Karimnagar district, 193 (87.7 percent) do not own property. Among the 27 (12.3 percent) respondents who own property, the percentage share of Forward Caste respondents is relatively higher while Scheduled Tribe is nil. Further, degree holders can not be seen among the respondents who own property.

Thus, in all the three selected districts, many women are far away from the ownership of property. Inter-district variation in this regard is marginal. The educational qualifications of the respondent did not show any impact on this aspect.

Domestic Work

Domestic work constitutes overall maintenance of the household. It requires so many forms of work - cleaning of house, vessels, washing of clothes, cooking, bringing water, collection of forest produce and fire wood, maintaining kitchen garden, looking after children and so much of drudgery work associated with the maintenance of house. This involves physical work as well as concentration and devotion of mind. Without expecting any rest, women would perform this work irrespective of their age, health etc. Women's domestic work is very crucial for the sustenance of the family particularly of rural poor. No family can survive without the domestic work performed by women. But, as capitalist economies recognise it only when the work possess exchange value. Since the domestic work though possess use value do not possess exchange value, it is not recognised either by the family or by the society. Still, women have to spend time in performing domestic work irrespective of their participation in the work which possess exchange value.

(i) Hours Spent on Domestic Work : In Khammam, out of 300 selected respondents 124 (41.5 percent) spend 5-6 hours per day, 106 (35.3 percent) spend 3-4 hours per day. However, 38 (12.7 percent) respondents are forced to spend more than 6 hours per day. While 32 (10.7 percent) spend less than two hours per day. The percentage of respondents who spend less than 2 hours is relatively higher among Forward Caste respondents. The respondents who could study upto Intermediate can not be found in the range of more than 6 hours per day. All the degree holders spend 3-4 hours per day on domestic work.

In Warangal, 133 (44.3 percent) spend 3-4 hours per day while 113 (37.7 percent) spend 5-6 hours per day on domestic work. Where as 46 (13.3 percent) respondents spend less than 2 hours per day and 14 (4.7 percent) have to spend more than 6 hours per day. The Forward Caste respondents are relatively higher in two extreme ranges of 1-2 hours and more than 6 hours. Moreover, the respondents who could study upto Intermediate and beyond can not be seen in the range of more than 6 hours per day.

In Karimnagar, 123 (55.9 percent) respondents spend 5-6 hours per day while 44 (20 percent) spend 3-4 hours per day and 34 (15.5 percent) will spend more than 6 hours per day where as 19 (8.6 percent) spend less than 2 hours per day on domestic work. No significant caste-wise variation is observed. However, in the range of more than 6 hours per day, the respondents who could study upto Intermediate and beyond can not be seen.

In all the three districts selected, the majority of respondents were spending 3-6 hours per day and inter-district variation is marginal in this regard. Further, in all the three districts, the higher the level of educational qualifications of the respondent, the lower will be the number of hours spent on domestic work. The phenomenon of higher educational qualification and consequent requirement of less number of hours on domestic work reflects relatively better economic position of the respondent. This trend is also uniform in all the three selected districts.

(ii) Nature of Domestic Work : In all the three selected districts, all the respondents irrespective of their age, caste, category and educational qualification will perform cleaning of vessels, house, washing clothes and cooking. While 25-30 percent of the respondents have to bring water from distant places. While 20-25 percent are involved in firewood collection and less than 15 percent respondents maintain kitchen garden. The requirement of firewood collection and bringing water from distant places indicates relatively lower economic position of the respondent. Though all the respondents are economically poor, they are not equally poor.

(iii) Assistance in Performing Domestic Work : In Khammam district, 106 (35.3 percent respondents could get assistance from husband while 91 (30.4 percent) perform domestic work on their

own and others assistance can be found in the case of 55 (18.3 percent) respondents. Of course, children also extend support for 48 (16 percent) respondents. However, assistance from husband in this regard is relatively lesser among Scheduled Caste and Scheduled Tribe respondents. Degree holders get assistance either from husband or from Children.

In Warangal district, 91 (30.3 percent) respondents could get help in performing domestic chores from husband and it is followed by 90 (30 percent) from children while 61 (20.3 percent) from others but 58 (19.3 percent) could not get any assistance from any one in this regard. The assistance from husband is relatively negligible among Scheduled Caste respondents. Further, it is relatively higher among respondents who could study upto Intermediate and beyond.

In Karimnagar district, 80 (36.4 percent) respondents out of 220 selected will do domestic work on their own while 67 (30.5 percent) would get help from husband and 37 (16.8 percent) from children and 36 (16.4 percent) from others. The help from husband is relatively lesser among Scheduled Caste respondents while it is relatively higher among respondents who could study upto Intermediate and beyond.

In all the three districts nearly 30 percent respondents perform domestic work on their own while 30 percent used to get assistance from husband. It is to be noticed that in all the three districts, the help from husband is relatively lesser among Scheduled Caste respondents and it is higher among respondents who are highly qualified. Thus, no inter-district variation is noticed in this regard.

Family Purchasing Priorities

In Khammam district, 101 (33.7 percent) out of 300 respondents selected give preference to savings and 77 (25.7 percent) respondents give priority to purchase goods which are exclusively used by male members of the family. While 74 (24.7 percent used to give importance for consumer durables and 48 (16 percent) respondents alone give preference for the expansion of trade. However, preference for the expansion of trade is relatively higher among Backward Class respondents. The caste and educational qualifications of the respondent did not play any significant role in this regard. Further, in majority cases, husband decides family purchasing priorities.

In Warangal district, 115 (38.3 percent) respondents give preference to save while 113 (37.7 percent) give priority to purchase consumer durables and 41 used to purchase goods which are exclusively used by the male members of the family and 31 (10.3 percent) respondents give preference for the expansion of trade. No Scheduled Tribe respondent gives preference for the expansion of trade. Similar trend can be noticed among degree holders too. Interestingly, in the case of majority of respondents, they themselves are deciding family purchasing priorities.

In Karimnagar district, 88 (40 percent) respondents give preference to save while 81 (36.8 percent) give priority to purchase consumer durables and 34 give importance to purchase goods which are exclusively used by the male members of the family but only 17 (7.7 percent) respondents give preference for the expansion of trade. Degree holders give preference only for savings. Further, in majority cases, husband decides family purchasing priorities.

In all the three selected districts, the first priority is being given to saving. Next preference goes to the purchase of consumer durables in Warangal and Karimnagar districts while it occupy third place in Khammam district. This, however, indicates the spread of consumerism even among rural poor. In all the three districts, least preference is given to the expansion of trade. The caste and educational qualifications did not play any vital role in the determination of family purchasing priorities. Moreover, this aspect is exclusively decided by husband in the case of majority of respondents in Khammam and Karimnagar districts while in majority cases the respondent herself is in a position to take decision in Warangal district. Thus, inter-district variation is observed in regard to the question of who decides family purchasing priorities.

Harassment

Women are subjected to the harassment by their own family members which is usually part of the domestic violence. This is significantly present in all the families irrespective of their caste, age, educational qualifications and earning capabilities.

In Khammam district, 66 (22 percent) out of 300 selected respondents are subjected to harassment by the family members. No caste-wise variation is observed. However, it is nil among Degree holders. As many as 56 (84.9 percent) respondents are harassed by husband. Further, wife-beating is a major problem confronted by the respondents which is followed by Dowry problem.

In Warangal district, 77 (25.7 percent) respondents are subjected to harassment in the family irrespective of their caste and educational qualifications. Further, 48 (62.3 percent) respondents are harassed by husband while 18 (23.4 percent) respondents are by their respective mother-in-law and the remaining are by their sister-in-law. Again, wife beating is a serious problem and it is followed by dowry issue.

In Karimnagar district, 57 (25.9 percent) respondents are victims of harassment by the family members. Among them, 40 (70.2 percent) respondents are harassed by the husband while 12 (21 percent) are from mother-in-law and 5 (8.8 percent) are from their sister-in-law. Even in this district, wife-beating is a serious problem and second position occupied by dowry problem.

In all the three districts, 20-25 percent of the respondents are subjected to the harassment and majority of them are harassed by the husband. Further, wife-beating and dowry are the two serious problems confronted by the women. In all these aspects, inter-district variation is marginal.

Protest Against Harassment

In Khammam district, out of 66 respondents who are subjected to harassment. 33 (50 percent) of them could protest it. Of them, 20 respondents have informed about the problem to their respective DWCRA groups. Since the group members meet regularly to discuss about the economic aspects of the programme, it will be utilised as a dias to discuss about their family problems as they could see uniformity in their problem. The DWCRA groups could initiate some action in the case of 16 respondents and could solve the problem in the case of 12 respondents.

In Warangal district, out of 77 respondents who are subjected to domestic violence, 49 could protest it and of them, as many as 52 could discuss about the problem in their respective DWCRA groups. They could initiate action in the case of 29 respondents and of them, they could solve the problem of 18 respondents.

In Karimnagar district, out of 57 who are the victims of harassment, 18 could protest it and of them, 16 could place it in front of their respective DWCRA groups. However, the groups could initiate action in the case of 10 respondents but could solve the problem only in the case of 3 respondents.

The protest is relatively lesser in Karimnagar district when compared to Khammam and Warangal districts. Similarly, the percentage of respondents who informed about the problem of harassment to their respective DWCRA groups is relatively lower in Karimnagar. Even in the case of initiation of action and solving the problem, Karimnagar stands last. Thus, inter-district variation is observed. However, in all the three districts one common phenomenon is observed i.e., women are no longer silent victims of the domestic violence. DWCRA has improved their confidence and as a result, they would like to face it as a group. They could identify commonality in their problem. The success rate might be lower but the confidence it has created is much larger. This will smoothen their path for attaining empowerment.

Social Awareness

Since DWCRA is a group activity, their regular meetings naturally improves social awareness of the respondents because in the meetings, they discuss their family problems as well as the social problems which they confront.

In Khammam district, 73 (24.3 percent) out of 300 respondents selected used to discuss about social problems also in their meetings. Usually they are related to their local area. Similarly, in Warangal district, 87 (29 percent) respondents utilise their regular meetings to discuss about social problems that they face in their locality. However, they are only 11 percent of the respondents in Karimnagar district. Thus, in all the three districts, atleast some of the respondents are seriously discussing about the social problems that are related to their locality. However, Karimnagar district stands last in this regard.

Social Activities

It is heartening to note that the respondents are also involved in social activities.

In Khammam district, 131 (43.7 percent) out of 300 selected respondents are involved in fighting against liquor consumption, 86 (28.7 percent) against social evils, 58 (19.3 percent) are in protesting attrocities. Further, as many as 205 (68.3 percent) respondents have actively participated in 'Janmabhoomi' programme of the state Government of Andhra Pradesh. However, the phenomenon of higher the educational qualification of the respondent, lower will be their participation in 'Janmabhoomi' is observed.

In Warangal district, 100 out of 300 respondents are involved in fighting against social evils and 99 are against liquor consumption while 89 are involved in protesting against attrocities. Further, 197 (65.7 percent) of the respondents have participated in 'Janmabhoomi' programme.

In Karimnagar district, 75 (34.1 percent) out of 220 respondents selected are involved in protesting atrocities on women while 69 (31.4 percent) are in fighting against social evils and 58 (26.4 percent) are against liquor consumption. Further, 79 (35.9 percent) have actively participated in 'Janmabhoomi' programme. The participation of Scheduled Caste respondents is relatively lesser. Further, Degree holders did not participate in this programme.

In all the three selected districts, the respondents are involved in any one of the social activities related to fighting against atrocities on women, social evils and liquor consumption. In regard to participation in 'Janmabhoomi' Khammam district stands first with 68.3 percent and it is followed by Warangal with 65.7 percent while the percentage of respondents who participated in this programme is only 35.9 percent in Karimnagar. Further, the participation of Scheduled Caste respondents is relatively lesser in this district. Thus, inter-district variation is observed. In Khammam and Karimnagar districts, Degree holders did not participate in 'Janmabhoomi'.

Political Participation

Political participation begins with the exercise of right to vote. In Khammam district, 294 (98 percent) out of 300 respondents selected are casting their vote. Of them, 179 (59.7 percent) respondents used to cast their vote on the basis of person while 121 (40.3 percent) respondents give preference to political party to which the contestant belonged to. Further enquiry has revealed that 174 (58 percent) respondents take decision on their own while 106 (35.3 percent) respondents are influenced by husband and 20 (6.7 percent) respondents are influenced by others. However, Degree holders could take independent decision.

In Warangal district, 298 (99.3 percent) respondents are exercising their right to vote and while casting their vote, 151 (50.3 percent) respondents give preference to person but 147 (49 percent) respondents used to elect on the basis of the political party. Further, 124 (41.3 percent) respondents could take decision on their own while 113 (37.9 percent) respondents are influenced by husband and 63 (21.2 percent) respondents are influenced by others while casting their vote. However, degree holders could take independent decision.

In Karimnagar district, 214 (97.3 percent) out of 220 selected respondents are exercising their right to vote. Of them, 135 (63.1 percent) gives preference to political party while 79 (36.9 percent) gives priority to person. Further, 102 (47.7 percent) are influenced by husband and 22 (10.3 percent) by others in taking decision as to vote casting but only 90 (42 percent) are able to take independent decision. It is to be noted that all the degree holders could take the decision on their own in this regard.

In all the three districts, the percentage of respondents who did not exercise their right to vote is marginal. the percentage of respondents who give preference to political party is relatively higher in Karimnagar district. Further, the percentage of respondents who could take independent decision in regard to vote casting is relatively higher in Khammam district. Thus, inter-district variation is observed in regard to political participation of the respondents. Interestingly, in all the three districts, degree holders could take independent decision in exercising their right to vote. Thus, the role of education in making the respondent independent in taking political decisions is significant.

Involvement in Local Politics

In Khammam, 63 (21 percent) respondents have involved in local politics. Of them, 32 are involved in canvassing, 20 respondents directly participated while 11 used to give encouragement. Degree holders did not involve in local politics.

In Warangal district, 57 (19 percent) could involve in local politics. Of them, 21 are involved in canvassing while self participation is by 19 respondents and 17 respondents used to encourage others. No participation of degree holders can be found.

In Karimnagar district, 30 (13.6 percent) respondents are involved in local politics. Of them, self-participation can be seen in 17 respondents, 10 are involved in canvassing while 3 used to encourage others. However, degree holders did not participate in local politics.

In all the three districts, the percentage of respondents who could participate in local politics is less than 21. However, Khammam district stands first while Warangal and Karimnagar occupied second and third positions respectively in regard to involvement of respondents in local politics. Though negligible, self-participation by the respondents is also seen in all the three districts. However, in all the three districts, degree holders are not interested in participating local politics. Thus, there is no any inter-district variation. The involvement of respondents in local politics though negligible is positive and indicates growing political awareness of the respondents which is one of the essential conditions of women's empowerment.

Achievement of DWCRA in the Opinion of Respondents

In Khammam district, 131 (43.7 percent) out of 300 selected respondents opine that they feel an improvement in both economic as well as social status while 98 (32.7 percent) respondents experience an improvement in their economic status only and 40 respondents are of the opinion that their social status alone has been improved but 31 (10.3 percent) respondents feel an improvement in their status within the family.

In Warangal district, 127 (42.3 percent) respondents felt an improvement in their economic status while 84 (28 percent) experiences an improvement in both economic and social status and 48 (16 percent) are of the opinion that their social status has been improved and lastly 41 (13.7 percent) respondents are experiencing an improvement in their status within the family.

In Karimnagar district, 84 (38.2 percent) respondents are of the opinion that their economic status alone has been improved but 79 (35.9 percent) respondents could observe an improvement in their economic as well as social status while 40 (18.2 percent) respondents find an improvement in their social status and 17 (7.7 percent) respondents could experience better position within the family.

Thus, the percentage of respondents who experience an improvement in both economic as well as social status is relatively higher in Khammam district while an improvement in economic status occupied first position in Warangal and Karimnagar districts. Keeping apart this minor variation among districts, in all the three districts, the respondents could experience an improvement in their status in one form or the other.

8

Conclusions and Recommendations

The conclusions drawn on the basis inquiry are presented in this chapter.

As it is mentioned in Chapter-I that the main objective of the present study is to examine the impact of DWCRA on Work, Income and Status of Rural Women in selected districts of Telangaṇa region of Andhra Pradesh viz., Khammam, Warangal and Karimnagar.

Sample Design

Three staged stratified random sampling technique has been adopted.

Initially, three districts viz., Khammam, Warangal and Karimnagar have been chosen first. This is followed by selection of 23 villages in Khammam, 20 villages in Warangal and 18 villages in Karimnagar. At the third stage, 300 respondents representing 19 trades from Khammam district, 300 respondents representing 24 trades in Warangal district, 220 respondents representing 19 trades in Karimnagar district are chosen. All the 820 sample respondents of DWCRA are administered by a structured questionnaire to elicit the information as to the impact of DWCRA on Work, Income and Status of rural women.

Caste-wise Distribution of Selected Respondents

Out of 820 selected respondents, as high as 492 belonged to Backward Classes, 133 to Scheduled Castes, 126 to Forward Castes and only 69 to Scheduled Tribes. Similar caste-wise distribution of sample can be found in Warangal and Karimnagar districts but in Khammam, second place in terms of number of respondents is occupied by Forward Castes while third place is occupied by Scheduled Tribes and Scheduled Caste respondents stand last in terms of their number.

Thus, in all the three selected districts, Backward Class respondents occupy first position in terms of their number.

Category-wise Distribution of Sample

Out of 820 selected respondents, 232 are Marginal Farmers, 163 are Rural Artisans, 143 are Small Farmers, 132 are 'Others', 111 are Agricultural Labour and lastly 39 are Non-Agricultural Labourers.

Marginal Farmers in terms of their number occupied first position in Khammam and Warangal districts while second position in Karimnagar district.

Rural Artisans occupy second position in Khammam district while third place in Warangal and Karimnagar districts.

In all the three districts, Non-Agricultural Labour occupy last position.

Characteristics of Selected Respondents

(i) Trade-wise Distribution of Selected Respondents : In Khammam district, Milch Animals stands first in terms of number of respondents, Tailoring occupy second place and Making of Pickles/ Edible items occupy third place.

In Warangal district, 45 respondents are found in Milch Animals, 26 in Chappals Making and third place is to Veg/ Fruit Vending with 18 respondents.

In Karimnagar district also Milch Animals Trade occupies first place with 70 respondents, second place occupied by the trade Petty Coats Making with 23 respondents and third place by the trade Basket Making.

In all the three districts the trade Milch Animals occupied first position. This, however, indicates the significance of Agriculture and Allied activities in rural India. As majority of the selected respondents belonged to the category of Marginal Farmers, they naturally prefer the trade Milch Animals as its sustenance requires some land base.

(ii) Trade and Caste-wise Distribution of Selected Respondents : In Khammam district Backward Classes respondents are found in 17 out of 19 trades selected, Forward Castes respondents in 14, Scheduled Tribe respondents in 8 and Scheduled Caste respondents in 5 trades.

In Warangal district, Backward Classes respondents are found in 20 out of 24 trades selected. The Forward Caste respondents are found in 9 trades, Scheduled Caste respondents in 7 and Scheduled Tribe respondents in only one trade.

In Karimnagar district, Backward Classes respondents are found in 17 out of 19 trades selected, Scheduled Castes in 8, Forward Castes in 7 and Scheduled Tribe respondents in 2 trades only.

In all the three selected districts, the scope of selecting various trades is relatively more wider for Backward Class respondents while Scheduled Tribe respondents stand last in this regard in Warangal and Karimnagar districts and Scheduled Caste respondents stand last in Khammam district.

(iii) Village and Caste-wise Distribution of Selected Respondents: In Khammam district, Backward Class respondents can be seen in 19 out of 23 selected villages while forward Caste respondents can be found in 14 villages and Scheduled Caste and Scheduled Tribe respondents are seen in 5 villages.

In Warangal district, Backward Class respondents can be found in 17 out of 20 villages, Forward Caste respondents in 9 villages, Scheduled Caste respondents in 6 villages while Scheduled Tribe respondents are seen in only one village.

In Karimnagar district, Backward Class respondents are found in 17 out of 18 villages selected, Forward Caste respondents in 6 villages, Scheduled Caste respondents in 8 villages while Scheduled Tribe respondents are seen in 2 villages.

Thus, in all the three selected districts, Backward Class respondents are distributed in relatively more number of villages and Scheduled Tribe respondents stand last in this regard.

(iv) Caste and Category-wise Distribution of Sample Respondents: In Khammam, majority of Forward Caste respondents are Small Farmers, majority of Backward Class respondents are Rural Artisans, while Scheduled Caste respondents are Agriculture Labourers and majority of Scheduled Tribe respondents belonged to the category of Marginal Farmers.

In Warangal district, majority of Forward Caste and Backward Class respondents belonged either to Small or Marginal Farmers while the majority of Scheduled Caste respondents are Rural Artisans and all the Scheduled Tribe respondents belonged to the category of 'Others'.

In Karimnagar district, majority of Forward Caste respondents are either Small or Marginal Farmers, the majority of Backward Class respondents are Rural Artisans, the majority of Scheduled Caste respondents are Agricultural Labour and the majority of Scheduled Tribe respondents are Rural Artisans.

Thus, in all the three selected districts, land base is relatively more for Forward Caste respondents.

(v) Trade and Category-wise Distribution of Selected Respondents: In Khammam district, Small and Marginal Farmers have significantly chosen trades related to Agriculture and Allied activities while Agricultural and Non-Agricultural Labourers preferred to select trades related to Business activity and Rural Artisans preferred trades related to Service Sector. However, all the economic category respondents are found in the trades Baniyans Making and Kiranam.

In Warangal district, majority of Small Farmers are found in Milch Animals but Marginal Farmers in Embroidery Work and Milch Animals, majority of Agricultural Labourers preferred 'No Trade' while Non-Agricultural Labourers preferred to chose the trades of Candle Making and Mushrooms. The majority of Rural Artisans who belonged Scheduled Castes have chosen the trade Chappals making.

In Karimnagar district, majority of Small and Marginal Farmers and Agricultural Labourers have chosen the trade Milch Animals and the majority of Non-Agricultural Labourers have preferred the trade Lace Work and finally as the majority of Rural Artisans belonged to Scheduled Tribes and therefore, they preferred the trade Basket making.

It is interesting to note that the majority of Small and Marginal Farmers have preferred the trades related to Agriculture and Allied activities in all the selected three districts. In Khammam district, majority of Rural Artisans belonged to Backward Class and therefore preferred Tailoring activity but the same economic category in Warangal mainly belonged to Scheduled Castes and therefore preferred Chappals-making while the same in Karimnagar mainly belonged to Scheduled Tribes preferred to select Basket Making.

This clearly reveals the inter-relationship between caste, economic category and selection of trade.

Inferences Drawn on the Basis of Analysis Related to Characteristics of Selected Respondents

(i) Majority of respondents in all the three selected districts have preferred the trades related to Agriculture and Allied activities especially Milch Animals.

(ii) The Backward Class respondents are found in relatively more number of trades.

(iii) The Backward Class respondents are distributed in relatively more number of villages.

(iv) The land base is continuously on the decline if one moves from Forward Castes to Scheduled Tribes.

(v) Strong inter-relationship between caste, category and selection of trade.

Socio-economic Background of the Selected Respondents

(i) Majority (>76 percent) of selected respondents are in the age group of 20-40 years.

(ii) Majority (> 73 percent) of selected respondents are either illiterates or studied upto primary level education.

(iii) Majority (> 85 percent) of selected respondents are married.

(iv) The primary occupation of the majority of respondents is Agriculture.

(v) Access to higher level education is relatively higher for Forward Caste andBackward Class respondents.

Caste and Size of the Family

(i) The size of the family is in between 3-4 for majority of respondents.

(ii) The size of the family increases as one moves from Forward Castes to ScheduledTribes.

Caste and House Possession, Assets and Savings

(i) Majority of selected respondents in all the three districts reside in Pucca houses.

(ii) Majority of Scheduled Tribe respondents in Khammam district reside in RCC houses because of Govt's assistance.

(iii) The position of assets weaken as one moves from Forward Caste to Scheduled Tribe respondents.

(iv) The ability to save is relatively higher among Forward Caste respondents and lesser among Scheduled Tribe respondents. Moreover majority of respondents irrespective of the caste preferred to keep their savings in chits.

Selection of Trade

In all the three selected districts, the majority of selected respondents are assisted by DRDA officials in the selection of trade.

Problems of Trade

(i) In Khammam district 85 out of 300 selected respondents face problems in regard to the procurement of raw material while 109 face problems in regard to sale of the product.

(ii) In Warangal district, 76 out of 300 selected respondents face problem in regard to the procurement of raw-material and 84 respondents face marketing problem.

(iii) In Karimnagar district, 59 out of 220 selected respondents face problem in regard to the procurement of raw-material and 79 face marketing problem.

(iv) Inadequate demand, transportation are the two major marketing problems.

(v) In Khammam 173 out of 300 selected respondents, in Warangal 108 out of 300 and in Karimnagar 83 out of 220 selected respondents could utilise the facility of DWCRA bazaars organised by DRDA to market their product.

Impact of DWCRA on Employment Generation

The employment generation by DWCRA is assessed on the basis of difference between Pre and Post-DWCRA employment. The analysis is made in relation to scheme, caste, category, educational qualifications and age of the respondent.

(A) In Khammam District

(i) 273 respondents were employed during Pre-DWCRA period and it has been increased to 300 during Post-DWCRA period.

(ii) The total days of employment per month was 4144 days during Pre-DWCRA period and it has been increased to 6986 days during Post-DWCRA period.

(iii) The average days of employment per month has increased from 15.17 during Pre-DWCRA period to 23.28 during Post-DWCRA period.

(B) In Warangal District

(i) The number of respondents who were employed during Pre-DWCRA period was 287 and it has been increased to 300 during Post-DWCRA period.

(ii) The total days of employment per month has increased from 4690 during Pre-DWCRA period to 7271 during Post-DWCRA period.

(iii) The average days of employment per month has increased from 16.34 to 24.23 during Post-DWCRA period.

(C) In Karimnagar District

(i) The number of respondents who were employed during Pre-DWCRA period was 184 and has been increased to 220 during Post-DWCRA period.

(ii) The total days of employment per month has increased from 2763 during Pre-DWCRA period to 4536 during Post-DWCRA period.

(iii) The average days of employment per month has increased from 15.01 during Pre-DWCRA period to 20.61 during Post-DWCRA period.

Thus, DWCRA has resulted in the

(i) rise in the employment to number of respondents.

(ii) rise in the total days of employment per month.

(iii) rise in the average days of employment per month.

(iv) Karimnagar district stands first in terms of generation of employment to number of respondents.

(v) Warangal district stands first in terms of generation of average days of employment per month.

Scheme-wise Analysis of Employment Generation

(i) Post-DWCRA employment has increased for all the respondents irrespective of the scheme in Khammam and Warangal districts, but it is negative in three schemes-Soft-Toys, Greeting Cards and No Trade in Karimnagar district.

(ii) Inter-scheme variation is noticed in terms of average days of employment generated per month in all the selected three districts but it is relatively lesser in Khammam and more in Karimnagar district.

Caste-wise Analysis of Employment Generation

(i) Total as well as average days of employment per month has increased for all the respondents irrespective of the caste in all the three selected districts.

(ii) Inter-caste and inter-district variation is noticed in this regard.

(iii) The DWCRA is relatively more successful in terms of generation of average days of employment among Scheduled Caste respondents in Warangal and Karimnagar and amongst ScheduledTribe respondents in Khammam district.

Category-wise Analysis of Employment Generation

(i) The total as well as average days of employment per month during Post-DWCRA period has increased for all the respondents irrespective of their economic category except for 'Others' in Karimnagar district.

(ii) Inter-category and inter-district variation is noticed.

(iii) Non-Agricultural Labourers stand first in Khammam and Karimnagar districts in terms of average days of employment generated during Post-DWCRA period while Rural Artisans stand first in this regard in Warangal district.

Educational Qualifications and Employment Generation

(i) The total as well as average days of employment per month during Post-DWCRA period has increased for all the respondents irrespective of their educational qualifications in all the selected three districts except the respondents who could study upto Intermediate level in Karimnagar district.

(ii) Illiterates are successful in Khammam and Karimnagar districts while Degree holders are successful in Warangal district.

(iii) Inter-district variation is observed.

Age-wise Analysis of Employment Generation

(i) The total as well as average days of employment per month during Post-DWCRA period has increased for all the respondents irrespective of their age in all the three selected districts.

(ii) Inter-age as well as inter-district variation is observed in this regard.

Employment Generation Exclusively by DWCRA

(i) DWCRA has generated employment positively in terms of days of work per month in all the three selected districts.

(ii) Inter-scheme as well as intra-scheme variation in this regard is noticed in all the three districts.

(iii) Employment generation for more than 11 days per month exclusively by DWCRA to the selected respondents is relatively higher in Khammam and lower in Karimnagar districts.

(iv) Intra-scheme variation is relatively wider in Warangal district.

(v) Inter-district variation is noticed.

Caste-wise Analysis

(i) DWCRA has generated employment positively for all the respondents irrespective of the caste in all the selected three districts.

(ii) Intra-caste variation in this regard is relatively wider among Forward Caste respondents in all the three districts.

(iii) Forward Caste and Backward Class respondents are relatively in a better position in this regard in all the three districts.

(iv) Inter-district variation is noticed.

Consequential Employment Generation

(i) It is positive in all the three selected districts.

(ii) More utilisation of services of family members.

(iii) Inter-scheme and inter-district variation is observed.

Impact of DWCRA on Income Generation

(i) In Khammam district, the average income per month has increased from Rs. 364.06 during Pre-DWCRA period to Rs. 972.70 during Post-DWCRA period.

(ii) In Warangal district, the average income per month has increased from Rs. 542.97 during Pre-DWCRA period to Rs. 996.06 during Post-DWCRA period.

(iii) In Karimnagar district, the average income per month has increased from Rs. 456.88 during Pre-DWCRA period to Rs. 776.59 during Post-DWCRA period.

Thus, DWCRA is a success in terms of generating income to the respondents. However, inter-district variation can be observed.

Scheme-wise Analysis of Income Generation

In Khammam District

(i) Milch Animals is relatively more successful in terms of generating income.

(ii) Rise in average income due to DWCRA is negative in the trade Woolen Works.

In Warangal District

(i) The trade Chappals making is relatively more successful in terms of generating income.

(ii) Rise in average income during Post-DWCRA period is negative in the trade Mushrooms.

In Karimnagar District

(i) The trade Tailoring stands first in terms of income generation during Post-DWCRA period.

(ii) Rise in average income is negative in the trades Embroidery Work and No Trade.

Thus,

(i) Inter-scheme and inter-district variation is noticed.

(ii) Khammam district stands first in terms of generation of income while Karimnagar district stands last in this regard.

Caste-wise Analysis of Income Generation

(i) The average income per month during Post-DWCRA period has increased for all the respondents irrespective of the caste in all the three districts except Forward Caste respondents in Warangal district.

(ii) Inter-caste and inter-district variation can be observed.

Category-wise Analysis of Income Generation

(i) The average income per month during Post-DWCRA period has increased for all the respondents irrespective of their economic category except Non-Agricultural Labour in Warangal and Others in Karimnagar district.

(ii) The category of Small Farmers occupied first position in terms of average income generation in Khammam district, while Rural Artisans occupied first position in Warangal and Non-Agricultural Labourers in Karimnagar district.

(iii) Inter-category and inter-district variation is noticed.

Educational Qualifications and Employment Generation:

(i) Post-DWCRA average income has increased for all the respondents irrespective of their educational qualifications in Khammam district while it is negative for the respondents who could study intermediate in

Warangal district and who could study beyond secondary education in Karimnagar district.

(ii) Degree holders are relatively more successful in terms of generating income in Khammam and Warangal districts while the respondents who could study upto Primary level education occupied this position in Karimnagar district.

(iii) No relation between educational qualifications of the respondents and the success of DWCRA in terms of generating income.

Age-wise Analysis of Income Generation

(i) The average income during Post-DWCRA period has increased for all the respondents irrespective of their age in al the selected three districts.

(ii) The performance of respondents who are in the age group of 41-50 years and above is relatively better in terms of income generation.

Income Generation Exclusively by DWCRA

(i) Income generation exclusively by DWCRA is positive for 292 out of 300 respondents in Khammam, 290 out of 300 respondents in Warangal, 194 out of 220 respondents in Karimnagar districts.

(ii) The performance of Khammam is relatively better in this regard.

Repayment : Repayment is regular by all the respondents in all the selected three districts irrespective of the scheme, caste, economic category, educational qualifications and age of the respondent.

Impact on Consumption Pattern of the Respondent

(i) Rise in the income from DWCRA has resulted in rise in savings of majority of respondents.

(ii) Secondly, they have given preference to the education of their children.

(iii) Negligible preference for the expansion of trade.

(iv) No inter-district variation is noticed.

Impact of DWCRA on the Status of Women

DWCRA will be a success only when it can improve the status of women. Mere economic success of the programme will not improve the status of women as it is determined by the socio-cultural factors determined by patriarchy. Therefore, an assessment in regard to the impact of DWCRA on the status of women within and outside the family assumes significance.

Women's Participation in Decision Making of the Household

Women's active participation in decision making related to the household naturally improves intra-household distributive rules in favour of women.

The data in regard to the participation of respondents in short-run decision making of the household related to daily expenses have revealed that:

(i) In Khammam, 61.7 percent respondents take decision on their own and it is 68.7 percent in Warangal and 44.6 percent in Karimnagar district.

(ii) No any inter-caste variation is observed.

(iii) Domination of husband is relatively higher in Karimnagar district in this regard.

(iv) Husband's domination is negligible when the respondent is educated at the level of intermediate and beyond.

Women's Participation in Long-run Decision Making of the Household

These decisions are called as long-run decisions because they have long-run implications on the household.

The decisions in regard to expansion of trade, purchase of consumer durables, education to the children, arrangement of marriages to the children, debt and repayment would come under this category.

(i) Husband's domination can be found in taking decisions in regard to expansion of trade, purchase of consumer durables and taking debt and repayment.

(ii) Joint decision is higher in regard to education of their children and arrangement of marriages.

(iii) Higher the level of education of the respondent upto the level of Intermediate and beyond, higher will be the joint decision.

(iv) Inter-caste variation in this regard is marginal.

(v) Husband's domination is relatively higher in Karimnagar district.

Among the long run decisions, the decisions in regard to expansion of trade and debt and repayment are significant as they decide the access to as well as control over resources by the respondent. Moreover, the trade belonged to the respondent. In these important decisions, the role of respondent is negligible which clearly indicates the prevalence of intra-household disparities in decision making of the household. Moreover, the wife is consulted (joint decision) when she is educated at the level of Intermediate and beyond. The independent earnings along with the level of education of the respondent improves her position in the family to some extent.

Further, though all the respondents earn income independently, more than 87 percent of the respondents do not own any property at all. This clearly explains lack of control over resources by the respondents.

Burden of Domestic Work

The gender-based division of labour in the household imposes the responsibility of domestic work on women which constitutes various activities connected to the maintenance of household.

(i) More than 75 percent of the respondents in all the three selected districts spend more than 3-4 hours per day on domestic work.

(ii) The respondents who could study upto Intermediate level and beyond can not be found in the range of more than 6 hours per day on domestic work. The access to higher level education itself indicates relatively better economic position of the respondent. This lessens the hours to be spent on domestic work.

(iii) Inter-district variation is marginal in this regard.

(iv) 25-30 percent of the respondents have to bring water from distant places and 20-25 percent of the respondents are involved in firewood collection. These two aspects indicate the relatively lower economic position of the respondents among the selected women.

(v) 30-36 percent of the respondents could get assistance from household in performing domestic work.

(vi) Husband's assistance is relatively lesser among Scheduled Caste respondents.

(vii) Husband's assistance is relatively more among Degree holders.

However, overall responsibility of domestic work lies on the shoulders of women.

Role of Women in Deciding Family's Purchasing Priorities:

(i) In majority cases, the husband decides family's purchasing priorities in Khammam and Karimnagar districts.

(ii) First preference to savings and this is followed by the purchase of consumer durables and next the goods which are exclusively used by the male members of the family. Further, least preference is observed on the expansion of trade.

Domestic Violence

(i) Domestic violence is visible in the case of 20-25 percent of the selected respondents.

(ii) Wife-beating and Dowry are serious problems confronted by the respondents.

(iii) In majority cases, women are subjected to the harassment by husband only.

Protest Against Domestic Violence

As members of DWCRA groups, the respondents can not be passive towards domestic violence. The group activity raised their self-confidence and they began to discuss and initiate action against domestic violence. This is one of the significant positive trend created by DWCRA towards the attainment of women's empowerment. This qualitative phenomenon can not be quantified but it gradually smoothens the path for women's emancipation.

Social Awareness : The regular meetings of DWCRA became the dais for discussing family as well as social problems especially local problems that they confront.

Political Participation

As the political participation begins with the exercise of right to vote, the data are elicited on this aspect.

(i) 98 percent of selected respondents in Khammam, 99.3 percent in Warangal, 97.3 percent in Karimnagar district exercise their right to vote.

(ii) 40.3 percent respondents in Khammam, 49 percent in Warangal and 63.1 percent in Karimnagar give preference to political party to which the contestant belonged to.

(iii) 58 percent of selected respondents in Khammam, 41.3 percent in Warangal, 42 percent in Karimnagar district take decision independently in this regard.

(iv) Degree holders in all the three selected districts are taking decision independently in this regard which clearly denotes the role of education in making the women active even in regard to political decision making.

(v) 21 percent of selected respondents in Khammam, 19 percent in Warangal and 13.6 percent in Karimnagar district are involved in local politics. In all the three districts, Degree holders are away from local politics.

(vi) Self-participation in elections is negligible.

Thus, political awareness is basically confined to exercising right to vote. Recently, they show enthusiasm to participate in political decisions. DWCRA and its group activity plays a positive role in making women self-confident in this direction which is recognised as one of the important conditions for women's empowerment.

Achievement of DWCRA in the Opinion of Respondents:

All the respondents experienced an improvement in their status either in economic form or in social form or in both. Few have experienced a better position within the family.

The study has proved that:

(i) There is a direct relationship between success of trade and economic status of women;

(ii) There is no significant relationship between success of trade and change in the intra-household gender specific distributive rules in favour of women; and

(iii) There is a positive relationship between economic status of women and political participation especially in terms of exercising right to vote.

Recommendations

The present inquiry has clearly revealed that the DWCRA is a success especially in terms of generating employment and raising level of income of rural women. This has resulted in the rise in their level of consumption. Though marginal, an improvement in gender relations is also noticed. Moreover, the DWCRA has resulted in raising the social as well as political awareness of the rural women. It has raised their self-confidence, mobility and awareness through independent earnings and group activity. However, the following recommendations are made to make the programme more effective in attaining its objectives.

(i) Provision of training in various skills is necessary to make the rural women efficient in producing quality goods.

(ii) Enlargement of marketing net-work is required to increase the sale of products.

(iii) Frequent organisation of DWCRA bazaars at the District, State and National level is required.

(iv) Interaction among DWCRA groups should be initiated by DRDA.

(v) NGO's may be encouraged to initiate and develop inter-link among DWCRA groups.

(vi) Meetings of DWCRA groups at the District and State level should be organised to share their experiences with each other.

(vii) DWCRA groups are to be encouraged to take up programmes to increase their social awareness and make them active in participating in decision-making related to the household and society.

(viii) Awareness programmes are to be organised to raise their political consciousness as well as active political participation.

(ix) Measures are to be taken to achieve an improvement not only in quantitative terms but also in qualitative terms i.e., effective participation of women in decision making to be achieved.

All these recommendations are made to make the DWCRA more effective to make the rural women economically independent, socially conscious and politically active to reduce rural poverty and to improve gender relations which is expected to smoothen the way for attaining women's empowerment.

Bibilography

Books

Amarthya Sen : Poverty and Famines: An essay on Entitlement and Deprivation, Clarenden Press, Oxford, 1981.

Amarthya Sen : Inequality Re Examined, Oxford Univeristy Press, New Delhi, 1999.

Charan Singh : India's Poverty and its Solutions, Asia Publishing House, Bombay, 1959.

Dilip, S. Takur : Poverty, Inequality and Unemployment in Rural India, Some Conceptual and Methodological Issues in Measurements, B.R. Publishing Corporation, Delhi, 1985.

Dilip, K. Basu (ed) : Social and Economic Development in India - A Ressaessment, Sage Publications, New Delhi, 1986.

Deepa Mathur : Women, Family and work, Rawat Publications, New Delhi, 1995.

Hanumappa, N.G. : Dimensions of Rural Poverty in India, New Delhi, 1979.

Kurien, C.T. : Poverty, Planning and Social Transformation, Allied Publishers, 1978.

Kamble, N.D. : Poverty with in Poverty, Sterling Publishers, Pvt., Ltd., New Delhi, 1979.

Kalpana Kannabhiran (et al) : Sarihaddululeni Sandhyalu : Feminist Politics, Action, Question, Swetha Publications, July, 1995.

Mishra, A.P. : Rural Poverty in India : Problem in Planning and Strategy for Poverty Alleviation, Deep and Deep Publications, New Delhi, 1988.

Michel, P. Todaro : Economic Development in the Third world, Orient Longman, UK, 1989.

Mittal Mukta : Women Power in India, Anmol Publications, Pvt., Ltd., New Delhi, 1995.

Manuja Devi, K. : Rural Women-Poverty Alleviation Programme, Anmol Publications, Pvt., Ltd., New Delhi, 1997.

Marilyn (et al) : Speaking Out: Women, Economic Empowerment in South Asia, Vistar Publications, New Delhi, 1999.

Misra Seth : Women and Development : The Indian Experience, Sage Publications, New Delhi, 2001.

Mohini Giri : Emancipiation and Empowerment of Women, Gyan Publishing House, New Delhi, 1998.

Nirmala Benarjee and Devaki Jain : Indian Women's Experience of Development, ICSSR, New Delhi, 1990.

Neera Desai (ed) : A Decade of Women's Movement in India, Himalaya Publishing House, 1993.

Parikh, K. and Sudershan, S., (ed) : Human Development Structural Adjustment, Macmillan, New Delhi, 1993.

Pruthvi Raj (et al) : Women and social change, Anmol Publications, Pvt., Ltd., New Delhi, 1995.

Sunderan, I.S., : Anti Poverty Rural Development in India, D.K. Publications, New Delhi, 1984.

Sankuntala Narasimham : Empowering Women : An Alternative Strategy from Rural India, Sage Publications, New Delhi, 1999.

Tarlok Singh : Poverty and Social Change, Orient Longman, New Delhi, 1969.

Thimmaiah, G. (ed) : Studies in Rural Development, Chugh Publications, Allahabad, 1979.

Articles

Archana Sood : Development of Rural Women-Perception and Outcome, Kurukshethra, Vol. XLII, No. 12, Sep-1994, pp.15-18.

Aasha Kapur Mehta : Recasting Indicies for Developing Countries, A Gender Empowerment Measure, *Economic and Political Weekly*, Vol. XXXI, No. 43, 1996, pp. WS 80-85.

Balasaheb Vikha Patil and Gurucharan Singh : Implementing IRDP Effectively, Kurukshetra, Vol. XXXIX, No. 10, July, 1991. pp. 26-28.

Bina Agarwal : Work Participation of Rural Women in Third World; Some Data and Conceptual Biases *Economic and Political Weekly*, Vol. XX, No. 51 & 52, 1985, pp. A 155-64.

Chinnadurai, R. : Possibilities of High Income Activities for Women, Kurukshetra, Vol. XLII, No. 12, Sep, 1994, pp. 11-14.

Demery, L and T. Addison : The Impact of Macro Economic Adjustment on Poverty in the Presence of Wage Rigidities, *Journal of Development Economics,* 1993, pp. 603-32.

Dev, S.M. : Economic Reforms and the Rural Poor, *Economic and Political Weekly,* Vol. 30, No. 33, August 19, 1995, pp. 2085-88.

Dev, S. M., Suryanarayana, M.H., and Parikh, K.S. : Rural Poverty in India : Incidence and Issues an Policies, Asian Development Review, Vol. 10, No. 1, 1992, pp. 35-66.

Deolankar, Vivek : Status of Women Enterpreneurs, Khadi Gramodyog Vol. XXXI, No. 8, May - 1985, pp. 331-335.

Devaki Jain : Valuing Work : Time as a Measure, *Economic and Political Weekly,* Vol. XXXI, No. 43, (1996) pp. 46-57.

D.S. Dhillon and B.N. Hansra : On Making DWCRA Effectively, Kurukshetra,Vol. XXXIX, No. 12. Sep, 1991, pp. 15-19.

D.K. Ghosh : Awareness of IRDP Beneficiaries : A Study Kurukshethra, Vol. XXXIX, No.12, Sep - 1991. pp. 15-19.

Darunee Tantiwiramanand : Changing Gender Relations in Thailand: A Historical and Cultural Analysis, *Indian Journal of Gender Studies,* Vol. 4, No.2, July-Dec, 1997. pp. 167-195.

Dwaraknath, H.D. : Rural Development and Poverty Alleviation Programme, Kurukshethra Vol. XLIII, No. 4, Jan, 1995, pp. 22-23.

Gandhi, A.C. and Ravali, R.D. : Impact of Rural Development on Economic Status on Women, Rural India, Kurukshethra, Vol.49, No. 1 & 2, Jan-Feb, 1986, pp. 16-18.

Gupta, S.P. : Economic Reform and its Impact on Poor, *Economic and Political Weekly,* Vol. 30, No. 22, June 3, 1995, pp.1295-1313.

Hanumantha Rao, CH : Integrating Poverty Alleviation Programmes with Development Strategies - Indian Experience, *Economic and Political Weekly,* Vol. 27, No. 48, November 28, 1992, pp. 2603-7.

Ifthikhar Ahmed : Technology and Feminisation of Work, *Economic and Political Weekly,* (1994) Vol. XXIX, No. 18, pp. W 534-38.

Indira Hirway, Darshini Mahadevia : Critique of Gender Development Index - Towards an Alternataive, *Economic and Political Weekly,* (1996) Vol. XXXI, No. 43, pp. WS 80-85.

Joy R. Ranadive : Gender Implications of Adjustment Policy Programme in India. Significance of the Household, *Economic and Political Weekly,* (1994) Vol. XXIX, No. 18, pp. WS 12-18.

Jyothi Rani, T. and Rajaiah, B. : Female Population, Literacy and Employment some Observations, *The Indian Journal of Social Work,* Vol. XLIX, No. 3, July, 1998. pp. 245-251.

Jyothi Rani, T. and : Ravinder Reddy, K. Performance of DWCRA in Khammam Dist. - A Study, Conference *Journal of AP Economics Association,* Khammam, 2001.

Jyothi Rani, T. and : Ravinder Reddy, Impact of DWCRA on Rural Women -A Comparative Study in Telangana" *Conference Journal of AP Economic Association,* Rajahmundry, 2002.

Kumud Sharma : Gender, Environment and Structural Adjustment, *Economic and Political Weekly,* (1994) Vol. XXIX, No. 18, pp. WS 5-11.

Kishore, C. Samal : Poverty Alleviation after Liberalisation: Study of a Tribal Block in Orissa, *Economic and Political Weekly,* (1998) Vol. XXXIII, No. 28, pp. 1846-1857.

Kusam Lata Tiwari : Women and Development, Kurukshethra, Vol. XLIII, No.11, Aug, 1995, pp. 53-55.

Malyadri, P. Gowrappa, K. and Baswaraja, M. : Alleviating Poverty through IRDP, Kurukshethra, Vol. XL, No. 10, July, 1992, pp. 22-24.

Manimekalai, N. and Rajendran, R. : Self-Employment through DWCRA, (A Case study) Kurukshethra, Vol. XLI, No. 10, July, 1993, pp. 5-9.

Mukul Mukharjee : Towards Gender Awareness Data Systems : Indian Experience, *Economic and Political Weekly,* (1996) Vol. XXXI, No. 43, pp.WS. 63-71.

Nandita Shah and Others : Structural Adjustment, Feminisation of Labour for and Organistional Strategies, *Economic and Political Weekly,* (1994) Vol. XXIX, No. 18, pp. WS 39-48.

Nandita Datta, A and Sachidanand Sinha : Gender Disparities in Social well-being: An Overview, *Indian Journal of Gender Studies,* Vol. 4, No. 1, Jan-Jun, 1997, pp. 51-62.

Peter Waterman : Hidden from Her Story, Women, Feminism and New Global Solidarity, *Economic and Political Weekly,* Vol. XXVII, No. 44, Oct 30, 1993.

Prathap Reddy, K. and Buchamma, K. : How far has IRDP Helped Alleviate Poverty, (A Study of Karimnagar District in A.P.), Kurukshethra, Vol. XL, No. 3, Dec-1991, pp.5-12.

Pranab Mukharjee : Developing New Strategy for Women's Development, Kurukshethra, Vol. XL, No. 5, Feb, 1992, pp. 19-22.

Premkumar, N. and Rahul Kumar, A. : How does DWCRA Scheme Operation: (A Case Study), Kurukshetra, Vol. XL, No. 5, Feb, 1992. pp. 24-29.

Pradhani, M.A. : Poverty Eradication Programmes and Rural India, Kurukshethra, Vol. XLIII, No. 4, Jan, 1995, pp.18-21.

Rajagopal : Linkages in IRDP: Lessons from Some States, Kurukshethra, Vol. XXXIX, No. 7, April, 1991. pp. 4-8.

Reddy, A.R., Suresh Reddy, Y. and Mohan Reddy, P. : Women and Rural Development (A Study of DWCRA in Cuddappah District), Kurukshethra, Vol. XLII, No. 12, Sep, 1994, pp. 19-22.

Seetharam, M. : Development of Rural Women-Problems & Alternatives, Kurukshetra, Vol. XL, No. 4, January, 1992, pp. 28-30.

Sivashankaraiah, M. and Ramappa, P. : Impact of DWCRA on Rural areas (A Study), Kurukshetra, Vol. XLI, No.10, July, 1993. pp.5-9.

Suman Singh and Manisha Goel : Bottle Necks in the Implementation of the DWCRA Programme, Kurukshethra, Vol. XLII, No. 12, Sep, 1994, pp. 23-25.

Sarmistha Choudhury : Awareness of Rural Women and their Development: (A Study), Kurukshethra, Vol. XLIII, No. 12, Sep, 1995, pp. 44-48.

Sunderam and Suman Singh : Assessment of DWCRA Programme on Modalities of Operation, Kurukshethra, Vol. XLIII, No. 11, Aug, 1995, pp. 96-99.

Seetha Prabhu, K. Sarkara, P.C. and Radha, A. : Gender Related Development Index for Indian States-Methodological Issues, (1996) Vol. XXXI, No. 43, Economic and Political Weekly, pp. WS 72-79.

Sujatha Gothoskar : Women, Work and Health : An Interconnected Web-Case of Drugs and Cosmetics Industries, *Economic and Political Weekly,* (1997) Vol. XXXII, No. 43, pp. WS 45-52.

Tendulkar, S.D. and Jain, L.R. : Economic Reforms and Poverty, *Economic and Political Weekly,* Vol. 30, No. 23, June, 10, 1994, pp. 1373-77.

Uttambhai, H. Patel : Crossing the Poverty Line through IRDP, Kurukshethra, Vol. XLII, No. 12, Sep-1994, pp. 30-31.

Reports

Asian Development Bank : The New Reform Programme, Internal Document, October, 1992.

Asian Development Bank : Asian Development Outlook, Oxford University Press, Oxford, 1992.

Alternative Economic Survey 1991-98 : (7 years of Structural Adjustments), Alternative Survey Group, Rainbow Publishing Limited, New Delhi.

Alternative Economic Survey 1998-2000 : (Two years of Market Fundamentalism) Alternative Survey Group, Rainbow Publishing Limited, New Delhi.

Bourgignon, F.J. de Melo and J. Morrison : Poverty and Income Distribution During Adjustment : Issues and Evidence from the OECD Project, World Development, Vol. XIX, No. 11, pp. 1485 - 1508, 1991.

Bussink, W.C.F. : Poverty Redressal in India - Past and Future, Poverty Reduction in India-options and Perspectives, Ministsry Foriegn Affairs, the Hague, pp. 19-53, 1991.

Delhi Science Forum : Alternative Economic Survey : 1996-97, 1997, New Delhi.

Ghosh, A.K. : Economic and Restructuring, Employment and Safety Nets, in ILO ARTEP, 1992, pp. 94-102. 1992.

Govt.of India : Towards Equality, Report of the Committee on Status on Women in India, Department of Social Welfare, Ministry of Education and Social Welfare, December, 1974.

Human Development Report-2000 : Published by Oxford University Press, New York.

Human Development Report - 2001 : Making New Technologies Work for Human Development, Published by Oxford University Press, New York.

ILO/ARTP India : Employment, Poverty and Economic Policies, New Delhi, December, 1992.

Jyothi Rani (et al) : Evaluation of IRDP 1996-97 in Khammam District, A Report Submitted to DRDA, Khammam, April, 1998.

Kundu, A. : Poverty and Unemployment in Urban India : Trends, Issues and Perspectives, Procedings of the Conference on Poverty and Employment, Institute of Applied Manpower Research, New Delhi, 1985.

Kanbur, R. : Measurement and Alleviation in Poverty, in IMF Staff Papers, Vol. 36, 1987, pp. 60-85.

Killick, T. : Structural Adjustment and Poverty Alleviation, Standing Committee on Poverty Alleviation, UNCTAD/PA/7, May 18, 1994.